Taiwan's Modernization

Americanization and Modernizing Confucian Manifestations

Other books by the same author (in the order of publication date)

Economic Dynamics: Growth and Development
Synergetic Economics
Knowledge and Value: Economic Structures with Time and Space
Japan versus China in the Industrial Race
Confucianism and Industrialization
Capital and Knowledge: Dynamics of Economic Structures with Non-constant Returns
Adam Smith and Confucius: The Theory of Moral Sentiments *and* The Analects
A Theory of International Trade: Capital, Knowledge, and Economic Structures
An Economic Theory of Cities: Spatial Models with Capital, Knowledge, and Structures
Singapore's Modernization: Westernization and Modernizing Confucian Manifestations
A Theory of Interregional Dynamics: Models of Capital, Knowledge, and Economic Structures
The American Civilization Portrayed in Ancient Confucianism

Taiwan's Modernization

Americanization and Modernizing Confucian Manifestations

Wei-Bin Zhang

World Scientific
New Jersey • London • Singapore • Hong Kong

Published by

World Scientific Publishing Co. Pte. Ltd.
5 Toh Tuck Link, Singapore 596224
USA office: Suite 202, 1060 Main Street, River Edge, NJ 07661
UK office: 57 Shelton Street, Covent Garden, London WC2H 9HE

British Library Cataloguing-in-Publication Data
A catalogue record for this book is available from the British Library.

TAIWAN'S MODERNIZATION: AMERICANIZATION AND MODERNIZING CONFUCIAN MANIFESTATIONS

ISBN 981-238-351-4

Printed in Singapore by World Scientific Printers (S) Pte Ltd

Preface

In *Managing in a Time of Great Change* (1998: 208–9), one of the most important contemporary management thinkers, Peter Drucker, observes:

> Yet every single one of the younger overseas Chinese ... was confident that his group could successfully solve its problems and yet maintain its basic Chinese character. "They will change details, but they won't change the fundamentals any more than the Japanese changed theirs when they modernized," said a Taipei lawyer ... "And it will work!"

One might wonder why contemporary Chinese are loftily claiming "won't change the fundamentals" after they have experienced Western domination in many aspects since the Opium War. One might tend to interpret this as a continuation of unjustified racial pride, if not stupidity. Some Chinese are aware of the continuation of Chinese civilization as Chinese societies are experiencing Westernization (more properly, Americanization in the case of Taiwan). Nevertheless, there are only a few studies about whether the Chinese assertion is justifiable. This book demonstrates why Chinese people claim to be continuing the essence of Chinese culture at the same time as they are conscious of becoming Westernized. We demonstrate that Taiwan has actually provided an important case study not only of the capitalist spirit of overseas Chinese, but also for possible implications of Confucianism for modernization.

This book is part of a broad examination of Confucianism and its implications for modernization of the Confucian regions covering Mainland China, Taiwan, Hong Kong, Macao, Vietnam, Japan, South Korea, North Korea, and Singapore. In *Japan versus China in the Industrial Race* (Zhang, 1998), I examine why Japan could have rapidly become industrialized and why China had been so slow in its take-offs. It is shown that

Japan followed the Confucian principles when faced with economic, political, and military challenges from the West, and that China had been against the Confucian principles. For instance, one difference between Japan and Mainland China is that Japan accepted the classical Confucian principle of determining one's social position by education and merit after the Meiji Restoration, and China denied this Confucian principle before the economic reform. In *Singapore's Modernization* (Zhang, 2002), I look at some cultural sources of Singapore's rapid economic growth and the characteristics of its democratization. In *Confucianism and Modernization* (Zhang, 1999a), the Confucian principles are summarized in contemporary terms (see also Chapter 2 of this book). It is indicated that the important elements, except for the voting processes of the masses, of democracy can be identified in Confucianism. Instead of voting, Confucian tradition uses examination systems to select the right men for government. In *Adam Smith and Confucius* (Zhang, 2000), I compare the ethical, social, and economic principles advocated by Adam Smith and Confucius. Adam Smith has been the most influential thinker in developed economies in modern times. Confucius was the most influential thinker in the Confucian regions (except Singapore) before the Opium War. After comparing their opinions about the fundamental issues related to man, society, and government, it is concluded that Smith and Confucius were similar in principles, but different in "sentimental emphases."

In this book, the name Taiwan is used interchangeably with the Republic of China on Taiwan and the ROC.

Acknowledgments

I am grateful to Juliet Lee Ley Chin and Kim Tan for effective co-operation and to an anonymous referee for important comments. My great indebtedness to many scholars, whose research has provided the foundation upon which this book was written, cannot be acknowledged here, except in places where their names are cited in the text. I am very grateful to the multi-cultural environment, created by students and staffs from over 60 countries gathered on Japanese soil, at the Ritsumeikan Asian Pacific University.

I take great pleasure in expressing my gratitude to my wife, Gao Xiao, who has been supportive of my efforts in completing this book and helped to format the manuscript.

Contents

Chapter 1

Introduction

Ever since Max Weber (1864–1920) proposed the assumption that culture determines the history of economic development, the neoclassical economic growth theory equipped with advanced mathematics has tried to convince its students that culture does not matter in long-term economic performance. Nevertheless, modern economic history has demonstrated that culture does matter in economic development. After World War II, the Confucian regions have witnessed economic growth rates unprecedented in world history. "Economic miracle" is the common term used to describe these regions' experience. The six fast-growing Confucian economies (Japan, Taiwan, Korea, Singapore, Hong Kong, and Mainland China) experienced an annual per capita growth (in international purchasing power parity) of about 5% from 1965 to 1995 (Rowen, 1998: 2). The rapid industrialization of these regions has transformed their social and political spheres. There are some common patterns of economic development among the Confucian regions. They have experienced rapid urbanization, a steady decline in the population employed in agriculture, and changes in lifestyles. New social and political forces have emerged that transformed traditional societies into post-industrial or industrial societies.

If Weber was right, that is, if culture determines everything, one might ask why it does not work in a consistent way. Why have the Chinese, for instance, been so unproductive for so long at home and so industrial abroad? And why have the Mainland Chinese recently ameliorated their economic conditions so rapidly? We maintain that neither a single cultural equation (as Weber has argued) nor a single economic force (as the neoclassical growth theory presumes) can fully explain economic performance. To approach socio-economic dynamics, we need a multi-interdependent equations approach. Weber must have missed, if our theory of high-dimensional dynamics is sound, some dimensions that play a key role in determining socio-economic dynamics. We hold that these neglected dimensions should include economic conditions, political and socio-economic geography, and politics.

Rather than the one-directional cause-and-effect between culture and economic development, we hold that both culture and economic development interact with each other (Zhang, 1998). In general, we presume a relationship of "parallel" significance in economic conditions and ideology in socio-economic dynamics. According to the synergetic approach, one factor (such as ideology) may be "enslaved" by economic conditions during a period of history. Similarly, economic dynamics may be enslaved by ideology during another period. That is, during some brief period of history, "the economic determinism" is "approximately" valid; during some other period, "the cultural determinism" is not misleading. If we consider history as a continuous organic whole, there are no permanent masters and slaves between cultural and economic conditions. This infers that neither Weber's nor Marx's explanation of history is telling when we consider history as an organic whole, even though their theories may be sound if we limit our historical study to a specified period. Thus, we do not deny the possible validity of Weber's opinion for a specified historical period. However, we hold that Weber's argument is not generally cogent. From the synergetic viewpoint (Zhang, 1991), Weber's theory, like that of Marx, should be a special case of general socio-economic theory.

1.1 Taiwan's Economic Miracle and Rapid Democratization

Taiwan is unique among Chinese communities. On the one hand, it operates in a purely Chinese environment. On the other hand, it has been faced with threats from Mainland China since the end of China's civil war in 1949. Taiwan has embarked on its own distinct, divergent path of development in a modernized Confucian style. During these past decades, Taiwan has witnessed a whirlwind of turbulent events, including periods of internal political strife and suppression, rapid economic development, military crises, and the attainment of political stability and democratization. Taiwan has become a Chinese society with a democratically elected government that has taken a route different—perhaps only in timing—from the rest of Mainland China in Westernization and modernizing Confucian manifestations.

When the Kuomintang (KMT) moved its headquarters to Taiwan, the Taiwanese people had suffered from Japanese colonization and the KMT's cruel mistreatments. Most of Taiwan's Japanese-built industry and infrastructure were destroyed by American bombing raids or had been siphoned off to Mainland China by nationalist Chinese government agencies. The KMT, reeling from its defeat at the hands of the Chinese Communists, was infamous for its corruption and ineptitude. However, after it assumed full control of the island in 1949, the KMT accelerated the economic development and started a rapid democratizing process. Like the defeated Japanese soldiers who built a modern Japan after World War II, the defeated KMT soldiers from Mainland China concentrated their energies on modernizing Taiwan together with the Chinese who had immigrated to the island earlier. The human capital and political experiences that the KMT had accumulated from governing Mainland China and domestic wars benefited Taiwan's modernization.

During the first half of the twentieth century, Taiwan achieved little growth, at least in per capita terms. Even by the early 1960s, the economic conditions and income levels were not different from those in African countries (Maddison, 1989: 15). Its high growth rate was maintained through the 1970s and beyond. From humble beginnings, it has become the world's most dynamic exporter of manufactured goods. Its spectacular growth has been brought about largely through increased factor inputs (high investment, rising participation rates, and inter-sectoral transfers of labor). Until the last few years, the Taiwanese economy had experienced rapid growth, stable prices, low employment rate, and relatively equitable income distribution. Instead of foreign debts, Taiwan has accumulated one of the world's largest foreign exchange reserves. It has experienced structural changes through the stages of import substitution, export promotion, and rapid technological upgrading. The economic structural gravity has shifted from agriculture to labor-intensive light manufacturing industry, and then to capital- and skill-intensive manufacturing industry and services. From 1952 to 1962, Taiwan's economy was dominated by the agricultural sector, and the average growth rate of the Gross Domestic Product (GDP) was 7.93%. The rapid economic growth was partly due to an expansion in the export of agricultural products, processed agricultural products, and textiles. From 1963 to 1980, the annual growth rate of the GDP was 10%. During this period, the exports of agricultural products decreased, while those of manufactured products increased.

From 1981 to 1995, the annual growth rate of the GDP was 7.52% (Yu, 1999: 142). With exports of US$111.7 billion and imports of US$103.6 billion in 1995, Taiwan was the fourteenth largest country in the world in terms of trade. With rapid economic growth, Taiwan also experienced rapid improvements in living standards in terms of education, housing, sanitation, and transportation and communications. The life expectancy increased from 58.6 years in 1945 to 74.5 years in 1995. Its educational record has been exemplary. Taiwan had maintained its faith in education at a time when Western nations and many developing countries were becoming increasingly disenchanted with it. In 1945, 28.3% of adolescents attended high school; in 1995, 94.4% did. In 1945, 11.3% of youths attended colleges and universities; in 1995, it was 45.3% (Kuo, 1999: 43). Taiwan has set an example of how a small country can be transformed from being an underdeveloped economy into a developed one within a short span of time. As discussed later, Taiwan has designed its developmental policy according to its own geographical, historical, political, and economic circumstances.

As demonstrated by Zhang (1999a), the Confucian values are similar to democratic values. If one refers to traditional Confucian values as a belief in hard work, thrift, honesty, self-discipline, high regard for education, respect for enterprise, and concern over family stability, then they are exactly the same traditional Western values that enabled the West to dominate the world politically, economically, and culturally. Confucianism shaped the social fabric, forged status consciousness, and provided the system of role enforcement in Chinese communities before modern times. Confucianism may affect Taiwan in two ways. First, it directly affects social and economic behavior and institutional structures. The "overemphasis" on children's education in Taiwan, for instance, might be due to Confucian values and tradition. Second, it affects perception and value structures. How decisions are made and how behavior is culturally interpreted by, for instance, the Taiwanese may be strongly influenced by Confucianism. We maintain that Taiwan has succeeded in industrialization because it has accepted Western philosophical and ethical principles (which are similar to Confucian principles). We will show that Taiwan has applied the value system of the West, but its manifestations in Taiwan are different from those in contemporary Western societies. The reader may wonder how this can be done. We maintain that a few basic principles may have various manifestations, in the same way as described by Sun Tze in *The Art of War*: "There are not more than five musical notes, yet the combinations of these five give rise to more melodies than can ever be heard." In the West, social and economic institutions have changed constantly and exhibited a great variety in modern times. Irrespective of their differences in structures and operations, Western democratic institutions are commonly considered to have the same set of philosophical and ethical principles common to Western civilization. We maintain that Taiwan has produced manifestations of the Western value system that are unique to its historical conditions. Taiwan has modernized Confucian principles by applying them in the spirit of the west, rather than according to the traditional technological and economic conditions of Mainland China.

1.2 Common Patterns of Industrialization in the Confucian Regions

Economic development results from the complex interactions of multiple forces. The Zeitgeist, for instance, that a region, a race, or a state collectively holds, may be the key factor determining its economic evolution during a certain period of history. According to the modern nonlinear economic theory, there is no unique correspondence between culture and economic development in long-term economic evolution. The theory shows that "historical memory," initial conditions, and international environment (which are neglected or treated as trivial factors in the mainstreams of traditional economic theory) often play a deterministic role in paths of economic development. The economic "miracles" of the Confucian regions have been examined from various perspectives. For instance, in the cultural approach, the success of these regions is often attributed to Confucianism. There is no definite reason to conclude that democracy certainly leads to economic development. This is also true of Confucianism. Historically, China was poor during the late Qing dynasty when it was claimed to be Confucian. The divergent paths taken by China and Japan since the Opium War until China's economic reform cannot be explained only by cultural or ideological differences between the two economies (Morishima, 1982; Zhang, 1998). If one uses cultural values as the only factor to explain industrialization of the two economies, one would conclude, as Weber (1951) did, that the traditional Chinese culture should be more suitable for capitalism and industrialization than the traditional Japanese culture. The modern economic history exhibits the opposite.

Although their take-offs began at different times, Japan, South Korea, Singapore, Hong Kong, Taiwan, and Mainland China exhibited some common patterns of growth. Each region embarked on rapid economic growth by introducing market mechanisms with strong government intervention. Their rapid growth was also preceded by a period of state planning. Immediately after the Meiji Restoration, the Meiji government directly owned and managed a very large share of the Japanese economy. After failures in state planning, the government started decentralization. Both Korea and Taiwan were under the absolute control of Japan before they started industrialization. In Singapore, government intervention has been strong. Mainland China planned its economy before economic reform was started in 1978. Hong Kong is an exceptional case in that, during its period of rapid economic growth, it was run by the British and the Chinese people worked under the auspices of British laws and economic institutions. If we consider Hong Kong as "part" of the United Kingdom, we gather that the "order parameters" for social harmony and economic efficiency were stable. When it was handed back to China, Hong Kong was already industrialized under the British.

None of the regions experienced a catastrophic transformation from a planning economy to a market economy. If one reads what Mencius said about "socialism," "capitalism," and a "market economy with government intervention," one may gain an insight into the dynamic mechanisms of social and economic transformations in the Confucian regions. Mencius (390–305 BC) pointed out that

> The principle of the philosopher Yang was: "Each one for himself." Though he might have benefited the whole empire by plucking out a single hair, he would not have done it. The philosopher Mo loves all equally. By rubbing his whole body from the crown to the heel, he could have benefited the empire; he could have done it. Zimo holds a medium between these. By holding that medium, he is nearer to the right. But by holding it without leaving room for the exigency of

> circumstances, it is like holding one point. The reason why I hate holding to one point is the injury it does to the way of the right principle. It takes up one point and disregards a hundred others.
>
> Those who are fleeing from the errors of Mo (socialism) naturally turn to Yang (capitalism), and those who are fleeing from the errors of Yang naturally turn to orthodoxy (Confucianism for Mencius, democratic policy and market economy with government intervention in the modern sense). When they turn, they should at once and be simply received.

Neither socialism nor capitalism will find a lasting home in the (educated) Confucian mind. According to Mencius, the validity of Keynes' economic theory is dependent on the situation at hand. It has become evident, from modern economic theory, that Keynesian economics is valid only under special circumstances.

Before reaching the industrial stage, each Confucian region is governed by authoritarianism. Overall, the authoritarian government seems to be popular in the rapid growth period. As a region becomes industrialized, authoritarianism tends to lose the publicity it enjoyed earlier. This common preference for "first economic development and then cultivation and democracy" can be found in one of the sayings of Confucius:

> When Confucius went to Wei, Ran You acted as the driver of his carriage. Confucius observed, "How numerous are the people!" Ran You said, "Since they are thus numerous, what more shall be done for them?" "Enrich them," was the reply. "And when they have been enriched, what more shall be done?" Confucius said, "Teach them."

We get hints on the dynamic processes of industrialization and democratization in the Confucian regions by referring to Confucius' attitude towards the timing of economic development and personal development of the masses. Since the contents of traditional education (which are mainly concerned with ethical and cultural issues) are different from those in modern education (which are mainly scientific and technical in nature), we may expect that even if it is economically oriented, a modern government influenced by Confucianism should emphasize science and technology because they are intrinsic to economic development. The shift in economic production means that it is necessary to implement policies for economic growth and mass education, while at the same time providing a livelihood for the people. The industrialization of the Confucian regions was initiated with the rapid spread of education for the masses.

There is a common belief among the (industrial or industrializing) Confucian regions that a meaningful democracy can hardly be achieved without economic growth. Mencius' saying hints at the source of this belief:

> They are only men of education who, without a livelihood, are able to maintain a fixed heart. As for the people, if they do not have a livelihood, they will not have a fixed heart. And if they do not have a fixed heart, there is nothing which they will not do in the way of self-abandonment, of moral deflection, of depravity, and of wild license. ... Therefore, an intelligent ruler will regulate the livelihood of the people, so as to make sure that, above, they shall have sufficient wherewith to serve their parents and, below, sufficient wherewith to support their wives and children; in good years, they shall always be abundantly satisfied and, in bad years, they shall escape the danger of perishing. After this, he may urge them, and they will proceed to what is good for, in this case, the people will follow after that with ease. ... It never has been that the rulers of a state where such results were seen—the old wearing silk and eating flesh, and the black-haired people suffering neither from hunger nor cold—did not attain to imperial dignity.

According to Confucianism, a society can hardly achieve consensus on socio-economic development if its people do not receive an education. A democratic system comprising different political parties and voting strategies tends to result in social instabilities and harmful consequences if the uneducated masses do not have a livelihood. According to Confucianism, the people's livelihoods, rather than an ideology or religion, is the cornerstone of the state. The book of *Great Learning* records that:

> In the *Book of Poetry*, it is said, "The imperial domain of a thousand *li* is where the people rest. ... The twittering yellow bird rests on a corner of the mound." Confucius said, "When it rests, it knows where to rest. Is it possible that a man should not be equal to this bird?"

Confucius maintains that the central task of government is to provide its people good living conditions. As living conditions are improved, education should be made available to the people. The Confucian model of economic development and personal development explains why the people in some Confucian regions are obedient to their authoritarian governments, which provided economic freedom, but not political freedom, in the initial stages of industrialization. However, the mind is fickle. As soon as industrialization is underway, each region embarks on a rapid process of democratization. As living conditions improve, education becomes accessible, values change and discernment increases in society, the people's desire for democracy becomes obvious.

The people in each Confucian region began to despise authoritarianism as soon as the economy became industrialized. The people trusted "capable" and authoritarian leaders when they were not well educated. This is particularly true when leaders succeeded in providing social stability and improving the economic conditions. Nevertheless, as people become well-informed, educated, and prosperous, they tend to judge human affairs themselves rather than simply accept whatever the authorities say. As society progresses, an authoritarian leader who was respectable and praiseworthy in the initial stage of industrialization may become despised in an industrial society.

1.3 The Principles of Confucianism

> I hate the manner in which purple takes away the lustre of vermilion.
>
> *Confucius*

Confucianism is commonly perceived as an ethic, a humanistic and rational view of the world based on relationships in the family and clan, respect for ancestors, obedience to heads of family and clan, loyalty, and benevolence towards one's inferiors (Hall and Ames, 1987; Slote and De Vos, 1998). The common perception of obedience neglects the individualistic aspects of (classical) Confucianism (Hall and Ames, 1995, 1998; Zhang, 2000), which arises from observing the behavior of Chinese in modern times. It is reasonable to expect Chinese communities with little education and under foreign control to center their life around the nuclear family, extended family or clan. However, similar to that, one will get a distorted picture of Karl Marx if one interprets Marx's theory, based on Mainland China's modern history. One may provide misleading interpretations of Confucianism, based on observation of "concrete loyal identities" in overseas Chinese communities. In Confucianism, loyalty means to follow the way or be true to one's conscience. Blind obedience to the head of the family or the leader of an organization is never justified in ancient Confucianism. The family is never treated as the "calculation center."

To show the impact of Confucianism on Taiwan's modernization, there is a need to explain Confucianism. It is held that modernization in the Confucian regions followed Confucian principles and "modernize" them according to changed conditions. This argument implies that the Confucian regions need not reject Confucianism in order to modernize, even though it is necessary to modernize the Confucian principles to provide a solid foundation for modernization. Recent studies (Morishima, 1978, 1982; Tu, 1996; Zhang, 1998, 1999a) have shown that the economic success of Japan and "the four little dragons" (Singapore, Hong Kong, South Korea and Taiwan) in the Confucian regions are strongly influenced by the proper application of Confucian principles under Western influence.

One might ask how it is possible for Taiwan to have followed the Confucian principles and, at the same time, modernized these principles. As an analogy, we observe that a plant grown from the same seed may manifest different forms in different environments. One can hardly find the "perfect form" of a plant in nature. Similarly, different types of society might be formed. A belief system may have multiple manifestations. For instance, while Japan, Korea, and Mainland China claimed to be Confucian, their practical ethics, human relations, and behavioral patterns were different. Similarly, when we call the Western countries democratic, this does not mean that their institutional structures and voting processes are identical (Lipset, 1990, 1996). Stromberg (1996) has demonstrated the non-existence of an authoritative history of democratic thought in Western civilization.

Recently, the concept of "illiberal democracy" was introduced to distinguish the Western form of democracy from that in Asia. Bell and Jayasuriya (1995: 3) argue that

> Western political thinkers generally share a belief that "all persons are by nature equal," a principle of equal respect for the moral status and intrinsic worth of each person ... Needless to say, this principal commitment to equality has been imperfectly applied in practice ... but at least at the level of theory most Western thinkers since the birth of liberalism in seventeenth century England begin with an assumption that the interests of each member of the community matters, and matters equally—the common doctrine of Judaism and Christianity that we are all equally God's children—help to explain the taken-for-granted, uncontroversial status of an egalitarian premise.

They also observed that the social and political systems of the West systematically excluded large numbers of individuals from political power and a fair share of the benefits of social co-operation. But they concluded that "in East Asia … the moral and political status of each person has traditionally varied both in theory and practice in accordance with a person's unchosen position within a hierarchical family unit." This is a partial, if not queer, interpretation of Confucianism. According to Confucianism and Taoism, all individuals are equal by nature. No individual is born to rule and none is born a slave. Social mobility based on one's efforts and education were practiced for many centuries in East Asia. Bell and Jayasuriya failed to appreciate the essence of Confucianism, notwithstanding their understanding of contemporary Chinese behavior.

As an ethical system, Confucianism has evolved over the years. After the death of Confucius, it underwent a complex process of development. After Confucius passed away, Mencius and Hsun Tzu established two rival schools of thought based on Confucius' teachings. During the Han dynasty, various pseudo-scientific reasoning and cosmological speculations were grafted onto Confucianism. The Neo-Confucianists of the Sung dynasty (AD 960–1279) were influenced by Taoism and Buddhism, and lent Confucianism a philosophical impact hitherto unknown. According to Chang (1963), a comprehensive account of Confucianism through the ages may be described from the four periods in its history: (1) Confucianism as one of the many schools of thought in the age of the "Hundred Schools"; (2) Confucianism in as the most privileged and authoritative school of thought during the Han dynasty (206 BC–AD 220); (3) its eclipse by Buddhism and Taoism; and (4) its rebirth as Neo-Confucianism. Confucianists from different periods held divergent viewpoints of the same issue. For instance, various assumptions were made about human nature since Mencius. The key concepts, such as *jen*, were interpreted in different ways. Before Confucius' time, *jen* was interpreted as the specific virtue of benevolence. For Confucius, *jen* meant the universal virtue. Confucius termed it as the source of all goodness. During the Han dynasty *jen* was interpreted as love, affection, and living together. Han Yu (AD 768–824) considered *jen* as universal love. The Neo-Confucianists of the Sung dynasty interpreted *jen* variously as impartiality, consciousness, union with Heaven and Earth, the character of love, and the principle of the mind. The dynamics of Confucianism is shown in Fig. 1.1. In modern times, there are various interpretations of Confucianism. Some modern Chinese intellectuals believed that China's inability to modernize is due to Confucianism.

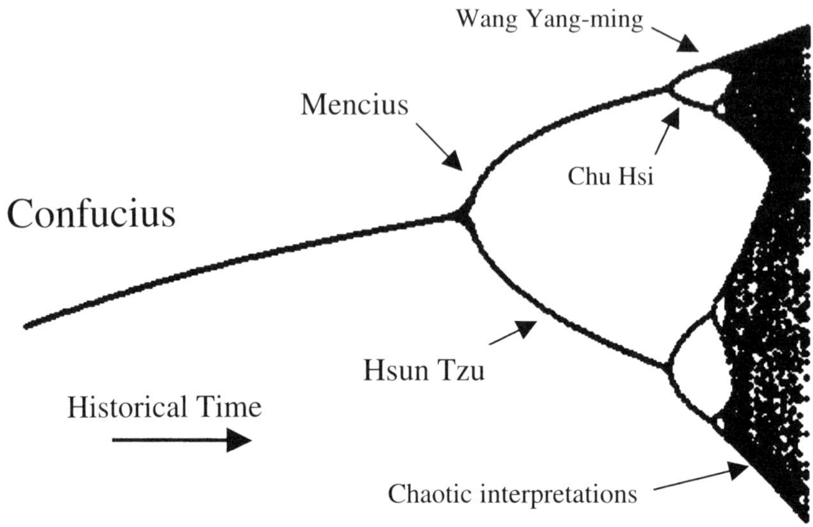

Figure 1.1 Dynamics of Confucianism in history.

Having analyzed the various schools of Confucianism, we summarize their main Confucian (ethical, political, and economic) principles (Zhang, 1999a): (1) free will and rationality (which lays the foundation for the Confucian regions to be rational, adaptable, and progressive, as well as to embrace the sciences with little cultural conflicts); (2) natural equality and social inequality (which provides the basis for human equality and social mobility); (3) self-cultivation through education and equal opportunities in education (which is the key factor in explaining the social appreciation of knowledge and education, as well as the emphasis on education); (4) the welfare of the people and the policy of benevolence (which provides a sustainable basis for industrialization and democratization of the Confucian regions); (5) a hierarchical social structure supported by talent and merit (which is essential for establishing social order according to virtue, merit, and education); (6) mutual obligation, rather than law, in maintaining social justice (which explains why the cost of social negotiation is relatively higher than legal costs in the Confucian regions); (7) the rectification of names (which means that one should only receive what one is socially or economically "worthy of"); (8) the dynamic interaction between market forces and government intervention (which implies that the two polarities, socialism and capitalism, of rational economic thought hold limited appeal to Confucianists); (9) love with different degrees of intensity (which does not promote "inflation of love," in Freudian expression, and extreme social welfare in the economic sense); (10) respect for hard work and appreciation of frugality (which are important to sustain economic development); and (11) an emphasis on social harmony and the justification of rebellion against corrupt governments.

1.4 Modernizing Manifestations of Confucianism

There is often confusion over Confucian principles and their manifestations, such as the actual forms of filial piety, propriety, and ceremony. Confucianism does not hold that there is a unique correspondence between a principle and its manifestations under various circumstances. For instance, Ch'eng Hao (AD 1032–1085), a famous Confucian scholar, had said (Chan, 1973: 540): "Loyalty and faithfulness are spoken of with reference to man. Essentially, they are concrete principles." In Confucianism, it is the essence or principle, rather than a concrete manifestation, that one's mind should be loyal to. This principle may help us to understand why Confucianism has been able to change its manifestations according to the prevailing historical conditions. Special customs based on Confucianist principles for an agricultural economy may be invalid in an open industrial economy; but the Confucianist principles may still be valid in the new environment. In this sense, traditional studies on Confucianism and its impact on economic development may have limitations in explaining the possible impact of Confucianism on sustainable economic development and (long-term) modernization of the Confucian regions, in the sense that the special manifestations of the Confucian principles may have little to do with reality; however, the Confucianist principles may strongly influence the Confucian regions in their globalizing processes.

An ideology may have different manifestations under different historical circumstances. For instance, based on the same democratic principles, the United States and Canada have designed different institutional structures according to their own geographical, cultural, social, political, and economic conditions (Lipset, 1990, 1996). Aristotle (384–322 BC) has argued for the possibility of different manifestations of the same principle: "There is certainly more than one form … of democracy." Democratic institutions change over time within the same culture and vary between countries within the same time frame. Similarly, a concrete rule may "serve" different ideologies. For example, John Locke's *Second Treatise of Government* is considered the first fully developed natural rights theory congruent with subsequent human rights ideas. However, Locke sought to protect only the rights of propertied European males. He did not consider women, savages, servants, and laborers as individuals with rights (Donnelly, 1999). As pointed out by Donnelly, in the last two centuries, the West has increasingly expanded its recognition of human rights. For instance, the right to vote was restricted to only a small propertied elite in many European countries in the nineteenth century. The petition for the rights of working men and women often led to violent conflicts in nineteenth and early twentieth century Europe and North America. Hence, we can see that the manifestations of human rights ideas vary over time even in the same civilization.

It is held that the basic principles of Confucianism summarized above should enable the Confucian regions to sustain economic development and become democratic. But this does not mean that traditional institutional structures and concrete human relations designed under these principles in agricultural economies are suitable for industrial civilization. For instance, the traditional ideal of "the five generations under the same roof" can hardly become an ideal of family life in contemporary industrial economies. The so-called "generation gaps" implies that there is a lack of appreciation and mutual understanding among the members under the same roof. Although the basic moral principle that one should take care of one's children as well as parents has not changed with time, the way of caring and concrete reciprocal relationships are changeable in rational civilization when socio-economic conditions are changed. To always follow the basic principles and to adjust one's behavior according to changed environment is an important character of Confucianism. The *I Ching* says "The superior man produces his changes as the leopard does when he changes his spots: their beauty become more elegant. Small men change their faces: they show themselves as prepared to follow their ruler." It is argued that the "spots," the traditional manifestations of the Confucian principles, are replaced by the modern democratic manifestations, but the essence of Confucianism remains the same in different times (Zhang, 1999a).

Confucianism is manifested differently in traditional economies of China, Japan, and Korea. Benevolence is a common term in both China and Korea, but it is almost not mentioned in Japan. Loyalty is highly valued in both Japan and Korea, but is not so high on China's list of virtues.

Moreover, even a particular concept may be interpreted differently in various cultures. For instance, the meaning of loyalty is not the same in China as in Japan. In China, loyalty means being true to one's own conscience. In Japan, its normal meaning is essentially a total devotion to one's lord. There have been many studies about how each of the Confucian regions is Confucian in modern times (e.g. Smith, 1959; Jansen, 1965; Morishima, 1982; Zeigler, 1988; Lu, 1994; Tu, 1996; Ranis et al., 1999). There has also been an increasing concern regarding the impact of Confucianism on the industrialization of the Confucian regions. As the orthodox philosophy for Chinese civilization for many centuries, Confucianism has influenced the Chinese mind on both conscious and subconscious levels. Confucianism has influenced the Chinese mind in many ways, through Confucian teachings, arts (which were inspirited by Confucianism), literature, poetry, customs, and ceremonies. The mind affects action. The connection between Confucianism and action (including political and economic decision-making) is found in the mind in modern times. Modernized manifestations of Confucianism would be reasonably different among varied Confucian regions. According to cultural tradition, historical conditions, and economic geography, different Confucian regions would modernize various manifestations of Confucianism in different speeds. For instance, it is reasonable to observe that faced with threats from Mainland China, Taiwan has democratized more rapidly than the other Chinese regions. As a multi-racial state surrounded by non-Confucian nations, Chinese Singaporeans have emphasized law more strongly than other Chinese regions. Tu (1996: 2) observed that intellectual historians had a tendency to stress the common heritage and shared spiritual orientation, while anthropologists tended to make broad generalizations and detailed descriptions of the local scene. Japanologists tended to minimize the prominence of Confucian thought in Japan's modern transformation. Sinologists accepted the relevance of Confucian ethics in the economic ethos and political culture of Taiwan, Hong Kong, Singapore, and overseas Chinese communities for granted.

Another way to illustrate changeable manifestations of the principles under changed socio-economic circumstances is to compare two thinkers who hold similar principles but have different viewpoints about what are suitable social and economic institutions for societies in their own times. To further explain the necessity of modernizing manifestations of the Confucian principles, we compare Confucius and Smith.

As analyzed by Zhang (2000), Confucius and Smith held similar viewpoints related to the fundamental issues about man and society, but the "manifestations" of their general principles are quite different. Adam Smith was baptized on 5 June 1723 at Kirkcaldy, a few miles from Edinburgh, Scotland (Lux, 1990; Ross, 1995). Confucius was born in 551 BC in Shantung Province in Mainland China (Fung, 1952, 1953; Chan, 1973; Chen, 1990). Smith lived in an age when his country was expanding both domestically and internationally. Adventurous spirits tended to have positive social consequences. At this time, wealth was created through the expanding market for transatlantic trade with North America and the Caribbean islands. Confucius lived in a period that was characterized by wars among states. In his time, wars raged unchecked. There was very little law and order save what each man could enforce by his own arm, his armed followers, or his powers of intrigue.

The thoughts of Smith and Confucius about some fundamental issues related to man and society are compared by Zhang (2000). It was found that they had similar opinions about the free mind, the ideal man and the common man, human relations among different men, the ideal society (one with little government intervention), the great and the rich, possible role of justice and propriety in maintaining a just society, passions and learning, and the influence of social and intellectual environments on man. For instance, Confucius' gentleman is almost identical with Smith's superior prudent man, even though they employed different "arts of virtue." Both Confucius' and Smith's "ideal man" possesses similar desirable qualities. The ideal man is a symbolic man who possesses almost imaginary good characteristics. The man should cultivate himself and provide happiness to others. He follows what is natural and right, and obeys the ordinances of Heaven. He is social, but does not join some clubs for special purposes. He lives a simple, frugal, and virtuous life rather than being covetous of money or power. He is peaceful and quiet. He is careful and slow in speech, but earnest and quick in action. He studies extensively, but always keeps himself under the restraint of virtue. He practices earnestly what he has learned and is constantly seeking good sources of knowledge. Knowledge is applied to practical problems, rather than used as empty talk and decoration. If he finds the truth, then no matter what conditions he lies under, he should be satisfied. In summary, Smith's and Confucius' perfect men are not supposed to be found in reality. They employ imaginary men to discuss moral issues. The conceptions of the prudent man in Smith's moral philosophy and that of the gentleman in Confucius' philosophy are like the mathematical conception of positive infinite in one-dimensional space: no one knows where it is, even though the mathematician is convinced of its direction and usefulness. The mathematical conception is the consequence of man's intelligence. It is useful, even though it may or may not exist in reality.

The sentimental centers in both Smith's and Confucius' moral philosophy are quite different: Smith is more concerned with the nation than Confucius, while Confucius is more concerned with the family than Smith. The two rational thinkers are quite different when they make "practical choice." For instance, Smith appreciates the hero, while Confucius values the gentleman-scholar; Smith chooses justice as a way to maintain social order, while Confucius prefers propriety, education, and the doctrine of rectification of names; Smith admires passions, while Confucius asks for education and cultivation; Smith signifies the fortune (associated with birth), the rich and the great for maintaining social order, while Confucius sets up moral examples; Smith is concerned with national economic growth and wealth accumulation, while Confucius worries about the welfare of the people; Smith recognizes the significance of popular arts for common people's happiness, while Confucius treats arts as a tool for masses' moral education and a way for gentleman's cultivation and leisure; Smith treats children as a center of family life; while Confucius emphasizes taking care of the aged. It is argued that the differences of the two rational thinkers on practical choice are partially because they lived in different social and economic environments. Since contemporary social and economic conditions are different from those that Smith and Confucius experienced, it is reasonable to see that their "practical preferences" or "situational judgments" are rarely relevant for modern societies. But their common ideas about the ideal man, the desirable reciprocity for human life, and ideal society have had and will continue to have lasting impacts on the two rational, Western and Confucian, civilizations.

Smith is influential mainly due to his ideas about economic liberty. But the idea of economic liberty is historically not new to China, both in theory and in practice (Chen, 1911; Ch'u, 1965; Chao, 1986; Hu, 1988; Brook and Blue, 1999; Deng, 1999). In fact, if the reader notices that Confucianism strongly inspired Quesnay, this feeling of déjà vu may not be surprising (Zhang, 1999a, 2000). In Chinese tradition, the idea that economic agents should freely produce and sell what they want is characterized as non-active policy; Smith terms it natural liberty. It is also important to mention that Smith and Confucius are quite different in their visionary ways of perceiving the world. Smith is Newtonian, while Confucius is I-Ching-influenced. According to the Newtonian vision, there is a single-patterned society with unique stable equilibrium. The *I-Ching*-influenced mind is different from the Newtonian mind. To further illustrate this difference, let us consider socialism and capitalism. In the viewpoint of Confucianism, socialism and capitalism should be important for constructing theories and providing insights into actual functions of social and economic systems (according to Confucius, "I set it forth from one end to the other"), but are not good to characterize actual economies because the actuality lies between the two extremes. In other words, even if an economic system can attain its goals with socialism (capitalism), the extreme situation is only momentary and will soon move away from it. In recent years, the socialist economies have collapsed, while governmental intervention in the capitalist economies has steadily increased. This structural transformation between socialism and capitalism is due to internal mechanisms of social evolution. Socialist collapse is due to enforced stability and femininity (strengthened *yin*), while increased government intervention in capitalist systems is due to inherited instability and masculinity (strengthened *yang*). Neither the *yin* nor the *yang* is desirable from the Confucian point of view. Only a mixed economic system is sustainable with justice in the long term. However, the desirable degree of mixture is not prefixed—this further implies that the Keynesian economics should also be temporarily valid. If one reads what Mencius (371–289 BC) says about first "state planning," then "market," and finally a "mean way" as mentioned before, one may gain insight into the Confucian mind about social and economic transformations. In fact, as pointed out in Zhang (1998, 2003), though the traditional Chinese vision of social evolution is in conflict with the Newtonian vision of change, it has a close relationship with the nonlinear dynamic vision. The traditional Chinese culture perceives social change as a complicated dynamic interdependence of various forces with uncertain patterns. The *yin–yang* principle symbolizes this vision. The recognition that Confucianism cannot be explored by the Newtonian vision partially explains why the Chinese rationality had not converged to the traditional Western rationality in the last century. My works on nonlinear science, theoretical economics, and Confucianism show that the Confucian mentality is converging to the modern rationality because of the recent development of nonlinear sciences, computers, and rapid globalization. Traditional Chinese vision has much more similarity with the modern nonlinear scientific vision than with the traditional scientific vision (e.g. Haken, 1977; Nicolis and Prigogine, 1977; Capra, 1983; Prigogine and Stengers, 1984; Gleick, 1987; Zhang, 1991; Waldrop, 1992; Mainzer, 1996). It is argued that nonlinear science provides a common ground for cultural communications between the Western and Confucian civilizations.

Chapter 2

History Before 1945

Taiwan sits astride the Tropic of Cancer. It is separated from Mainland China by the Taiwan Straits, about 100 miles from the coast of the mainland. Shaped like a tobacco leaf, the island is about 250 miles long and 80 miles in width. No part of Taiwan is more than 50 miles from the sea. Its area is 13,884 square miles. More than half the island is mountainous, with some 60 peaks over 10,000 feet in elevation. The island has considerable forests in the central and eastern mountain regions, but few other natural resources other than coal. Taiwan's most important natural resource is its agricultural land. Only one-fourth of its total area is arable. Subtropical climate allows the cultivation of several crops a year. The western half of the island is an alluvial plain, a heavily cultivated region where most of Taiwan's inhabitants live. In addition to the island of Taiwan, there are a few small offshore islands under the control of the ROC. They include, for instance, the Pescadores Islands (Penghu) in the Taiwan Straits and the Quemoy (Kinmen) and Matsu islands. There were six million Taiwanese Chinese when Chiang Kai-shek and his two million followers fled the mainland and escaped to the island during the period 1948–1950. By the end of 1997, Taiwan's population was 21.4 million. There are nine different types of aboriginal people in Taiwan with a total population of about 370,000, or about 1.7% of Taiwan's population in 1995. These aboriginal inhabitants of presumably Malayo-Polynesia origin were tribes who lived by hunting and slash-and-burn agriculture. Except the aborigines, the population is made up of almost entirely of ethnic Chinese. Most of Taiwan's people live on the plains, giving the island a population density of 590 persons per square kilometer, the second highest in the world.

2.1 Taiwan Under the Dutch

Large-scale migration of the Chinese to the island did not take place until the seventeenth century, notwithstanding the Chinese knowledge of the existence of Taiwan as early as in 605. As early as the fourteenth century, the Chinese and the Japanese arrived in the island as merchants, fishermen, and deer hunters. The first Chinese settlers on Taiwan were landless adventurers and semi-retired pirates. The first Europeans to reach Taiwan were Portuguese navigators. They arrived off the coast of Taiwan and named the island "Ilha Formosa" (beautiful land). The Portuguese attempted to make Taiwan a trade center in the early 1600s. They departed soon after establishing a settlement in the north. The Dutch supplanted the Portuguese. To penetrate China by sea, the Dutch occupied Taiwan from 1642 to 1662 as a foothold in the China market (Shepherd, 1993). Dutch rule was indirect. The Dutch government's chartered agent, the Dutch East India Company, first colonized the southwester part of the island in 1624. The Company appointed a colonial governor and had full powers of taxation and control over people in Taiwan. The Dutch pacified the deer-hunting aborigines and recruited Chinese labor from the mainland for rice and sugarcane agriculture. It was estimated that when the Dutch arrived in Taiwan in 1624, the Chinese population was 25,000 (Davidson, 1903). In the 1650s, the Chinese population increased to 100,000. Many Chinese moved to Taiwan during the Dutch period, during which China was experiencing the dynastic change from the Ming (1368–1644) to the Ch'ing (1644–1911). Apart from the social turmoil in the mainland and social stability in Taiwan, another important factor that induced the Chinese to immigrate to the island was that the Dutch East India Company encouraged the Chinese to settle in the island to promote agriculture.

The Dutch exercised effective control over Taiwan. The Chinese peasants were classified into reclamation groups. Each group was led by local headmen who were supervised by the Dutch. Each Chinese received a piece of land after reclamation. The selling and leasing of land was forbidden. The Chinese worked the crown land as tenant farmers and were not free to choose their residents (Campbell, 1903). By 1642, the Dutch established the capital near the modern city of Tainan and maintained there a garrison of more than 2000 soldiers and some 600 officials (McBeath, 1998). Chinese peasants were recruited from the mainland.

When they arrived in Taiwan, the Dutch supplied them with seeds, farm implements, and oxen to cultivate in the virgin land. The Dutch also helped the Chinese to construct irrigation systems and provided security against aboriginal attacks. Instead, the Chinese were obligated to pay the Dutch both rent and taxes, through selling agricultural products (rice and sugar) to the Dutch company. The Dutch dominated trade in Taiwan, through imposing heavy taxes in the form of customs on the Chinese and Japanese commercial competitors. The Dutch in Taiwan procured lavish profits from the triangular trade with China and Japan and from various taxes. In 1653, the Dutch revenue from croplands was sufficient to cover the annual expenditures of the company in Taiwan (Ka, 1995: 12).

In 1656, the Dutch reported 5578 ha of land under rice, 1573 ha under sugar cane, and 36 ha under other crops. Rice production supplied the local needs. Sugar was the prime export commodity of the island. The Dutch rule stimulated the economic development of the island. It was estimated that a substantial share of Taiwan's sugar production was exported by the Dutch to Persia: 260 metric tons (MT) in 1640, 299 MT in 1652, and 428 MT in 1661 (Iwao, 1955). Under the administration of the Dutch East Indian Company, the island became a meeting place for Dutch, Chinese, and Japanese merchants. Raw silk, silk piece goods, and porcelain were imported from China and re-exported to Japan and Java. European merchants also traded with China and Japan via Taiwan. For the Dutch, Taiwan was important for its strategic location and as an entrepôt. Taiwan exported small quantities of rice and sugar. Besides farming, hunting was the other major economic activity, which facilitated the export of deerskins. However, with the extinction of the deer population in the later 1600s, the trade ended. The Dutch made, overall, little efforts to develop the island.

Dutch rule ended in 1662 when the Ming loyalist Cheng Ch'eng-kung (called Koxinga in the West) and his army of 25,000 (who represented the last major force still loyal to the Ming dynasty) drove the Dutch out of Taiwan. His Fukienese soldiers retreated to Taiwan to escape from the conquering Ch'ing dynasty. They turned Taiwan into a rebel Chinese region, developing fortifications to support the Ming and attack the mainland. Cheng carried out large-scale military colonization on aboriginal land to settle his army. Under Cheng's administration, Chinese people were attracted to the island by free land and the exemption of land tax for

3 years. Cheng turned his soldiers into farmers and encouraged farmers to settle in Taiwan. Under Cheng's rule, arbitrary taxes were imposed on tenants. Officials and local strongmen were allowed to encroach the land (except the crown land) of aboriginal peoples as their own private land (Hsu, 1980). Agricultural development was accelerated, and sugar refining and salt production were increased. They brought Chinese laws, customs, and traditions to the island. However, the military forces on the island failed to resist a large naval invasion by the Manchu. In 1683, when Cheng's heirs surrendered to the Ch'ing and Taiwan came under the rule of the Manchu empire as part of Fukien province, the Chinese population on the island was estimated at between 200,000 and 350,000. In 1684, when the Manchus began to administer Taiwan, the total cultivated land was 17,898 ha.

2.2 The Ch'ing Dynasty

The Manchus founded China's last dynasty, Ch'ing (1644–1911), in 1644. The Manchus were originally nomadic people of northeast Asia, settled in north and central Manchuria. The Manchus were tribesmen who lived by hunting and gathering. But in southern Manchuria, where they bordered on the Ming (1368–1644) and where the group that conquered China originated, the Manchus had adopted agriculture and lived a more settled life. They were strongly influenced by Chinese culture; in the late Ming, they adopted Chinese social organization. They adapted to the Chinese order shortly after conquering China. The Manchus formed a number of tribal states and had a tribute relationship to the Ming emperors. After having united several tribes under his personal rule, in 1616 Nuerhachi (1559–1626) proclaimed himself emperor of north Manchuria and set up his capital at Mukden (now Shenyang). When he died in 1626, he had laid the foundations of Manchu power. His immediate successor, his ninth son, Abahai, proclaimed the "Great Pure" (Ch'ing) dynasty in 1636.

The Manchus seized Beijing in 1644. But it was not until 1683 that the Manchus were able to complete the subjugation of the entire country. The Manchus did not claim any revolution. They came to Beijing, announcing to suppress the anti-Ming rebels and secure for China peace and order. This persuaded most local officials in the North to accept the new dynasty. The transition from the Ming to the Ch'ing had little effects on the basic structure of Chinese society at the local level. Local society functioned according to its traditional mechanisms. To preserve ethnic identity, the Manchus banned intermarriage between Chinese and Manchus. The Manchus were not engaged in commerce or in common labor.

The Manchus wanted to govern the entire China, and at the same time to maintain their own political, military, and social identity as a dominant alien minority. They might be absorbed or overthrown by China's millions. Manchus constituted about 2% of the population of the empire, just enough to provide the imperial clan, the top supervisors, and garrisons for China. The Ch'ing regime was from the beginning not purely Manchu but a Manchu–Chinese synthesis. To maintain their power, the Manchus made concessions to Chinese institutions and accepted (many aspects of) the Chinese way of life. They ruled China in the Chinese way with the co-operation of the Chinese, even though they maintained secret service systems to protect their own dominant position. The state bureaucracy was fairly small and extended only down to the county level. It did not penetrate into the countryside. Control over rural areas was usually maintained via a process of negotiation between county magistrates and local leaders. The three ingredients of the Ch'ing rule were ultimate military force, ultimate political power, and Manchu supervision of Chinese collaborators in the administration. They maintained power by obtaining the support of the Mongols, the co-operation of the Chinese elite, and the tacit assent of the Chinese populace.

Administration during the Ch'ing dynasty was supervised by six ministries (Six Boards) responsible for personnel administration, revenue, rites and rituals, war, justice, and public works. The Six Ministries each had two presidents, one Chinese and one Manchu, and four vice presidents, two Manchu's and two Chinese. The Ch'ing completed the dual control system by appointing equal numbers of Manchus and Chinese to the Board of Censors. China was divided into 18 provinces, which were under the control of governors-general and governors. There was also a racial balance of power. When a Manchu was appointed governor-general, the governors under him were usually Chinese, and vice versa. Provincial governors, under the direct control of the emperor, had a large measure of autonomy. The rule of avoidance required that the officials had to supervise provinces other than those in which they were born and raised. The rule of circulation demanded that the officials were frequently transferred and scrambled in different mixes in order to avoid the development of permanent cliques or alliances between officials and the local upper class.

Nuerhachi and his immediate successor, his ninth son, Abahai, promoted the study of Chinese and utilized Confucianism as the state's ideology. Chinese Confucianism promotes individual self-control and dutiful conduct to one's superiors. The Manchu dynasty used traditional Chinese culture to rule and administer China. The Ch'ing scholars were mainly concerned with the Chinese cultural heritage; they created no new standards of thought or major schools of philosophy. They were careful interpreters and diligent editors of traditional learning. The Manchus used Neo-Confucianism as state ideology to win control over the intellectuals, the habitual ruling class in China, and through them the people. Emperor Kangxi's Sacred Edict of Sixteen Maxims was to be read by all subjects, and was full of supposedly Confucian ideas of loyalty, obedience, duty, morality, and propriety. The Manchu turned Confucianism from a code of ethics into a system of thought control. Chinese scholars had reviewed written history and literature to bring together great works of art under the pressure of the Manchu. But the Manchus' real purpose was to screen out anything critical or disagreeable and then burn it. Scholarship was especially dangerous under emperors Yongcheng and Qianlong, both of whom carried out mass censorship of intellectuals. The great "art patron" Qianlong destroyed some 2600 titles. Since then, scholars in China avoided dangerous subjects such as politics and economics. The Manchu book-burners and witch-hunters were still much in power as an institution by the end of the nineteenth century. Under Manchu control, the Chinese had lost the ability to think, not to mention the inability to properly appreciate Confucianism.

In most areas of governmental and intellectual organization, the Manchus followed Chinese precedents. Political life was monopolized by the bureaucracy so that the Chinese masses had little to do with it in any case. The imperial government was confined to the upper layer of society and was not present in the villages. Society as a whole was connected not by communications but through orders from the top down. The common Chinese had little sense of duty towards national development or racial identification. The Manchus developed a very sophisticated controlling network over the whole society. The situations were vividly described by

Williams, an American missionary long resident in China, in 1895 (Grieder, 1981) as follows:

> The great leading principles by which the present administration preserves its power over the people, consist in a system of strict surveillance and mutual responsibility among all classes … . It is like a network extending over the whole face of society, each individual being isolated in his own mesh, but responsibly connected with all around him. … The effect … upon the masses of the people is to imbue them with a great fear of government, both of its officers and its operations; each man considers that safety is best to be found in keeping aloof from both. This mutual surveillance and responsibility, though only partially extended throughout the multitude, necessarily undermines confidence and infuses universal distrust, while the object of complete isolation, though at the expense of justice, truth, honesty, and natural affection, is what the government strives to accomplish and actually does to a wonderful degree. The idea of government in the minds of the uneducated people is that of some ever-present terror. … Thus, with a state of society sometimes on the verge of insurrection, this mass of people is kept by check by the threefold cord of responsibility, fear and isolation.

In the eighteenth century, Chinese contact with the West was limited to commerce through the port of Guangzhou under the Canton System. By the 1820s, the expansion of the Chinese market for opium reversed the balance of trade. By 1828, opium was responsible for 90% of the value of all foreign goods imported to China. By 1834, opium accounted for 51% of British imports into China. The situation was becoming intolerable for China. In 1839, the imperial court decided to enforce a ban on opium. In March 1839, an imperial commissioner, Lin Zexu, arrived at Guangzhou. Lin demanded the foreigners to hand over all the opium, over two million pounds, which they had stored in Guangzhou. The British merchants saw this demand as being unjust and refused to hand over the contraband drug. Lin then put them under house arrest. Eventually, the merchants gave in and Lin then destroyed the opium. The British insisted on their right to sell opium in China in the name of free trade. They used these efforts as an excuse for war and expansion in China. The conflict led to the Opium War (1839–1842) in which China was defeated. The defeat led to the first of many unequal treaties forced on China. Manchu prestige was greatly reduced by the defeat in the war. Between 1826 and 1850, there were frequent floods in many of the regions along the valleys of the Yellow and Yangzi rivers. In the 1840s, there were serious famines in south China and unrest in almost every part of the country. In the 1860s, British and French forces burned the summer palace. Since then Manchu power slowly concentrated in the hands of Empress Dowager, who plotted her way to the top and prevented the reform efforts of a few officials. She was concerned with consolidating her own power, wealth, family, and the Manchu dynasty against political opponents. She was not sympathetic to modernization. China's defeat in war at the hands of Japan in 1894–1895 further stimulated foreign interests in the partitioning of China. At the dawn of the twentieth century, the dynasty made a serious attempt of implementing reforms of Chinese institutions. However, the timing was poor. The dowager urged a full-scale return to traditional ways to solve China's problems, in the hope of avoiding the collapse of the Manchu rule. The last-minute efforts of the Manchu rulers to save themselves failed miserably. The Empress died in 1908. The 2-year-old Emperor Puyi ascended the throne. The power of the central government rapidly diminished. In 1911, an army coup in Wuhan seized the control of the city and the heads of many other provinces declared their loyalty to the revolutionaries. The revolution of 1911 toppled the Ch'ing dynasty.

2.3 Taiwan Under the Manchus

After 1683, Taiwan became a prefecture (*fu*) of Fukien Province of the Ch'ing dynasty. In the early years after the Ch'ing court took over Taiwan, it had no strong intention to be extensively involved in Taiwan. It only adopted regressive policy stances in defense and prohibition of immigration. Public affairs were mainly handled by the local elites. Although the Ch'ing emperor claimed ownership of all land in the island, tenure rights were granted to his subjects as long as they paid taxes. Tenant farmers of the Cheng family and its lords became owners of the land that they had possessed during the Cheng period. It was free for landowners to transmit landownership to their sons and to sell and purchase land in the Ch'ing period. If peasants became tenants to landlords, they were bound by a commercial contract (Ka, 1995: 16). Distribution of land was relatively even in the mid-1680s. The land tax on the peasants was lighter during the Ch'ing period than during Dutch and Cheng rule. Economic activities were carried out under quasi-public and market-oriented mechanisms. People from different birthplaces enjoyed co-operative relationships partially because of easily available land and "loose" human networks.

As virgin lands were widely available, Taiwan was a pure market-oriented agricultural economy in transactions of land, capital, and labor. As population increased and paddy-rice farming technology became care-intensive, local political and economic powers became more consolidated, based on the landed economy.

In the early years of Manchu control, Taiwan saw much higher levels of social uprisings. As argued by Shepherd (1993), because these uprisings did not seem to threaten imperial control over Taiwan, the government would not make direct and full-scale intervention based on the rationale of minimizing costs. It was difficult for the Ch'ing court to extend effective authority over the remote island. In order to maintain social stability on the island with a rebel tradition, the Ch'ing did not encourage the island to develop. Residents in Taiwan were not eligible for official position and military service. The Ch'ing court directly sent the army and officials from the mainland in rotation for short periods. Chinese immigration was forbidden until 1875. The government also restricted trade between Taiwan and the mainland. Despite these restrictions, there was large-scale illegal Chinese immigration from the mainland.

From the seventeenth century onwards, immigrants from the mainland began to settle in Taiwan. Toward the end of the seventeenth century, Chinese peasants began to migrate to Taiwan in large numbers. In the next two centuries, population, cultivated land, and output increased slowly but steadily. The immigrants brought with them the techniques used for the cultivation of rice and sugarcane. These crops became the major products for local consumption and export. In 1811, the *pao-chia* system of mutual responsibility, holding both the village and the family responsible for the conduct of their members, was introduced to Taiwan. The system required each household to register its members. In the 1811 registration, a Chinese population of 2,003,861 was recorded. Table 2.1 shows the Chinese population and cultivated land in Taiwan for the period 1650–1905. Table 2.1 is based on the estimation made by Ho (1978). As shown in Table 2.1, the population of Taiwan increased dramatically from 1650 to 1905. These increases were mainly due to immigration from Mainland China. Large-scale immigration from Mainland China started from the early eighteenth century. Before Taiwan became a Japanese colony, it had already been a society composed mainly of descendants of mainland immigrants and a small percentage of the indigenous population. Chinese immigrants

Table 2.1. The Chinese population and cultivated land in Taiwan

	ca. 1650	ca. 1680	1811	1887
The population	100,000	200,000–350,000	2,003,000	3,200,000
Cultivated land (ha)	7187	17,898	–	350,575

mainly came from Kwangtung and Fukien. During the 1730s, the rapid increase of population led to the adoption of more care-intensive type of paddy-rice farming. Double cropping in paddy-rice farming began to spread. There was also a significant increase of irrigation facilities and the adoption of wide varieties of seeds. The care-intensive type of paddy-rice farming prevailed widely after the 1780s. Most immigrants were quite mobile and did not have strong incentives to become sedentary. Moreover, ethical or family lines tend to co-operate among themselves in the alien environment. There was frequent co-operation among different ethnic groups in land reclamation. Partially because of the government's restrictions on marine transportation and immigration, during the seventeenth and the first half of the eighteenth century, the Chinese population remained predominantly one of male settlers without family ties. Household network organizations in Taiwan were neither extensive nor well organized.

In the late 1780s, most of the island's lowland areas or better lands in the west and north were fully opened. The increase in population and limited land enforced the adoption of the more intensive farming methods and strengthened competition for land, water, and other limited resources. Social rivalry was becoming more intensive. The increase of care-intensity in farming activities tended to result in smaller-size family farms. Moreover, the declining availability of land made inheritance the major source of access to land. As population pressure increased and resources became less available, the cohesiveness of local groups and local discord increased. Family or household network groups became increasingly important for economic security and resource sharing.

The care-intensive type of paddy-rice farming had significant implications for how economic transactions and human relations were arranged. Because of the scarcity of easily convertible land, Taiwan had to rely heavily on household networks for engaging in economic activities. Members of the family were engaged in care-intensive type of paddy-rice farming. They shared the common concern about benefits, costs, and insecurity of the family. The family was generally blood-based. Filial piety was the basis of Taiwanese social organization. There was a cluster of norms based on filial piety about relationships between the children and their parents in the Chinese family. Children should please, follow, and support their parents while the latter are alive, and should mourn and ritually serve them after death. A Chinese proverb says: "people rear sons to provide for old age." The filial piety in Taiwan means serving and "obeying" one's parents.

The traditional Chinese household in South China was characterized as an extended family. Chinese immigrants brought this institution to Taiwan. The household was a decision-making and basic survival unit that was economically, socially, and politically self-sufficient. All members of the family had to pool their economic resources and share security with other family members. In particular, male members of the household gave their first loyalty to their own family instead of other social institutions. In general, socio-economic performance would make almost no attribute for one to be included or excluded from the same family. The head of the family (i.e. father) was ideally an absolute autocrat within the family. The male descendants of the same generation had equal rights within the family hierarchy. Because of the unchallenged power, the authority of the household head tended to be personalistic, unpredictable, and less obligatory. The Chinese household tended to last no more than one generation. When the household head passed away, sons divided the family estate on an equal basis. The original family was terminated. Rights and obligations were equally distributed among the branches of the original family. The newly formed families were not obliged to maintain mutual support for each other. Outside of the family, the traditional Chinese tended to be opportunistic and prone to establishing human networks on calculations of the benefits and costs of social and economic exchange.

Taiwan's economy was based on traditional agriculture. The economy was not highly integrated or commercialized. In the middle of the nineteenth century, Taiwan was opened to foreign trade only through the treaty ports. Taiwan was opened to the world market after the imperial powers imposed on China the treaties of T'ien-chin (1858) and Peking (1860). After 1878, export of camphor, tea, and sugar was increased. About 20% of the population was engaged in export-oriented production. European and American merchants came to Taiwan to buy camphor, tea, and sugar and to sell manufactured goods. Penetration of foreign capital and expansion of the market brought about structural changes in Taiwan's economy. For instance, by the end of the late nineteenth century, sugarcane was crushed by stone mills (worked by two or three buffaloes) and each mill was set up and jointly owned by farmers to produce their own produce. However, in the late nineteenth century, sugarcane milling was steadily taken away from sugarcane growers by mills set up with foreign merchants and big landowners. The extending market and growing production increased the growth of multiple and large-scale economies. These developments enabled a few merchants to monopolize trading, money lending, milling, and land-intensive activities. In 1887, in response to the French threat to Taiwan, the Manchu government upgraded Taiwan from a prefecture to a province. A capable official, Liu Ming-chuan, was appointed its governor (1886–1891). He implemented many institutional changes. Immigration was encouraged. From 1884 to 1891, the government subsidized immigrants' travel expenses across the Taiwan Strait. In 1887, it was estimated that there were 3,200,000 Chinese on the island. To control Taiwan, Governor Liu reinforced the *parochial* system. The household registration system enabled the government to conduct a thorough cadastral survey that disclosed tax evasion. Nevertheless, Liu's reform failed to help him to get the support of the local powerful groups. He was finally dismissed in 1891 (Ka, 1995: 34).

Since the late 1860s, the Ch'ing court became more involved in public affairs in Taiwan. The administrative efforts of the court were significantly increased. It tried to incorporate and suppress strong local household network groups through divide-and-rule policies or direct threat of severe penalty. The imperial court also began to offer Taiwan a higher quota of official degrees allotted for Taiwan's young scholars and to increase the grant of other economic or commercial privileges (Wang, 1998: 90). Instead of mobilizing their resources and sharing security in structural and consolidated ways, local household network groups started to interact upward with the state or with other elite of similar social and political standings. They tended to highly appreciate degrees, positions, and privileges granted by the state. They also began to build various economic and political relations, particularly based on marriage ties, among the gentry class itself.

In more than 200 years it governed Taiwan, the Manchu government showed little interest in developing Taiwan. Nevertheless, Taiwan experienced some economic changes within a traditional Chinese context. Population grew steadily and more areas were brought under cultivation. It did not have an integrated transport system and national economy was not well integrated. Although the population increased, per capita income did not increase. The only significant attempt by the government to promote economic development was made by a few enlightened officials by the end of the nineteenth century. They recognized the need to modernize Taiwan. Liu Ming-Chuan initiated numerous economic projects such as the construction of a north–south railroad, the laying of a cable line from Taiwan to Fukien, the dredging of Keelung and Kaohsiung harbors, a cadastral survey of the island, the establishment of a shipping company, and the revival of the coal industry (Ho, 1978: 23). The 8 years of Liu's administration (1884–91) represented the only serious effort by the Manchu government to modernize the island. However, the projects initiated by Liu were only partially completed. Peking offered neither political nor financial support to Liu's ambitions. All of Liu's projects could not be completed under the Manchu government; the Japanese eventually completed all of his projects.

2.3 Taiwan Under Japanese Colonial Rule

The Japanese arrived in Taiwan on May 29, 1885, after defeating the Chinese in the Sino-Japanese War of 1895. In the middle of the nineteenth century, Japan was forced to open its doors to foreign trade and establish diplomatic relations with the Western powers, which had already achieved structural changes from agricultural economies to industrial ones. In contrast to China, a milder foreign challenge provoked a stronger domestic response in Japan. During the early Meiji era, foreign pressure on Japan was relatively weak. By 1868, the Western powers had got what they mainly wanted from Japan and Japan ceased to be much of a problem in their eyes. No foreign wars or outside interventions threatened Japan. In the early Meiji era, the government tried its best to avoid foreign conflicts, partly because of its relative weakness. Aggressive pursuit of Japan's interests was combined with a strong sense of restraint. In the 1880s, military and political progress made many Japanese feel the need for a more positive and aggressive foreign policy. But around this time Japan had little need of an economic colony because its own modern industries were still in their infancy. As industrialization progressed, Japan felt the urge to build a colonial empire in order to secure raw materials, new markets, or overseas investment opportunities. Viewing the colonization process and its profits, Japanese leaders wanted to engage in an aggressive, expansionist policy abroad. In 1875, the government decided to open Korea as the Americans had opened Japan earlier. Traditionally, Korea had been a tribute state of the Ch'ing dynasty. Except for some regular tribute missions to Beijing, the Koreans had little interaction with the outside world. In 1875, the Japanese sent a gunboat expedition to Korea. They forced the Koreans to accept the same kind of unequal treaty system that they tried to shed themselves. The Treaty of Kangwha, signed in January 1876, opened a number of ports to trade and gave the Japanese certain extraterritorial rights in the new treaty ports. By the early 1890s, the Japanese army wanted Korea free from Chinese rule and firmly under Japanese domination. The competition for power over Korea between the declining Ch'ing dynasty and the burgeoning new Japan resulted in the Sino-Japanese War of 1894–1895. Through this war, the tiny Japanese island kingdom showed the world the results of its efforts to build national wealth and strength. The great Ch'ing empire was forced to admit defeat. The peace terms exacted by the Japanese in the Treaty of Shimonoseki, signed in April 1895, included that the Ch'ing (1) recognized the independence of Korea; (2) ceded to Japan the territories of Taiwan and the Pescadores Islands; (3) ceded control over the Liaotung peninsula; (4) agreed to pay an indemnity of 364 million *yen*; and (5) agreed to a commercial treaty that gave Japan the same extraterritorial rights and most-favored status that the European powers enjoyed.

Different from the Dutch, whose only purpose was to enrich themselves through trade, Japan ruled Taiwan directly. Japan wanted Taiwan to become its agricultural colony to supply food and a market for Japanese industrial products. In early years, the Japanese did not have sufficient economic and military means to maintain order in Taiwan. It took them 8 years to fully control Taiwan (Kerr, 1974). Taiwan became a heavy burden on Japan's budget in the early colonial period. During the period 1895–1902, the subsidies to Taiwan's military expenses and civil administration amounted to 7% of Japan's government expenditure budget. The financial burden of the military rule made the Japanese public to favor the sale of Taiwan to any available buyer, such as China. To reduce the financial burden on Japan, the colonial government came to rely heavily on the land tax in Taiwan. In 1896, the colonial government guaranteed protection to owners of land rights to make them report their land possessions and carry out their tax obligation. Until 1898, the colonial government devoted most of its energy to military suppression. Between 1898 and 1906, the government adopted policies that led to financial independence for the colony and a suitable environment for economic growth. It also monopolized the production and sale of opium and camphor. Net profits from the production and sale of opium were huge from 1898 to 1907 (Ka, 1995: 54). By 1905, the central government no longer subsidized Taiwan's civil administration.

The Japanese colonial government adopted highly centralized control and dominance. Under the auspices of the colonial government, farmer associations and rural credit associations were established to provide technical assistance and financial services (Gold, 1988: 104–9). The colonial government strictly controlled the economy. Financial institutions under its control were set up to absorb the capital earned by indigenous landlords and entrepreneurs. These capitals were invested in the mostly Japanese-controlled industries in Taiwan or in Japan. The huge amount of capital accumulated did not improve the economic security of the Taiwanese economic elite. Lacking the institutional trust, most of the Taiwanese elite had to rely on friends or family members. In the early years of colonization, there was a rapid development of lineage network groups for pooling resources and sharing economic security. However, the Japanese soon recognized the political implications of such lineage networks and made attempts to stop their further development. The Japanese colonial policy and public administration weakened the traditional patterns of social and economic interactions between both intra- and interhousehold network groups. The Japanese controlled Taiwan through garrison troops, the education system, and the traditional Chinese form of a neighborhood collective responsibility system (called *pao-jia*). They established an efficient administrative apparatus for managing the island. They surveyed the population and land, standardized measurements and the monetary system, and established monopolies for trading and manufacturing goods. In the *pao-jia* system, all members of the neighborhood were held correctively responsible for local security. If one member of the neighborhood was found guilty of a crime, all members of the neighborhood were punished. The Japanese forced all schools to use the Japanese language. By 1950s, most Taiwanese elites fluently spoke both Japanese and Taiwanese. Many Taiwanese accepted Japanese values, dresses, and manners. Some Taiwanese adopted Japanese surnames. The Japanese included many Taiwanese into the colonial bureaucracy (Bullard, 1997: 40).

By the time the Japanese began to occupy Taiwan, Chinese settlers had occupied plains and established a booming agrarian economy producing rice and sugar. In the course of half a century of colonial rule, Taiwan became a food supplier in a new division of labor with Japan. The transition from a neglected Chinese province to a Japanese colony brought about an economic structural change from a closed economy to an open one. As a part of the progressive Japanese economy, colonization brought a substantial inflow of material, human capital, and technology. During the colonial period, the productive capacity was expanded. Different from the Manchu government that controlled a large territory with rich resources, the colonial government was keen about developing Taiwan as a part of its own resource-poor island. As shown in Table 2.2, which is based on Ho (1978: 27), Taiwan experienced economic growth and structural change during the colonial period. The first Japanese census conducted in 1905 recorded 2,899,458 Chinese (excluding Japanese and aborigines) on the island, among whom 2,492,784 came from Fukien, 397,195 from Kwangtung, and only 506 from other parts of Mainland China. From 1910 to 1940, Taiwan experienced growth in total product and population. Between 1906 and 1943, the death rate was reduced from 31.3 to 17.6 deaths per 1000 and the birth rate was almost constant, about 40 births per 1000. The growth rate of per capita output was approximately 19% per decade during the colonial period. The agricultural sector employed

Table 2.2 Taiwan's economic development, 1910–1940

	Population (million)	Net domestic product (1937 = 100)	Export volume index (1925 = 100)	Import volume index (1925 = 100)
1910	3.29	37	39	49
1920	3.66	40	44	68
1930	4.59	79	122	136
1940	5.87	93	196	172

about 70% of the total labor force, while the non-agricultural sector employed 30%. During the colonial period, Taiwan's economic growth was mainly owing to the development of agriculture; Taiwan's industry, except food processing, experienced almost no change. To integrate Taiwan's social and economic systems within Taiwan and with Japan, an efficient transport system was developed within Taiwan and between Taiwan and Japan.

In early years of the occupation, the Japanese public criticized the colony as a luxury and proposed selling Taiwan. However, it did not take long for the Japanese to recognize that Taiwan's economy could be developed as a part of Japan's economy. Japanese capitalists hesitated to invest in Taiwan because of limited resources or unfavorable conditions for investment. To improve investment conditions and speed up economic growth of the colony, the colonial state improved infrastructure. The Japanese decided to build extensive and expensive infrastructure to improve investment conditions in Taiwan. The colonial government invested heavily in various types of island-wide social infrastructures (e.g. the provision of social order and public health) and physical infrastructures (e.g. transportation, communication, and rural infrastructures such as harbor improvement, electricity, roads, irrigation, and energy supply systems). Japanese colonization introduced an integrated market in Taiwan. Railways, telegraphs, telephones, and the adoption of market reforms speeded up market integration. The colonial government emphasized the development of transport and communication, allocating about 40–60% of its developmental expenditures and fixed investment to this sector. When the Japanese arrived at Taiwan, the island had almost no roads or railways. By 1908, the two important ports, Keelung and Kaohsiung, were connected by rail. The Japanese also introduced modern banking and financial institutions. By the late 1920s, five modern banks with more than 50 branch offices were serving Taiwan (Ho, 1978: 29). In 1920, it had 637 km of public railways and 3553 km of roads and in 1940, 907 and 12,076 km, respectively. The Japanese government also paid great attention to human resources. During the colonial period, the average life span of Taiwanese increased significantly. The literacy rate, which was measured by the ability to read and/or write Japanese, among Taiwanese raised from 1% in 1905 to 12% in 1930 and 27% in 1940 (Ho, 1978: 33–5).

To make Taiwan a profitable colony, the colonial government was responsible for improving productivity and retaining direct control over the economy. It abolished the first-tier land rent and introduced modern farming technology such as the adoption of new varieties of crops and fertilizers. Under the guidance of the colonial government, the island was developed as an agricultural appendage to Japan. Initially, the Japanese Empire wanted to develop Taiwan into a sugar producer. When taking over Taiwan, the Japanese found that the structure of small-scale family farms within a layered network of tenancy relations was not suitable for establishing large-scale sugar plantations. The colonial government decided to use small-scale cultivators to supply cane to Japanese-owned refineries. Family farming persisted in Taiwan even under colonial rule. However, the industrial boom around the time of World War I increased the demand for rice in Japan. This led the Japanese Empire to develop plans to expand the role of imports of rice from Taiwan and Korea. The cultivation of Japanese-style rice in the two colonies was promoted. Imports from the two colonies increased from around 5% of domestic production in 1900 to over 20% by the 1930s (Francks, 1999: 74). Taiwanese farmers had to supply more rice to meet increased demand. Japan extracted substantial profits from the island through a triangular relationship connecting Taiwan's agricultural and non-agricultural sectors and Japan's economy. Taiwan's agricultural sector exported rice and sugar to Japan, and its non-agricultural sector imported Japanese manufactured goods to sell, along with commercial services, to the agricultural sector. Taiwan's economy became more productive and commercialized through the colonial government's efforts. By the 1930s, Taiwan became an open and dualistic economy with a large peasant agriculture existing side by side with a small, modern, non-agricultural sector. Since the government helped the agricultural sector with technological change and management, the two sectors were not isolated from each other. The agricultural sector often received new inputs and advanced technology from the non-agricultural sector. The sector already started modernization in the colonial period.

2.4 Taiwan was Returned to the Chinese on October 25, 1945

At the Cairo Conference of December 1943 and at the Potsdam Conference of July 1945, it was agreed that following the defeat of Japan,

Taiwan would be returned to China. As Chiang Kai-shek and the KMT were internationally accepted as governing the Republic of China, it was to KMT forces that the Japanese formally surrendered control of Taiwan on October 25, 1945. Most of the colonial officials, soldiers, and residents were repatriated to Japan soon after. The KMT military administration on the island initially "plundered" the island for valuables to support its battle with the communists on the mainland. When it reigned over both the mainland and the island, the KMT treated brutally the people both on the island and in the mainland. After it lost the mainland to the communists in 1949 and escaped to the island, it had to modify its behavior. When reigning over the mainland, the KMT could survive by plundering people. Nevertheless, after having lost the mainland to the communists, the KMT could no longer survive on the island without rapid economic development. For mere survival, the KMT had to be concerned with rapid economic development.

Chapter 3

Government and Democratization

> Do not regard seniority but advance the worthy and able; dismiss the incompetent and incapable without delay; ... develop the common people without waiting to compel them by laws. ... Yet, although a man be the descendant of a king, duke, prefect, or office, if he does not observe the rules of proper conduct and justice, he must be relegated to the common ranks.
>
> *Hsün Tzu (298–238 BC)*

The KMT was corrupt and disregarded people's livelihood when ruling the mainland and the island. The defeat of the KMT government by the communist Red Army was a lesson to the KMT leadership. The KMT was compelled to listen to what Mencius taught the Chinese more than 2000 years ago: "The carrying out his kindly heart by a prince will suffice for the love and protection of all within the four seas, and if he does not carry it out, he will not be able to protect his wife and children. The way in which the ancients came greatly to surpass other men, was no other than this: simply that they knew well how carry out, so as to affect others, what they themselves did." The KMT was aware that it was defeated by the communists not because of weak military capacity but because of the corruption within. Having lost power over the mainland, the KMT had to improve economic efficiency and morality in the resourceless island for survival. But China's modern history records that the winner of the Chinese civil wars, Chairman Mao, thrust the Mainland Chinese into abject poverty. The KMT would teach the Chinese Communist Party (CCP) how to manage a modern Chinese economic system 30 years after the CCP had driven the KMT to the island.

One might wonder how the KMT, having failed in its efforts to rebuild Mainland China from the early 1920s to the late 1940s, could be successful in modernizing Taiwan. What Mencius commended lends a helping hand to clarifying the behavior of the KMT after being defeated by the communists. When King Hui of Liang (who suffered from the shame of being defeated by Qin and Chu) consulted Mencius about how to protect his state from invasions of Qin and Chu, Mencius replied:

> With a territory which is only a hundred li square, it is possible to attain the Imperial dignity. If your Majesty will indeed dispense a benevolent government to the people, being sparing in the use of punishments and fines, and making the taxes and levies light, so causing that the fields shall be ploughed deep, and the weeding of them be carefully attended to, and that the strong-bodied, during their days of leisure, shall cultivate their filial piety, fraternal respectfulness, sincerity and trustfulness, serving thereby, at home, their fathers and elder brothers, and, abroad, their elders and superiors—you will then have a people who can be employed, with sticks which they have prepared, to oppose the strong mail and sharp weapons of the troops of Qin and Chu. The rulers of those states, rob their people of their time, so that they cannot plough and weed their fields, in order to support their parents. ... Those rulers, as it were, drive their people into pit-falls, or drown them. Your Majesty will go to punish them. In such a case, who will oppose your Majesty? In accordance with this is the saying, "The benevolent has no enemy."

Given the island's limited resources and incessant threats from the CCP, the KMT, which was mainly composed of "foreigners" in the early years of its settlement in Taiwan, had to change its governing strategy. According to Confucianism, to conduct benevolent policy is an optimal way for the new immigrants to make a living on the island.

3.1 The Confucian Ideal Government: The Government for the People

> If a truly royal ruler were to arise, it would still require a generation, and then virtue would prevail.
>
> *Confucius*

To apprehend the Chinese, at least educated Chinese, one needs to know the Confucian ideal and possible implications of the ideal for modernization of Chinese societies. The dominant theme in Confucian political ideology is not power but ethics. The rationale for the existence of the state is not to serve some personalized God or concrete ideology. The state is seen as a mechanism for maintaining moral order and securing people's living conditions. The government is not a means to use people for some special purpose. It is a body of organizations whose end is to serve the people. The ruler's duty is to work for the welfare of the people. Confucius maintains that the best policy of the government is to maintain peace and establish order in society. He proposes five methods—respecting people's business and sincerity, loving people, taxing properly, and operating economically—for the government to win the trust of the people and make them contented and tranquil. People obey the ruler only if the ruler behaves in a proper way. If the ruler fails to behave in a just way toward the people, the ruler's authority should be rejected.

In Confucian tradition, the essential purpose of government is to promote welfare of the people, not to serve the special interests of any minority or a special group of power holders. A ruler is good only when he can and will enjoy (suffer) when his people enjoy (suffer). It is the duty of government to provide benevolent policies. On the other hand, it is the duty of people to carry out their tasks. "The people are the most important element in a nation"; assures Mencius, "the spirits of the land and grain are the next; the sovereign is the lightest." The duty of the state is not to order people to do what it desires, but to provide people what they desire. The government should behave in such a way that the people's welfare is improved. "There is a way," Mencius, points out, "to get the empire; get the people, and the empire is got. There is a way to get the people; get their hearts, and the people are got. There is a way to get their hearts; it is simply to collect for them what they like, and not to lay on them what they dislike." We may argue that democracy in modern times is to establish such a government. Regarding the happiness of the people as the most important business of society and thinking of the love of the people as the way to hold power, Confucian tradition holds that society should not be ruled by force but operated in the kingly way or the way of moral power. "When one by force subdues men," assures Mencius, "they do not submit to him in heart. They submit because their strength is not adequate to resist. When one subdues men by virtue, in their hearts' core they are pleased, and sincerely submit, as was the case with the seventy disciples in their submission to Confucius." Since a good government takes the welfare of its people as the main purpose of governing, society under such a government should attract people from both near and far away. Confucius said: "Good government obtains," "when those who are near are made happy, and those who are far are attracted." The goodness of the government is judged by its people's happiness and other people's feet. We read from the *Book of Rites*, a Confucian classic, "Through the perception of right produced by ceremony, come the degrees of the noble and the mean; through the union of culture arising from music, harmony between high and low. By the exhibition of what is to be liked and what is to be disliked, a distinction is made between the worthy and unworthy. When violence is prevented by punishments, and the worthy are raised to rank, the operation of government was made impartial. Then come benevolence in the love of the people, and righteousness in the correction of their errors; and in this way good government held its course." Once, Fan Chi asked Confucius about benevolence. Confucius replied: "It is to love all men." He then asked about knowledge, to which Confucius replied: "It is to know all men." Fan Chi wondered what Confucius meant by these answers. Confucius further explained: "Employ the upright and put aside all the crooked—in this way, the crooked can be made to be upright." Fan Chi still could not understand Confucius and then asked Zixia about what the master meant. Zixia replied: "Truly rich is his saying! Shun, being in possession of the empire, selected from among all the people and employed Gaoyao, on which all who devoid of virtue disappeared. Tang, being in possession of the empire, selected from among all the people, and employed Yiyin, and all who were devoid of virtue disappeared." In Confucian tradition, it is through establishing good tradition and selecting benevolent politicians to important positions that a country can become civilized.

3.2 Sun Yat-sen's Three Principles of the People

> The faults of men are characteristic of the class to which they belong. By observing a man's faults, it may be known what kind of man he is.
>
> *Confucius*

Sun Yat-sen (1866–1925) was a Cantonese raised in Hawaii and Hong Kong. He spent his entire life in a period of chaos. Having been brought up along the coastal province and in overseas Chinese communities, he developed an open mind acceptable to different ideas. He was also well informed about the modern Western world. His own ideas had profound influences on Taiwan's political socialization and modernization. Although his proposals were sketched for the entire China, his political, social, and economic doctrines found fertile soil on the island after the KMT had been defeated in the mainland.

Sun Yat-sen is often called a muddled politician, an opportunist with generous but confused ideas, a theorist without great originality or intellectual rigor (Bergère, 1998). However, he is recognized as a Founding Father by both the CCP and the KMT in Taipei and Beijing. This queer situation reflects the intellectual poverty of the Chinese in modern times. A reason for both the CCP and the KMT to identify the same father with confused ideas is given by Dr Sun's own sayings: "The Chinese revolution cannot be said to aim at liberty. The individual should not have too much liberty, but the nation must have complete liberty of action" (Barlow, 1987: 87). The reality may not be fully explained by a theory, but an acclaimed founder should not have a messy mind for national construction. "I know," states Confucius, "how it is that the path of the Mean is not walked in: The Knowing go beyond it, and the stupid do not come up to it. I know how it is that the path of the Mean is not understood: The men of talents and virtue go beyond it, and the worthless do not come up to it. Everyone eats and drinks. But there are few who can distinguish flavors."

In 1894, Sun Yat-sen founded the Revive China society in Hawaii. In October 1895, the society attempted its first uprising in Canton. It tried other risings in South China. In 1905, Dr Sun and other nationalists formed the Alliance Society. The successful uprising in Wuchang led to the fall of the Ch'ing dynasty in 1911. However, Dr Sun and his supporters were not strong enough to seize power. The fall of the Ch'ing dynasty gave way to a warlord era, which was characterized by decentralization of political power and lack of effective leadership. There was no clear way of actualizing political legitimacy. Political power passed into the hands of military men or those who could hire them. The revolutionaries lost power within the framework of the republic government to the opportunistic Yuan Shikai, the leading general of the new armies of the late Ch'ing. In 1912, Yuan became the president of the republic. He tried to govern the country through his ties to military subordinates around the country, but his power was not strong. In 1915, he declared his intention to become emperor, which obtained little support and led to immediate rebellion. Yuan died a few months later. Immediately after Yuan's sudden death in 1916, political power passed into the hands of the warlords. There was no real political center after the death of Yuan.

The Russian Revolution and the communist movements in Europe at the close of World War I brought the Marxism–Leninism outlook to the attention of Chinese activities and convinced them of its truth and inevitable triumph. In the 1920s, Marxism became the pre-eminent outlook of Chinese thinkers and revolutionaries. The KMT was founded in 1912, but banned in 1913. Dr Sun restarted it in October 1919. On January 1, 1923, he issued a Nationalist Party manifesto, based on his *Three Principles of the People: Nationalism, Democracy, and the People's Livelihood*. Nevertheless, at this time the party organization was still weak. The situation was changed in the next 2 years with Soviet aid. After the first KMT Congress in January 1924, the KMT followed Soviet organizational principles, which helped Chiang Kai-shek and the future leadership of Taiwan to consolidate extensive powers. Dr Sun died on March 12, 1925. After his death, his military commander, Chiang Kai-shek, took control of the KMT. The rise of Chiang Kai-shek became the most important factor in the development of the KMT after Sun's death. Chiang Kai-shek was a master of the subtle art of political maneuvering. He applied the traditional Chinese methods to maintain power, building up a network of client relationships based on loyalty to himself while encouraging rivalry between his subordinates. He manipulated the cliques not only within the party and the military, but also within the civil service and the business community.

Sun establishes a 'theoretical' basis and practical programs for China's modernization. He designs the process as follows: (1) in the first phase of modernizing China, revolution would be carried out and power might be acquired by military means; (2) in the second phase, called the period of political tutelage, all Chinese peoples would be taught democratic ideology; and (3) in the third phase, constitutional democracy would be established. In reality, the first phase was not completed until 1949. Many leaders in Taiwan viewed the period after 1950 as a "Period of Political Tutelage." This period lasted until 1991, when the Constitution was placed into full effect by terminating "Temporary Provisions Effective During the Period of Mobilization for the Suppression of the Communist

Rebellion." Dr Sun highly valued nationalism because he was living in a time when (Sun, 1983: 5–6):

> The Chinese people have only family and clan groups; there is no national spirit. Consequently, in spite of four hundred million people gathered together in one China, we are in fact but a sheet of loose sand. We are the poorest and weakest state in the world, occupying the lowest position in international affairs; the rest of mankind is the carving knife and the serving dish, while we are the fish and the meat. Our position is extremely perilous; if we do not earnestly promote nationalism and weld together our four hundred millions into a strong nation, we face a tragedy—the loss of our country and the destruction of our race. To ward off this danger, we must espouse Nationalism and employ the national spirit to save the country."

In his doctrine, nationalism means an equal and independent status for China in the world and an equal status for all ethnic groups in China. Nationalism also means the restoration and renaissance of traditional Chinese culture. Democracy means that all Chinese people have civil liberties. His economic development plan was presented as (Sun, 1922):

> Industrial development in China should follow two distinct lines: private enterprises and government enterprises. All those that could be entrusted to the private sector, or those for which private operation is more appropriate than government operation, should be open to the private sector, encouraged by the state and protected by law. In order for private enterprises to develop in China, the hitherto suicidal tax system should be immediately eliminated, the monetary disorder should be immediately corrected; bureaucratic barriers should be removed and, most important, communications and transportation systems should be improved.

He tried to combine traditional Confucianism and Western science. The centers in his ethics were benevolence and harmony between the ruler and the ruled. He advocated a free economy with proper government interventions so that national wealth could be rapidly accumulated and equitably distributed.

In genuine Confucianism, opinions of the minority should be respected. Confucius' pupil, Zigong, once asked the master what he thought of a man who was loved by all the people of his village. Confucius replied: "We may not for that accord our approval of him." Zigong further asked the master what he thought of a man who was bated by all the people of his village. Confucius replied: "We may not for that conclude that he is bad. It is better either of these cases that the good in the village love him, and the bad hate him." To belong to the majority does not necessarily mean to be right; to belong to the minority does not necessarily mean to be wrong. "When the multitude hate a man," Confucius signifies the cautiousness in judging men, "it is necessary to examine into the case. When the multitude like a man, it is necessary to examine into the case." Confucius never says that there is a unique/common ideology (or religion) acceptable to all peoples. For Confucius, education is to enable one to understand but not to only simply repeat what one is taught.

Some aspects of Dr Sun's doctrines might not be suitable for sustaining a democratic society (Bauer and Bell, 1999). An Israeli historian observed (Barlow, 1987: 69): "If Sun Yat-sen had one consistent talent, it was for failure. Yet he remains a natural hero because the more than quarter of a century in which he was active was the darkest period of modern Chinese history, and without his memory it would seem even darker." The Chinese proverb jests: "A common man can become famous because there is no capable and virtuous man in China." The tragedy of modern Chinese history is that almost all significant social positions of China from the late Ch'ing dynasty until not long ago had been occupied mostly by trivial or cunning men.

3.3 The KMT on Taiwan Before 1950

> If a man takes no thought about what is distant, he will find sorrow near at hand.
>
> *Confucius*

The political history of China from the 1920s until the end of World War II was mainly the growth and development of nationalism and communism, characterized by dynamic struggles and co-operation between the KMT and the CCP (founded in 1921). The KMT ruled China during the late 1920s. Between 1921 and 1927, the relations between the KMT and the CCP were amicable. The KMT announced the formation of a national government on July 1, 1925, at Nanjing. But the Nanjing government was officially established as a national government on October 10, 1928. By 1928, the KMT government at Nanjing had become the strongest force in China after its victories in the Northern Expedition against the warlords.

From 1927 to 1947, Chiang ruled the ROC as a military dictator in constant warfare against warlords, the Japanese, and the Chinese communists. Nevertheless, by the early 1930s, large portions of the country began to fall into Japanese hands. On September 18, 1931, the Japanese army attacked the Manchurian capital, Mukden (Shenyang). Chiang Kai-shek urged the provincial leaders not to fight the Japanese. The non-resistance policy allowed more and more of Manchuria to be taken away by the Japanese. The Mukden incident and the subsequent Japanese conquest of Manchuria created a national crisis. The KMT's Fourth Conference in November 1931 called for uniting all groups. While the Nanjing government was trying to win national unity, the CCP tried to develop its force in the border areas of several provinces. In February 1932, the Japanese declared the establishment of a new, separate state of Manchukuo with the last Ch'ing Emperor, Puyi, as chief of state. The state was recognized neither by the Western powers nor by Nanjing. The Japanese invasion provoked an extensive anti-Japanese movement in many cities. The Xi'an incident in December 1936 ended the Communist–Nationalist civil war within China. The Japanese took Nanjing on December 13, 1937. The Japanese allowed their army to ravage the city at will over a period of 6 weeks. The Rape of Nanjing resulted in the death and humiliation of tens of thousands of non-combatant Chinese. After the loss of Nanjing, the KMT government moved its capital to Chongqing. In March 1938, the Japanese established a puppet government, the Reformed government at Nanjing. After March 1939, the frontline between the Japanese and the Chongqing-led forces of Free China was largely stable until 1944. With the outbreak of the Pacific War after the attack on Pearl Harbor by Japan in December 1941, China declared war on Japan. When Japan surrendered in August 1945, the power of the CCP and the KMT was the opposite to what it had been in the late 1930s. The communists were spread over half the country with considerable popular support. The change in the relative strengths and in the administrative competence of the two parties set the stage for a full-scale civil war in 1946. In 1949, Chiang Kai-shek and his armies fled to Taiwan. On October 1, Mao Zedong stood on the Gate of Heavenly Peace in Beijing and proclaimed the establishment of the People's Republic of China. His easy victory would lead the New China to suffering from repeated national disasters, while Chiang's failure would teach him on how to deliver goods to his people. One might use

Confucius' judgment about Guan Zhong to evaluate Chiang Kai-shek's behavior in Taiwan:

> Zigong said, "Guan Zhong, I apprehend, was wanting in virtue. When the prince Huan caused his brother Jiu to be killed, Guan Zhong was not able to die with him. Moreover, he became prime minister to Huan." Confucius said: "Guan Zhong acted as prime minister to the prince Huan, made him leader of all the princes, and united and rectified the whole kingdom. Down to the present day, the people enjoy the gifts which he conferred. But for Guan Zhong we should now be wearing our hair unbound, and the lappets of our coats buttoning on the left side! Will you require from him the small fidelity of common men and common women, who would commit suicide in a stream or ditch, no one knowing about them?"

In September 1945, the ROC government organized the Political Consultative Conference representing a range of political parties. In December 1946, the National Assembly in Nanjing endorsed a constitution proposed in the 1945 conference. The new constitution, based on Dr Sun's teachings, came into force in December 1947. The National Assembly also passed the Temporary Provisions Effective during the Period of Mobilization for the Suppression of the Communist Rebellion. These measures provided many powers to the President of the ROC. The first Nationalist soldiers arrived in Keelung on October 16, 1945. Nearly 60,000 troops who were bedraggled in appearance and lacked discipline disembarked in Taiwan to accept the Japanese surrender on October 25, 1945 (Bullard, 1997: 41). Since there was an active civil war within the mainland, the troops send to Taiwan at that time were older veterans. The soldiers, most of whom were illiterate old farmers, came to Taiwan to accept the surrender of the Japanese occupation forces, to disarm them, and to see them off from the island. The Nationalist leadership did not consider using military forces to keep social order in Taiwan since the leadership believed that the return of Taiwan to its governing would be warmly welcomed by the Taiwanese.

On October 25, 1945, the ROC government established the Supreme Executive Headquarters as the administrative structure to recover and govern Taiwan after 50 years of Japanese colonial rule. On May 1, 1946, the government held elections throughout the island for village and town councils and the first Taiwan provincial assembly. No further elections followed until the fall of 1949. On October 11, 1945, General Chen Yi, a student who had returned from Japan and married to a Japanese wife, was appointed Governor General of Taiwan. Although Chen personally might not have been a corrupt official, his transitional government was composed of opportunists and carpetbaggers. Because the Japanese had ruled Taiwan for 50 years and Taiwan's social environments were different from those in the mainland, Chen Yi was given executive power and was able to make laws according to Taiwan's needs. Moreover, courts and judges were also under his supervision. Commissioners in Chen Yi's administration monopolized tea, sugar, tobacco, and alcohol production and the supervision of foreign trade. When he arrived at Taiwan, Chen Yi held the view that he did not need many troops in Taiwan because he was in a friendly Chinese population. He soon returned 5000 troops back to the mainland to fight against the communists. The troops remaining in Taiwan were generally corrupt and not disciplined and they did not properly behave. The earlier troops' misbehavior was even used as negative examples for later troop education programs. Moreover, because few Taiwanese people spoke Mandarin and few of the KMT officials and soldiers spoke Taiwanese, communication between the Taiwanese and mainlanders was difficult. The misbehavior of the mainlanders also caused the Taiwanese to be dissatisfied with them. The mainlanders did not give the Taiwanese proper respect. They were biased against the local population, viewing them as the Japanese's collaborators when they had resisted Japanese invaders during the 8-year Sino-Japanese War. Except those who had become members of the KMT on the mainland during wartime, few of the Taiwanese elites were appointed to join the government. The KMT extracted resources from Taiwan to support the civil war in the mainland, resulting in food shortages and high inflation. The Taiwanese people found the rule of the KMT no better than that of the Japanese (Copper, 1990: 26).

The initial response of many Taiwanese to the restoration of Chinese sovereignty over Taiwan was high-spirited. For most citizens of Taiwan, China was their ancestral home and source of culture. Most of them did not enjoy strict Japanese colonial control, even though they might have respected the efficiency of Japan's bureaucracy and security forces. They believed that various kinds of social, economic, and political discrimination against the Taiwanese (under the Japanese colonial rule) would be eliminated. The Taiwanese soon recognized the cultural gulf separating them from the mainlanders. The KMT did not prove to be a qualified ruler partly because of its lack of discipline. Moreover, the mainland-centered Chinese chauvinism of the administration placed enormous pressures on the Taiwanese (Chu, 1994). The predacious behaviors of early Nationalist officials (who would be "rewarded" by being forced to remain in Taiwan for the rest of their lifes) upset many Taiwanese. Bureaucratic corruption was the symbol of the KMT even in the mainland, not to mention on the island. As in the mainland, Nationalist officials required people in Taiwan to pay expensive permits for virtually every transaction. Corruption was widespread on the island after the KMT took control. Profiteers smuggled local goods and Japanese supplies to the mainland black market. "Conscript peasants from China stole or commandeered bicycles but," describes Kerr (1965: 136), "unable to ride, carried them on their backs."

The anti-KMT feeling of the Taiwanese erupted on February 28, 1947, when the police and agents of the Tobacco and Wine Monopoly Bureau (which controlled the production and sales of matches, alcohol, camphor, and tobacco) interdicted unlicensed sales of cigarettes in a crowded park. They apprehended a widow and confiscated her cigarettes and cash, and knocked her down when she objected. A mob formed and the police fired into the crowd, killing four people. Residents of Taiwan lashed against the KMT and other immigrants from the mainland. The 28 February incident immediately caused widespread rebellion all over the island, with the Taiwanese people asking for fairer treatment. Chen Yi regarded this as a pro-communist rebellion. Martial law was enforced and over 20,000 KMT troops were sent to Taiwan to repress the Taiwanese. Taiwan was thereafter subjected to a brutal period of repression, retribution, and mass executions. Troops sought a long list of suspects, including landowners, doctors, lawyers, editors, teachers, professors, and entrepreneurs. Some were beaten and killed on the spot. It was generally believed that over 20,000 people were killed, arrested, or disappeared (Ku, 1997: 140). For more than 30 years, information about the 28 February incident was officially suppressed. At the end of martial law in 1987, leaders opposed to the KMT highlighted this in their campaigns. The government also conducted investigations. In 1995, President Lee Teng-hui formally apologized to the families of victims, and the then Taipei city mayor, Chen Shui-bian, named the "2-28 Peace Park" to commemorate the incident. In the same year, the Legislative Yuan enacted legislation to compensate relatives of the victims. Just before the 50th anniversary in 1997, the Legislative Yuan declared February 28 a national holiday.

The February 28 incident had led to a deep mutual distrust and animosity between the Taiwanese and mainlanders. Under the KMT's brutal ruling, few Taiwanese would participate in political activities. Most Taiwanese withdrew from the political arena until recent years. Through the incident, the Nationalist authorities wiped out Taiwan's intellectual and managerial elites who were educated and trained during the Japanese colonial period and might threaten the KMT's control of the island. The suppression of the rebellion cowed the rest of the populace into submission. The suppression included the shutting down of local presses. The incident played a crucial role in the consolidation of KMT power in Taiwan. Taiwanese nationalists and leftists were liquidated, driven into exile, or silenced. In fact, the KMT behaved similarly in the mainland. Through the cruel repression, the KMT eradicated possible opposition and established its unchallenged authority in Taiwan.

3.4 Consolidation of Power in the 1950s and 1960s

> He who with a small state serves a large one stands in awe of Heaven .... He who stands in awe of Heaven will effect with his love and production his own kingdom.
>
> *Mencius*

After being defeated by the Communists in the winter of 1949, the Nationalists fled to Taiwan. The KMT had to undertake a self-examination and reformation for survival in the new conditions. It could no longer be corrupt and ineffective as it had been in the mainland. Taiwan was a small land almost without any natural resources, except land and forestry. As a loser in the mainland and "refugee" to the island, the KMT had to contrive its "occupation policies" to prevent a possible CCP invasion and seeking of native Taiwanese support. Rather than exercising military means to preside over Taiwan, the KMT altered its strategy of political and economic means to undermine Beijing and to recuperate the support of the Chinese people. Taiwan was schemed as a model province of Dr Sun's Three Principles of the People. The KMT finally resolved to follow the Confucian way: to raise the standard of living of the Taiwanese people, to improve the quality of their life, and to gradually implement democracy.

Initially, the KMT expected to reorganize and retake the mainland, viewing Taiwan as a staging ground. After the ROC government was enforced to settle in Taiwan, President Chiang Kai-shek pledged that his regime would continue to struggle against the CCP-dominated mainland and build Taiwan into a model province based on the Three Principles of the People. He wanted to recover the mainland by uniting China under the ROC's 1947 constitution. On May 19, 1949, the KMT passed the law the "Temporary Provision Effective During the Period of Communist Rebellion." These provisions, designed as supplements to the constitution, were subsequently extended to Taiwan. Chiang issued in January 1950 an emergency decree that applied the 1943 martial law to Taiwan. The KMT justified the two measures by holding that China's civil war had not yet ended. The two measures suspended many important articles of the ROC Constitution. The Temporary Provisions included limits on political participation at the national level, a virtual ban on the formation of new political parties, censorship of the press, and surveillance of political dissidents who advocated communism or Taiwanese independence. The temporary provisions provided the president unlimited power. The president could serve unlimited terms and had enormous power in the appointment of key government personnel. Martial law, which would last until 1987, was imposed by the KMT to contain the threat from the People's Republic of China as well as threat from the Taiwanese. The martial law was used to restrict civil rights and liberties protected by the constitution. Despite the imposition of martial law, the KMT tried to follow Dr Sun's teachings of "rule by the people." The KMT permitted the continuation of local elections. The KMT used the local elections to create a system of highly loyal grassroots organizations throughout the country. Since opposition parties were restricted, the government was able to maintain political stability. From 1949, Taiwan entered an era of authoritarian rule under the KMT and leadership of the Chiang family. In the first two decades, the KMT met with little opposition from its subordinates and successfully carried out the policy of restrictions on political participation at the national level but open local elections.

In 1928, the US was the first country to recognize Chiang Kai-shek's Nanjing government as the legitimate government of China. After the bombing of Pearl Harbor and the formal US entrance into World War II, the US considered the Nationalist regime one of the great Allied powers fighting the Axis coalition. The US and other allied powers in the Cairo

Declaration of 1943 promised the POC that Formosa and the Pescadores would be returned to China at the conclusion of the war. With strong US political support, the ROC became one of the five permanent members of the Security Council of the United Nations (UN), formed in June 1945. The initial reaction of the US government to the defeat of the KMT in the mainland was to distance itself completely from the ROC and to remain indifferent to an expected imminent communist attack on Taiwan. Two weeks after Chiang Kai-shek established his headquarters in Taipei, the US government considered Taiwan to hold no special military significance to US security. On December 29, 1949, the US National Security Council decided that "no further action would be taken to assist the Chinese Nationalists to hold Formosa" (Bradley and Blair, 1983: 533). On January 5, 1950, President Truman claimed that the US would "not provide military aid or advice to Chinese forces" on Taiwan (Lasater, 1993: 7). In the official US statement of the "United States Policy Toward Formosa" issued in January 1950, the US asserted that Taiwan was part of China and that the US would discontinue its sale of military supplies to the KMT (Ravich, 2000: 104). Nevertheless, North Korea's surprise invasion of the South on June 25, 1950, changed the United States' foreign policy towards Taiwan. Overnight, Taiwan became free China, the bastion of anti-communism in East Asia.

Following the outbreak of the Korean War in June 1950, the US dispatched the Seventh Fleet to the Taiwan Straits to prevent a communist takeover of Taiwan. At the same time, the US government decided to provide military aid to the KMT. The US government reversed its policy of not intervening in the Chinese civil war. This change of US policy not only saved Taiwan's inhabitants from the terror and destruction of war, but also prevented the possible annihilation of the KMT forces by the communists. The PRC viewed the US action as an act of aggression against China, while the KMT saw it as giving it a "second chance." As part of its strategy to pressurize, the US gave political, economic, and military aid to Taiwan. From 1951 to 1971, the US supported the ROC representation in the UN and opposed that of the PRC. Total US economic aid to the ROC from 1949 to 1965 was US$1.7 billion, while the total US military assistance to the ROC from 1949 to the mid-1970s was US$4.2 billion (Lasater, 1993: 10). American aid helped the KMT regime maintain its military strength and stabilize the shaky agrarian economy.

Before being defeated by the communists, the KMT had weak ties with the provincial people in Taiwan. When the KMT came to Taiwan isolated from the mainland, it behaved as a "foreign" occupying force. The party had few ties with "indigenous" Chinese elites and had to rely on the military and bureaucratic cadre relocated from the mainland. It was able to govern Taiwan with an authoritarian manner because it was buttressed by military and police power, a large state-owned enterprise sector, and control over the financial sector. In the 1950s, the ruling class of the KMT regime was mainly composed of Chinese mainlanders. They clung to the key positions in most of the state apparatuses such as the armed forces and the education system. Those Taiwanese islanders who held important positions in this period tended to be those who had spent much of their mature lifetime on the mainland (Chu, 1994). The Taiwanese business community shared little formal representation in the ruling party.

Taiwan offered few obstacles to Chiang's rule from 1949 until his death in 1975. He consolidated in his hands broad powers to appoint, transfer, and dismiss officials. He commanded the party, the army, the security agencies, and the government. No opposition to his own rule was allowed. He brought with him not only the wealthy from the mainland but also the intellectuals. Different from the yokel Chairman Mao, the urban playboy President Chiang fully understood the significance of the elite for modernization. He succeeded in selecting outstanding economic officials who developed Taiwan's early economic growth strategies. In Taiwan, he modeled himself into a symbol of virtuous authority through his austere habits and lifestyle as well as his concern for the people's welfare and the paternalistic obligations of the state. He earned the respect of the people of Taiwan; most of them mourned his death in 1975.

When arriving in Taiwan, the KMT was under the threat of military invasion. On the other hand, Taiwan was socially fragmented as a consequence of being a Japanese colony and maladministration in the years immediately after retrocession. Taiwan could not survive if the KMT failed to develop military, economic, and moral strength. The KMT leaders recognized that this could be accomplished through unity with political socialization. When Chiang Kai-shek arrived in Taiwan, he was faced with problems of unity and democracy. It seemed that liberal democracy might lead to conflict and disunity because most people were poor and not well educated. The KMT chose to modernize Taiwan in a controlled fashion from an authoritarian state with emphasis on education toward democracy. From 1949 to 1987, when martial law was in force, advocacy of Taiwan's independence was illegal. During this period, the KMT continued to use the island as a "temporary haven" from which to launch an assault to recover the mainland. The KMT subjugated the island to its own purpose to recover the island. During 1950–1952, the KMT carried out a fundamental reorganization in order to invigorate the party machine from its state of paralysis in the mainland. The reorganization of the KMT followed the following six principles (Long, 1991; Maguire, 1998): (1) the KMT was to be a revolutionary democratic party and become a clean party; (2) membership of the KMT was to include a wider social base including farmers, workers, youth, and the intelligentsia (the KMT lost the power to the CCP partly because of these groups' support to the CCP in the mainland); (3) the KMT party structure was to remain democratic centralist (this was to allow local elites and different interest groups to co-operate with the KMT, but under control of the KMT); (4) the KMT's party cells would serve as the core of organizational units (this served to concentrate the power in the KMT and hence the Chiang family); (5) the KMT would provide leadership in all spheres and would be involved in making all key decisions and policies (this meant that the party was the state, and vice versa); and (6) KMT members would have to subscribe Dr Sun's Three Principles of the People. The reorganization ended in October 1952 at the KMT's Seventh Party Congress. The KMT decided that its historical mission was political unification of China according to Dr Sun's Three Principles of the People.

During the reorganization period, the KMT reregistered members and purged those considered disloyal, suspected of enemy connections, or found guilty of corruption (Riggs, 1952: 38). After the reorganization, the KMT's power was highly centralized, with a hierarchy of party apparatus dispersed throughout the state structure and society. On June 10, 1951, the Executive Yuan ordered licensing restrictions for newspapers. Chiang Ching-kuo was given the task to introduce a political commissar system within the armed forces. This helped the party to control the army. Party membership was high in the civil service, the farmers groups, and the military. In the next two decades, many Taiwanese joined the party. By the 1970s, many Taiwanese had risen up in the party ladder, especially at county and municipal levels.

Between 1950 and 1952, the KMT made various institutional reforms, such as reforming land ownership, auctioning former Japanese enterprise assets to the public, abolishing the dual exchange rate and replacing it with a single one, providing tax credits and information that business people could use to invest. During this period, primary education was expanded, more technical and vocational schools were established, and the higher education system was promoted. The KMT's land reform policy won support from Taiwanese peasants. Their support helped consolidate the legitimacy of the KMT rule. Numerous locally held elections enabled the rural upper class to enter into the one-party political system. Many original landlords and original laborers became more active in local politics after the land reform (Tai, 1969).

Taiwan's policy-making system was highly specific. Each function of the state had a separate office, with an elaborate system of monitoring its responsibility. Competitive national examinations were the main mechanism for recruitment to specialized agencies and bureaus of the state. The specialized bureaucracy was highly competent and effective. To work in a national government office was the first employment choice of university graduates. The KMT organized the new Taiwan government around five branches: the Executive Yuan, the Legislative Yuan, the Judicial Yuan, the Control Yuan, and the Examination Yuan (Clark, 1989). The President (indirectly selected) was the top political official and appointed the leaders of the Executive Yuan, the Judicial Yuan, and the Examination Yuan. The Premier of the Executive Yuan, appointed by the President, functioned as the Prime Minister. The Executive Yuan, the Legislative Yuan, and the Judicial Yuan were adopted from Western political traditions. The Control Yuan and the Examination Yuan were adopted from traditional Chinese political systems. The Examination Yuan is responsible for selecting members of the civil service and the Control Yuan for enforcing standards of behavior among government officials. The Taiwan provincial government was responsible for administering all districts, cities, towns, and villages and the public affairs relevant to their security, prosperity, and quality of life. The duties of the Taiwan provincial assembly included: interpellation of provincial leaders and administrators; passing provincial statutes; approving the levy of provincial special taxes, temporary taxes, and surtaxes; deciding on the disposal of provincial properties; and approving the laws of the provincial government and provincially owned enterprises. Although the KMT limited political participation at the national level, it carefully institutionalized local elections to maintain Dr Sun's democratic principles. National politics was dominated by the mainlanders (roughly 15% of the population), while the Taiwanese controlled local and provincial Taiwan politics. Moreover, local Taiwanese politicians were mostly members of the KMT. The KMT strengthened the social and economic ties of the KMT state with local elites. Between 1951 and 1965, free elections were held for five provincial assemblies. Those provincial elections continued until 1995, when a pending constitutional reform stipulated revising the provincial government and freezing local elections. By the mid-1960s, local elections for the Taiwan provincial assembly and for lower national units had become routine. Voter participation was high. From the 1950s to 1970s, voter turnouts in the elections of magistrates, mayors, and provincial assembly members were often over 70% (Chou and Nathan, 1987). A considerable number of the non-KMT candidates were Taiwanese. Many were chairpersons of industrial or commercial corporations and some were professionals in medicine, law, or journalism. These successful people were able to finance their political ambitions. In 1969, the KMT permitted the reinstatement of national parliamentary elections. The elections brought in a number of native Taiwanese and foreign-educated parliamentarians.

3.5 Limited Liberalization in the 1970s

> The superior man thinks of virtue; the small man thinks of comfort. The superior man thinks of sanctions of law, the small man thinks of favors, which he may receive.
>
> *Confucius*

After 1971, the international environment changed in a way that made it increasingly difficult for the KMT to claim itself to be the only legitimate government of all China. These changes included: Taiwan's expulsion from the UN in 1971; the Nixon–Chou En-lai Shanghai Communiqué in 1972; the death of Chiang Kai-shek in 1975, and the American derecognition of Taiwan in 1979. By the end of the Vietnam War, the US changed its attitude toward the PRC. The US considered friendly relations with the PRC as a strategic asset in US–Soviet competition. In November 1969, the US Seventh Fleet ended its regular patrol of the Taiwan Strait. In October 1971, the UN General Assembly voted to seat the PRC as the legitimate government of China. Because of the UN vote and trends toward improved US–PRC relations, many nations switched diplomatic recognition from Taipei to Beijing. In February 1972, Nixon visited the PRC and met with Mao Zedong and other Chinese leaders. The two sides made important statements of policy of Sino-American understanding on the Taiwan issue. The February 28, 1972, Shanghai Communiqué read (Lasater, 1993: 12):

> The Chinese side reaffirmed its position: Taiwan question is the crucial question obstructing the normalization of relations between China and the United States; the Government of the People's Republic of China is the sole legal government of China; Taiwan is a province of China which has long been returned to the motherland; the liberation of Taiwan is China's internal affair in which no other country has the right to interfere; and all US forces and military installations must be withdrawn from Taiwan. The Chinese Government firmly opposes any activities which aim at the creation of "one China, one Taiwan," "one China, two governments" or advocate that "the status of Taiwan remains to be determined."
>
> The US side declared: The United States acknowledges that all Chinese on either side of the Taiwan Strait maintain there is but one China and that Taiwan is a part of China. The United States Government does not challenge the position. It reaffirms its interests in a peaceful settlement of the Taiwan question by the Chinese themselves. With this prospect in mind, it affirms the ultimate objective of the withdrawal of all US forces and military installations from Taiwan. In the meantime, it will progressively reduce its forces and military installations on Taiwan as the tension in the area diminishes.

In February 1973, the US and the PRC established liaison offices in each other's capitals. In December 1978, the PRC changed its policy toward Taiwan from "liberation" to "peaceful reunification." On December 15, 1978, the US and the PRC announced they would exchange diplomatic recognition on January 1, 1979. The US also claimed to terminate diplomatic relations with the ROC. However, the American people and the people of Taiwan would maintain commercial, cultural, and other relations without official representations and without diplomatic relations. To prevent the PRC from threatening Taiwan, President Carter signed the Taiwan Relations Act (TRA) into law on April 10, 1979. The TRA has become the principal legal framework for US–Taiwan relations. The TRA states that the US decision to establish diplomatic relations with the PRC was based on the expectation that the future of Taiwan will be determined by peaceful means. The TRA also states that the US policy in the Western Pacific is to provide Taiwan with arms of a defensive character and to maintain the capacity of the US to protect Taiwan's security.

The crisis perceived due to the US derecognition of Taiwan resulted in a decline in support for political liberalization. Having lost the hope to lead China, the KMT started its naturalization policy by recruiting more Taiwanese locals into the state apparatus. The political power of business expanded in the 1970s and 1980s. Large private groups emerged, resulting in increases in the organizational capacities of the private sector. In the late 1970s, there was an increasing demand for sources of political funding. The KMT government tried to establish close relations with the private sector because the government needed greater business representation in policy-making as Taiwan's economy was shifting toward more complex, capital-intensive, and technology-intensive industries. The barriers separating the KMT from the private sector blurred. The private sector and the government had common interests (Chu, 1994). They recognized the necessity for being actively involved in industrial upgradation. They favored economic growth first with little environmental considerations and preferred economic growth to social welfare spending. They also supported exclusion of organized labor from economic policy-making. The KMT's reliance on business grew even more intensely in the mid-1980s as Taiwan's democratization was speeded up.

Conflicts between Chinese mainlanders and Taiwanese islanders spurred Taiwan into being politically progressive and dynamic. The distrust of Taiwanese islanders towards the mainlanders and Taiwan's relations with the mainland were the key factors for Taiwan's politics to be self-organized toward democracy. By the late 1970s, there was a rapid increase in demand for political freedom from the newly formed middle class and a well-educated (American-influenced) public. There was a more open attitude toward the discussion of sensitive political issues on Taiwan. After several electoral victories, non-KMT politicians wanted to organize an opposition political party by the mid-1970s. In the 1977 local elections, some of non-KMT politicians even publicly termed themselves candidates without affiliation with the KMT. These *tangwai* politicians won 25–30% of the popular vote and gained about 25% of the seats in national by-elections (Chou and Nathan, 1987). There was a growing consensus within Taiwan that martial law had fulfilled its purpose of stabilizing the island and it should be ended. By the 1970s, the use of the Taiwanese dialect was no longer prohibited. Many Taiwanese writers started to publish in the Taiwanese dialect. These works were mostly concerned with the lives of the lower-class Taiwanese-speaking people in the rural areas and in the towns. The rise of this type of literature was considered a sign of the resurgence of Taiwanese identity (Chu, 1994).

The KMT's final authority rested in the hands of its two supreme leaders Chiang Kai-shek (1949–1975) and his son Chiang Ching-kuo (1975–1987). Throughout his life in Taiwan, Chiang Kai-shek made certain that his eldest son Chiang Ching-kuo would succeed him. He helped Chiang Ching-kuo to establish his power bases in the armed forces, the security, the party, and the government. By the early 1970s, Chiang Ching-kuo had already held the second most powerful position in the authoritarian hierarchy. They appointed key officials in the party, the government, the military, and the security forces (Tien, 1992). The extent to which either of the two Chiangs monopolized Taiwan's political and military power is seldom matched in other authoritarian systems in the world. Chiang Kai-shek acquired his supreme power in Taiwan partly because the mainlanders who followed him to Taiwan were largely his confidants and followers who shared with him the goal of recovering the mainland. For the minority mainlanders to control the Taiwanese, it was necessary to maintain "internal cohesion" within the mainlanders. Moreover, Chiang Kai-shek's policy and organizational methods provided the common interests of the first-generation mainlanders on the island. The authoritarian system provided Taiwan with more than decades of political stability that enabled the government to launch a steady course of economic development. Under their leadership, the structural configuration, and functional relationship of the KMT, the state, and organizations in the ROC political system were essentially corporatist. The party and state formed closely interlocked ties. The KMT determined key personnel appointment of the government administration and the representative institutions. The party directed the statue by establishing disciplined intra-governmental party branches. The party-state was the principal arbitrator that directed organized civil groups. Through legal means and political controls, the party-state intervened the election of leaders and activities of strategic groups.

In Taiwan, democratization was engineered by the leadership of the late Chiang Ching-kuo. He ruled Taiwan in a style different from his father. As premier and later as president, he regularly went out with the people in causal dresses—to schools, factories, hospitals, offices, and fields. He paid more attention to youth and brought officials still in their 30s and early 40s into leading positions. In the late 1970s and 1980s, he began to redefine the KMT's mission. According to his vision, the KMT should develop Taiwan as a democratic society that mainland China's leaders and elite eventually should adopt. He emphasized the strict rectitude of government officials and campaigned actively for honest and efficient government. He quickly discharged corrupt officials. He was respected for his concern with people's problems and welfare and for his use of people and personal integrity. In 1972, when he became premier, he started the process of Taiwanization of the ruling party and the central government. In his first term of premiership, native Taiwanese were appointed to top government positions such as vice-premier and governor of Taiwan Province. After he became president, he launched a major program of political reform. Taiwanese were appointed as vice-presidents. In the years of his presidency, 14 of the 31 members of the KMT Central Standing Committee were Taiwanese.

Chiang Ching-kuo also started recruiting Western-trained Chinese technocrats into positions of power and responsibility in the government and party. Many of these educated individuals used their positions to recommend and implement political reform modeled on Western democracies. A significant number of overseas Chinese experts in the social sciences from the US and other Western countries were appointed to high-ranking posts in Taiwan. After he became president, Chiang reduced sentences of political prisoners and released many. Although the regime continued to censor publications, monitor political activity, and conduct surveillance and arrests of dissidents, it began to show great tolerance to political opposition. Without true democracy, there is no true freedom. The 1979 Kaohsiung incident was an example. The incident started with a protest against President Chiang Ching-kuo's decision to suspend the national elections planned because of America's derecognition of Taiwan. The protest developed into a violent clash between the dissidents and the police. Several police officers and bystanders were injured. Fourteen *tangwai* leaders and 140 protesters were arrested. The Kaohsiung incident represented the last episode of summary arrests of organized opponents to the KMT regime.

3.6 Democratization in the 1980s

> He who acts with a constant view to his own advantage will be much murmured against.
>
> *Confucius*

The KMT's ideal was democracy. The ancient "Chinese democratic principle" is reflected in Mencius' sayings: "If people generally are not able to enjoy themselves, they condemn their superiors. For them, when they cannot enjoy themselves, to condemn their superiors is wrong, but when superiors of the people do not make enjoyment a thing common to the people and themselves, they also do wrong. When a ruler rejoices in the joy of his people, they also rejoice in his joy; when he grieves at the sorrow of his people, they also grieve at his sorrow. A sympathy of joy will pervade the empire, a sympathy of sorrow will do the same; in such a state of things, it cannot be but the ruler attain to the Imperial dignity." In modern times, it is through democratic processes that the people (who are highly educated and wealthy and have formed a high variety of tastes through life experiences) can find a leader who can simultaneously enjoy and sorrow with them. The Confucian criterion for electing politicians helped Chinese society to accept Western democratic processes when social and economic structures and preference structures of the people become mature. In the early years in Taiwan, under the KMT leadership the people elected their local leaders and representative bodies for villages, cities, districts, and Taiwan Province. The limited democracy helped the KMT to legitimize its governance of Taiwan and made it an effective alternative to China's communist dictatorship. The KMT helped local elections, but without allowing an opposition party to compete with the KMT. The KMT justified such practice as preventing communist subversion, mobilizing society against the Chinese communist regime, and giving Taiwan's citizens time to learn about democracy and practice it. However, since the late 1970s, Taiwan had become more liberal and more tolerant about the *tangwai* opposition. During the 1980s, developments in the mainland helped to make democratization in Taiwan politically acceptable. The success of economic reform in the mainland reduced the apparent threat of invasion. This was important for democratization in Taiwan.

President Chiang Ching-kuo made many positive contributions to Taiwan's rapid democratization. In March 1986, he described his new vision as follows (Myers, 1998: 31): "Our party advocates practicing the spirit of making our present world a perfect moral order and to carry out our ROC on Taiwan constitution to the mainland to initiate a democratic, constitutional government; do away with dictatorship and class warfare; really implement a way for our people to determine their destiny; return political power to the people; and to make them entirely equal before the law." He was gradually convinced that democratic reforms were needed to ensure the continuity of the regime after his death. If he was not determined to speed up democratization, Taiwan's political reform could hardly be so rapid because there were enough conservative-minded figures in the top ranks of the KMT. He attempted to create an independent political identity for Taiwan. His Presidency marked the start of a rapid transformation from a situation of confrontation between Chinese and Taiwanese identities. Before his death in 1988, over 70% of KMT membership and over 50% of party and government officials were Taiwanese. The KMT was no longer a party dominated by Chinese from the mainland. It was in the hands of Chinese born and raised in Taiwan. Moreover, during the final years of his chairmanship of the KMT, the Central Standing Committee was regularly involved in debating policy proposals (earlier most decisions on party policy were made by the chairman alone). In his last years, martial law was abrogated in 1987, allowing political parties to be formed and to compete in elections. The other instruments of dictatorial control were also soon lifted, allowing freedom of assembly, association, and press. The political exiles who had demanded freedom and independence returned from abroad or were released from detention. Before his death in January 1988, he broke the taboo on negotiating with the mainland and allowed visits to the mainland on humanitarian grounds. By this time, Taiwan initiated economic links with the mainland. In 1987, indirect trade was valued at US$1.4 billion (Klintworth, 1995: 305). Massive investment in China and the legalization of family visits to relatives in the mainland in 1987 brought about a rapid increase in the interaction between these two Chinese societies.

President Chiang Ching-kuo died on January 13, 1988. Before his death, he had instructed that no member of his family should succeed him. His death ended the Chiang dynasty in ROC's history. For decades, Chiang Kai-shek and Chiang Ching-kuo personalized the political power of the KMT party-state. With the death of Chiang Ching-kuo both the KMT and the state apparatus lost their power center. Chiang Ching-kuo was succeeded by Vice-President Lee Teng-hui. Lee was a native Taiwanese, born in a village outside Taipei in 1923. He joined the KMT only in 1972. He was educated in Taiwan, Japan, and the US with no previous mainland China experience. After completing high school in Taipei, he was admitted to Kyoto Imperial University in Japan during Taiwan's Japanese occupation. After the war, he studied agricultural economics at National Taiwan University and then obtained his master degree at Iowa State University. Lee received his doctorial degree in agricultural economics from Cornell University in 1968. His dissertation won the prize of the American Association for Agricultural Economics in 1969.

Lee was distinguished by a complete lack of affiliation to any of the numerous factions of mainlander or Taiwanese politicians. He did not have any power base besides his education, ability, the authority of his office, and his popularity with the public. These qualifications would enable him to be fair in selecting political partners and carefully listening to the opposition. Chiang Ching-kuo moved Lee into the cabinet in 1972 as minister without portfolio. Lee demonstrated his competence, expertise, and loyalty. In 1978, he became Taipei city mayor. In 1981, he got the governorship of Taiwan province. At the conclusion of his term as governor, Chiang selected him vice president. Lee assured the people in Taiwan that he would continue the policies of Chiang, including the democratization of Taiwan. In the Thirteenth KMT Party Congress in July 1988, Lee was elected as Chairman of the KMT, the first Taiwanese to hold that position. A new Central Standing Committee was also elected, with 16 Taiwanese and 15 mainlanders. Like Lee, almost half of the members had received advanced degrees in the US. When Lee formed a new Cabinet in the same year, among the 13 newly appointed members eight were Taiwanese. With the lifting of martial law in 1987, the government reformed the old constitutional foundation of authoritarian rule to become truly democratic. The constitutional structure was modified to consolidate the position of the President as the decision-making center with the premier as his chief of staff. The Legislature acquired some political power from other branches of the government.

By the mid-1980s, the KMT began to change its way to deal with the *tangwai* opposition. The KMT began to meet with *tangwai* leaders and hold discussions with them. The KMT negotiated with opposition leaders to extend its state apparatus to incorporate new political forces. On the other hand, the face-to-face negotiations also meant the KMT's *de facto* recognition of the *tangwai* politicians' organizational activities. Under such circumstances, the *tangwai* leaders declared the establishment of the Democratic Progressive Party (DDP) on the eve (28 September) of the 1986 parliamentary election. Prior to the creation of the DDP, Taiwan had maintained for almost four decades a one-party system. The KMT monopolized political power and public resources. On the one hand, democracy is KMT's principle. The central government's elected bodies had to be consistent with the ROC claim that they represented all of China, Taiwan only as one province. Otherwise, the ROC would lose the legitimacy in the eyes of international audiences. This problem was set aside by martial law provisions allowing those elected on the mainland to continue to hold office without reelection in Taiwan. The executive branch controlled policy with few checks and balances from elected representatives. The creation of the DDP in 1986 and scores of other parties since then has categorically changed Taiwan's party system. The 1986 election turned out to be the first electoral campaign in post-1949 Taiwan in which political dissidents were able to participate as a legal political party. Seven months after this election, martial law was lifted on July 14, 1987 (Chu, 1994). After martial law was lifted, the DDP legislators started to refuse to acknowledge the constitution of the Republic of China and to advocate Taiwanese separatism. They argued that Taiwan should be governed by a Taiwanese political party and the KMT should be stripped of its legitimacy since it came to power by the 1949 invasion.

The DDP was an alliance of the main political dissidents, *Tangwai*, in Taiwan. The main motive of the *Tangwai* was to form an opposition party in Taiwan. On September 28, 1986, the formation of the DDP was announced. The KMT did not suppress the new party. In January 1989, the ROC's Legislative Yuan passed the Civil Organization Law, which created an institutional framework within which the DDP and other opposition groups can co-exist and compete with the KMT. In its early years, the DDP was troubled by conflicts among factions within the DDP. Although the DDP supported the eventual independence of Taiwan, it advocated the normalization of the relations between Taiwan and the mainland through exchanges and conducts in the short term. On October 13, 1987, the DDP at its Central Standing Committee passed the resolution entitled "The Current Stage's Mainland China Policy of the DDP," which included the following main points (Wu, 1995: 237–8): (1) people should have freedom to travel between Taiwan and the mainland, to exchange postal and telecommunication services, and to sweep their ancestors' tombs; (2) interactions in cultural, academic, and economic fields, sports, and science and technology should be conducted on an equal basis; (3) both Taiwan and the mainland should abolish the policy of the use of force against each other; (4) Taiwan and the mainland should have exchanges on an unofficial basis in the short term, while the two sides should hold political negotiations in the long term. In addition to the above resolutions, on April 17, 1988, the DDP passed another resolution during its Plenary Meeting of the Second Party Congress, claiming that the DDP would advocate Taiwan's independence if the following situations occurred: (1) if the KMT unilaterally embarked on talks with the CCP; (2) if the KMT betrayed the Taiwan people's interest; (3) if the PRC used force to reunify Taiwan; and (4) if the KMT would not make attempts to bring about a genuine democracy.

With the end of martial law, a number of restrictions on the size and establishment of newspapers and magazines became ineffective. Numerous newspapers and magazines were founded. They published various opinions. Owing to the new competitive environment, even newspapers close to the KMT were forced to change editorial policies. There were also widespread private radio stations, which broadcasted in Fukienese or Hakka rather than Mandarin. There were public debates over topics that had previously been discussed only privately. People openly discussed topics such as a Taiwanese identity different from that of Mainland China and a Taiwanese state. In association with rapid economic growth and widespread education over the preceding three decades, Taiwanese society had experienced great changes. A prosperous middle class had emerged with great demand for political freedom. Taiwanese businessmen were economically successful and self-confident. In the 1980s, the business community became directly involved in politics. Young people were tied of old-fashioned ideology, elderly leaders, and tight controls. Many went abroad to study. After having been educated under the educational systems either in Taiwan or in the West and having spoken the same language for more than three decades under the same environment, the mainlanders and the Taiwanese were prepared to communicate with each other. The distinction between the Taiwanese and the mainlanders had become less salient.

Following four decades of rapid economic growth and urbanization, Taiwan's social structure had become highly differentiated. The proliferation of secondary associations rose from 2560 in 1952 to 13,400 in 1989. At the end of the 1980s, more than 60 parties had been established. However, only a few of them gained any political importance. In the 1980s, many of these associations, such as farmers' groups and trade unions, demanded changes in the arrangement of the state–society relations (Tien, 1992: 12). The party-state had lost control over some associations previously held under its grip. Some associations were closely linked with the opposition parties. There were many street demonstrations and social movements in protest against existing public policies and the conduct of the party-state by the late 1980s. Taiwanese no longer tolerated the authoritarian system and the KMT structure of political subordination over the civil society. In late 1988, KMT and DDP members of the Legislative Yuan fought over several bills such as proposals for the voluntary retirement of senior parliamentarians holding office since 1947 and for the legalization of new political parties. The Voluntary Retirement of Senior Parliamentarians Bill was proposed paying each retiring official a pension of NT$3.74 million (which later became NT$4.5 million). Despite DPP members' strong demand that a general election be held to force the lawmakers out of office without pension, the voluntary retirement bill became law on February 3, 1989. At this time, about 900 of the 1000 members of the National Assembly and about 200 of the 300 members of the Legislative Yuan were senior representatives "frozen" in office since 1947 (Lasater, 1993: 42). The voluntary retirement failed to convince all of the senior parliamentarians to retire. In fact, many stayed on, especially in the National Assembly responsible for electing the president and amending the constitution. In early 1989, the Legislative Yuan passed a Civil Organization Law legalizing the establishment of new political parties. The law still prohibited political parties from advocating Taiwan's independence and supporting communism.

The opposition DDP began to push for Taiwanese independence and for further democratization by ending the hegemonic position of the KMT. The DDP radicals attempted to move Taiwan in the direction of national independence. This ran counter to the positions of the KMT as well as the CCP, both of which had long insisted that Taiwan is an integral part of China. The diverging interests of the political parties, local factions, and other groups intensified political competition. In the 1989 election campaign, the KMT used program emphasizing prosperity, welfare, and security, while the DDP demanded for further democratization and political reforms. The DDP also argued for Taiwanese independence. On December 2, 1989, elections were held for 293 seats in the ROC national, provincial, and local government. The KMT and 15 other parties competed for seats. The DDP expanded its electoral base, getting about 28% of the vote. The elections were the first to be held since the lifting of martial law and the first after the parties opposed to the KMT had been legalized. The KMT suffered a painful loss. Its share of the votes was 60.9%, 9% lower than the preceding election.

3.7 Consolidation of Democracy Since 1990

> There are cases in which the blade springs, but the plant does not go on to flower! There are cases where it flowers, but no fruit is subsequently produced.
>
> *Confucius*

In *Democracy in America*, de Tocqueville (1948) observes: "It is evident to all that a great democratic revolution is going on among us, but all do not look at it in the same light. To some it appears to be novel but accidental; and, as such, they hope it may still be checked; to others it seems irresistible, because it is the most uniform, the most ancient, and the most permanent tendency that is to be found in history." Democratization and termination of martial law brought the surface ethnic and social divisions long held in check by martial law (Lasater, 1993). Since the lifting of martial law in 1987, the KMT has moved Taiwan rapidly toward the democracy written in the 1947 constitution and Dr Sun's Three Principles. Although martial law imposed in 1949 was lifted in 1987, it was replaced by a national security law that imposed severe prison sentences on those who called for independence or supported communism. The authorities believed that such a safeguard was necessary to maintain law and order. However, the opposition interpreted this restriction as a legal means to suppress opposition activities. It was argued that as long as Taiwan's judiciary was not truly independent of the KMT influence, Taiwan could not become a free society. Due to strong protests by the DPP and other dissident organizations, the government was forced to amend the national security law. Since 1991, it is no longer a crime in Taiwan to advocate independence or to express support for communism. In May 1991, when the National Assembly held a special session to make some constitutional revisions and to lay a legal groundwork for re-election of its entire membership, the Period of Mobilization for the Suppression of Communist Rebellion on the mainland was ended, with appropriate changes made in the ROC Constitution to reflect the end of the civil war between the KMT and the CCP.

Taiwan's politics since 1990 has been characterized by the rising of the DDP to power. In the early 1990s, several influencial groups competed against each other, for example, the KMT against the DDP, the Taiwanese against the mainlanders, elected members of representative institutions against technocrats and party cadres (Halbersen and Ferdinand, 1996: 10). By the end of 1991, there were over 60 political parties in Taiwan, although only the KMT and its principal opposition, the DDP, were politically powerful. By the early 1990s, there was a strong tendency for the Chinese KMT to become the Taiwanese KMT. The disproportionate role of Chinese mainlanders who had dominated both politics and government in Taiwan since 1945 was sharply reduced by the National Assembly elections in 1991 and Legislative Yuan elections in 1992. On November 27, 1992, the KMT expelled a nominated candidate, Chen Che-nan, from its party membership list, because Chen proposed organizing a Taiwanese KMT. Chen advocated "one China, one Taiwan" policy. The expulsion indicated the failure of the KMT leadership in maintaining consensus on its "one China" policy. The KMT was divided into the Old Guard and the reformers. The latter led by President Lee Teng-hui became the mainstream faction. The New KMT Alliance split away from the KMT in 1994 and formed the New Party (NP).

The NP advocated its old one-China policy, criticizing President Lee Teng-hui for attempting to change the line. It also severely attacked the "money politics" of the KMT. Its representatives are young and of mainlander background. The NP represented the interests of many of the original mainlanders and their descendants. NP leaders won impressive numbers of votes in elections in 1994. Its share of votes in the 1995 nationwide elections was 13.0%, while the KMT's share was 46.1%, and the DDP's share was 33.2% (Far Eastern Economic Review, December 14, 1995). In the early 1990s, no group appeared to have the absolute advantage in winning voters. Chaotic situations encouraged these groups to make efforts to grasp the opportunity.

The KMT had successfully ruled Taiwan because of its large and relatively disciplined membership and its strict control over the state and the society. However, after continued economic growth and spread of education over four decades, the society was changed. The KMT's ability to control the society had been significantly weakened by the early 1990s. Once democratization took off, calculations of different groups influenced its form and speed. Especially, rationally calculated interactions between the DDP and the KMT became increasingly significant for Taiwan's democratization.

In the mid-1970s, the *tangwai* utilized street actions, squabbles on the legislative floor, literacy offenses, US congressional pressures, and working through overseas Taiwanese lobbying to bargain position with the KMT. In the monopolistic position, the KMT considered political concessions as prices to pay in exchange for induced moderation of the opposition (Tien, 1992). In November 1990, DDP radicals formed a Taiwanese Independent Sovereignty Movement Committee to promote Taiwan's independence. The DDP adopted the name of the Republic of Taiwan for the 1991 National Assembly election campaign. The DDP campaigned for an independent Taiwan in the election. However, of the 225 directly elected seats, the KMT won 179 seats. The result indicated that the idea of an independent Taiwan failed to have wide electoral appeal. In the 1992 elections, the DDP had learnt its lesson from the failures of 1991 and began to call for "one China, one Taiwan," instead of independence. It was aware of the necessity to pay more attention to public policy and to play the role of a parliamentary party rather than that of a mass movement in order to achieve its goal of becoming the ruling party. The party adopted the campaign strategy that concentrated on issues of corruption in the KMT and the dangers of military rule and of privileges. It also tried to become popular by proposing social programmes. On the other hand, the

KMT targeted its campaign strategy on business groups. The DDP doubled its numbers in the legislature by winning 37 seats out of 125 contested seats. In the 1992 elections, the DDP's success at the polls also encouraged it to switch its role from a dissident to a participant in the formulation of the government policy. Only after a few years of its foundation in the autumn of 1986, the party successfully established itself as the island's major opposition party, at both national and regional levels. In the local elections for the posts of governor of Taiwan and the mayors of Taipei and Kaohsiung in December 1994, the KMT won the posts of governor and mayor of Kaohsiung, while the DPP candidate became the mayor of Taipei. In the December 1995 Legislative Yuan election, the DDP gained 33.2% of the popular vote. In the December 1995 elections, the KMT's share of the vote sank to its lowest level ever. The 1996 election was the first direct presidential election in any Chinese entity in recorded Chinese history. On March 23, 1996, Taiwan's voters went to the polls to decide Taiwan's president, vice president, and delegates to the National Assembly. The elections in Taiwan in 1994, 1995, and 1996 were interpreted as the final stage of democratization process in Taiwan (Copper, 1998).

According to Dahl (1993), a country is democratic if seven criteria of democracy are satisfied: selected officials in control of government decisions, free and fair elections, inclusive suffrage, the right to run office, freedom of expression, alternative information, and associational autonomy. These criteria are now commonly considered as the "minimum standards" for a consolidated democracy. Kuo (2000) demonstrated that by 1997 Taiwan fulfilled all the minimum standards. We now summarize Kuo's confirmation. In 1992, all the first-generation representatives resigned and new representatives elected by Taiwanese citizens were included. In 1996, Lee Teng-hui was elected as the President directly by the people. Thus by 1996, the control over government decisions about policy in Taiwan has been constitutionally vested in elected officials. Since 1987, the government has taken effective measures to reduce irregularities and improve the freedom and fairness of elections. It is generally agreed that Taiwan's elections have been conducted as freely and fairly as in any other democratic country. Inclusive suffrage had been less problematic for Taiwan even prior to 1987. Practically all the adult citizens on the island have the right to vote in all elections held by the government. The right to run for office has been guaranteed after 1987. Since 1987, most of the restrictions on freedom of expression have been removed and new standards and regulations have been put in place that are similar to those of democratic countries. With the lifting of martial law, Taiwanese citizens enjoy a degree of information freedom similar to other democratic countries. After 1987, restrictions on political and social organizations were lifted.

3.8 Taiwan's Relations with the PRC

> With those who do violence to themselves, it is impossible to speak. With those who throw themselves away, it is impossible to do anything.
>
> *Mencius*

After the ROC government retreated to Taiwan, Chiang Kai-shek rejected all proposals for negotiation with China. On January 1, 1950, the *Central Daily News* of the ROC reported: "President Chiang Kai-shek proclaims that in 1950 they will counterattack and recover the mainland." The PRC's original policy of national unification was to "liberate" Taiwan by military force. In the 1950s and 1960s, Beijing continued to threaten to use force against Taiwan and criticized US interference in China's "domestic affairs." During the period 1949–1958, there were intermittent fights in the Taiwan Strait between the two sides. In January 1955, the RPC launched a successful assault on the minor offshore island of Tachen. In August 1958, the PRC heavily bombarded Quemoy, a small offshore island near Fujian. Since then, the two sides entered into the "cold war period." Beijing and Taipei cho se to use the "hostile strategies" against each other for about 30 years.

Based on Bau (1992), we apply game theory to explain the political game between the two sides. During the period 1949–1978, the goal of Beijing was to "liberate" Taiwan, while that of Taipei was to recover the mainland. In order to achieve its goal, each side could choose either of co-operative and hostile "strategies." A strategy is said to be co-operative if it is characterized by a high degree of compromise and low degree of confrontation. A hostile strategy is characterized by a high degree of confrontation and low degree of compromise. As shown in Table 3.1, according to what strategies the two sides chose, there would be possibly four states for the relationship across the Taiwan Straits. The four states are the status quo (when the two sides chose co-operative strategies), the

Table 3.1 Interactions and preferences across the Taiwan Straits, 1949–1978

	Status quo	Confrontation	Beijing liberates Taiwan	Taipei recovers the mainland
The PRC	Desirable	Less desirable	Most desirable	Least desirable
The ROC	Desirable	Less desirable	Least desirable	Most desirable

confrontation (when the two sides chose the hostile strategies), Beijing liberates Taiwan (when Beijing chose a hostile strategy and Taiwan chose a co-operative strategy), and Taipei recovers the mainland (if Beijing chose a co-operative strategy and Taiwan chose a hostile strategy). We describe the preference orderings of the two sides as follows. The first choice of the two sides was to defeat the opposing side. Their second choice was to maintain the status quo (each side as *de factor* independent state) to have an opportunity to reunify China. The third choice was mutual confrontation, in which each side perceived itself as the possible loser in the game. The fourth choice is total loss to the opposing side. If we rank the preferences of the ROC and the PRC to each state in the order of most desirable, desirable, less desirable, and least desirable, we can assign the two sides' preference orders for the four states as shown in Table 3.1. The political game across the Taiwan Straight is thus described by the deadlock game in game theory. It is well known that the dominant strategy of Beijing and Taipei is hostile and the equilibrium state is the confrontation. It is also the Nash equilibrium since none of the two sides can be better off if they change their hostile strategies. The confrontation state is also stable since neither side can enforce the other to accept the outcome that is the best for the former and the worst for the latter and the two preference orderings of each side under the dominant strategy are better than those under the alternative strategy. The deadlock game was continued until Mainland China began to carry out economic reform and open policy in the late 1970s. As explained by Bau (1992), Mainland China would not play the deadlock game any more because of changed situations.

On January 1, 1979, the PRC and the US established full diplomatic relations. This led to a new era in the relations between two Chinas. In January 1979, Beijing sent a "Message to Compatriots in Taiwan" under the name of the Standing Committee of the Fifth National People's

Congress. The message suggested that the two Chinas should directly conduct "three links" (transportation, postal services, and trade) and "four exchanges" in academic, cultural, sporting, and technological endeavors. On September 30, 1981, Ye Jianying (1981), the Chairman of the Standing Committee of the PRC's National People's Congress, issued the following "Nine-Point" proposal for peaceful reunification of Taiwan: (1) the CCP and the KMT hold talks on a reciprocal basis to co-operate for the third time to accomplish the great cause of national reunification; (2) the two sides across the Taiwan Strait make arrangements to facilitate reunions and visits by relatives and tourists as well as academic, cultural, sports exchanges, and reach an agreement thereupon; (3) after the reunification, Taiwan can enjoy a high degree of autonomy as a special administrative region and can retain its armed forces, and the Central Government will not interfere with local affairs in Taiwan; (4) Taiwan's current socio-economic system will remain unchanged, so will its way of life and its economic and cultural relations with foreign countries; (5) people in authority and representative personages of various circles in Taiwan may take up posts of leadership in national political bodies and participate in running the state; (6) when Taiwan's local finance is in difficulty, the Central Government may subsidize it as is fit for the circumstances; (7) Taiwan Chinese who wish to come and settle on the mainland will be guaranteed that proper arrangements will be made for them, that there will be no discrimination against them, and that they will have freedom of entry and exit; (8) Taiwan's industrialists and businesses are welcome to invest and engage in various economic undertakings on the mainland, and their legal rights, interests, and profits are guaranteed; and (9) the reunification of the motherland is the responsibility of all the Chinese. On June 26, 1983, Deng Xiaoping, then the Chairman of the Central Military Commission of the CCP as well as the *de facto* leader of the PRC, made another proposal for the peaceful reunification of China (Wu, 1995: 22): (1) Taiwan will become a special administrative region after the reunification and may retain its independent nature and practice a system different from that of the mainland; (2) Taiwan may exercise independent jurisdiction; (3) Taiwan may also keep its own armed forces, so long as they do not constitute a threat to the mainland; (4) the mainland will station neither troops nor administrative personnel in Taiwan; (5) Taiwan will administer its political party, government, and armed forces; and (6) seats in the Central Government will be reserved for Taiwan. On September 26, 1984, Beijing put forward another policy for peaceful reunification called "one country, two systems." In early 1995, President Jiang Zemin made an eight-point proposal on reunification, which was consistent with Deng's formula in principle. Jiang explicitly stated: "Chinese will not fight Chinese." The above-mentioned proposals by Beijing since 1979 constitute the main framework of Beijing's policy toward Taiwan.

When the PRC began to approach Taiwan for peaceful reunification in 1979, the ROC showed strong distrust toward Chinese leaders. In 1979, when Beijing proposed "three communications and four exchanges" in the Message to Compatriots in Taiwan, the late ROC Premier Sun Yun-chuan called the proposal as "trickery and lies" (*The Washington Post*, January 12, 1979). On May 9, 1980, Taipei first responded to the PRC's proposals. Sun told a Japanese journalist during an interview that the reunification of China is the common wish of all Chinese people and China must be reunited based on freedom and democracy rather than under the Chinese communists' totalitarian tyranny. In March 1981, the KMT proposed "Reunification of China Under the Three Principles of the People" as a formal response to Beijing's proposals (Wu, 1995: 89). The ROC held that Dr Sun's Three Principles of the People represented the Chinese orthodoxy tradition, while the PRC's communism was a heresy that had destroyed Chinese culture. By the 1980s, following Dr Sun's Three Principles, the ROC had succeeded in developing Taiwan into the richest and freest province in 5000 years of China's history. Taiwan's policy means that a reunified China must be led by a democratic government (rather than by a regime based on a one-party dictatorship), and be based on orthodox Chinese culture and tradition (rather than on the heresy of Marxism–Leninism). When the nine-point proposal was proposed in 1981, Sun considered the proposal Beijing's intension to sow disorder within Taiwan (*New York Times*, October 3, 1981). In December 1983, President Chiang Ching-kuo called Deng Xiaoping's six-point proposal as "the endless united front tricks played by the Communist bandits are, to us, futile efforts that indicate they are at the end of their tether" (Wu, 1995: 74). ROC Premier Yu Kuo-hua considered the "one country, two systems" policy an attempt "to delude the free world, to produce an illusion of 'peaceful-existence' between the ROC and the Communist China ... If today we are not alert and natively discuss the so-called model, theory or system with the Communist bandits, it would only lead us to the limbo of self-destruction or to capitulate to the Communist bandits" (Wu, 1995: 74).

Since the PRC has changed its policy toward the ROC since 1979, Taipei has actually modified its policy toward Beijing from "counterattack and recover the mainland," to "using 30% military force and 70% political force" to recover the mainland during the 1960s and the 1970s, and then to "reunify China under the Three Principles of People" in the 1980s. The ROC's attitude and policy toward the mainland has become much less hostile after China began to carry out economic reform in the late 1970s. Significant policy change did not come until Chiang Ching-kuo decided to legalize indirect trade (with direct links prohibited) and transportation links with China in 1987. Chiang kept the "three nos" policy (no official contacts, no negotiations, and no compromise). Chiang's decision reflected the impact of China's success in economic reform. However, he warned that the ROC government had to be very cautious in dealing with the Chinese communists. He said that if Taiwan made a wrong decision, the PRC would take the chance to occupy the island. He held that reunification would be possible only if the PRC abandoned its ideology and embraced the Three Principles of the People. In July 1987, Taipei ended the travel ban to Hong Kong and Macao on tourist visas, which implied a relaxation of the policy restricting people from Taiwan to visit the mainland for family reunion or tourism. In July 1987, the KMT also began to allow the reprinting and sale in Taiwan of selected non-political and academic publications of the mainland and to permit mainland herbal medicine to be imported directly to Taiwan from Hong Kong wholesalers. In September 1987, the ROC government allowed people who were not public servants to enter the mainland for meeting their relatives. In June 1988, the KMT government decided to expand person-to-person contacts between the mainland and Taiwan and would reconsider its transportation, postal, and aerial policies toward the Chinese mainland. At the same time, the people of Taiwan were permitted to visit their relatives on the mainland. It was also possible for people to get permission to return to their homeland to pay their respects to their ancestors. In September 1988, the ROC government relaxed the restrictions on the visits of mainlanders to their sick relatives and suggested the possibility for public servants to be permitted to visit their relatives on the mainland.

In the early days of Lee Teng-hui's presidency, the government tried to follow Chiang's "three nos" policy. However, new needs for interaction merged as China's opening was speeded up and Taiwan needed more markets. In his 1990 inaugural address, Lee announced three preconditions for a complete opening up of economic, trade, academic, cultural, and scientific exchange with China (Leng, 1996: 47): (1) recognition by Beijing of the overall world trend toward democracy and the common hope of all the Chinese; (2) implementation of political democracy and a free economic system in China; and (3) no military threat against Taiwan and Taiwan's free development of its foreign relations on the basis of the one-China policy. These conditions were unacceptable to China. Two days after his announcement, Lee added that these conditions need not be necessarily met at the same time. By 1991, the two main factions of the KMT had repeated conflicts over the party's China policy. The non-mainstream faction, which considered China's unification as the ultimate goal, asked for broader economic and cultural exchange and favored the creation of a "Greater China Economic Circle." The mainstream faction asked for lifting the ban on direct transportation on condition that Beijing recognizes Taiwan as an equal political entity and abandons the option to use force to settle the reunification issue. In August 1992, the National Unification Council defined the term of "one China." According to this definition, "one China" means the Republic of China founded in 1911 with de jury sovereignty over all of China. Taiwan is part of China, so is Mainland China. Since 1949, China has been temporarily divided, and each side across the Taiwan Strait has been administered by a separate political entity. From 1988 to 1992, Lee Teng-hui used democracy to fight conservative forces within the KMT. From 1993, Lee used democracy to combat China's policy of unification under "one country, two systems." In his trip to Latin America in May 1994, Lee said (*Zhongguo shibao*, May 7, 1994): "The Chinese Communist regime says China's sovereignty is in its hands. I say, sorry, China's sovereignty is in the hands of all the Chinese people, including people in Taiwan. Since democratization, Taiwan's sovereignty has been in the hands of the Taiwanese people, not the PRC. The PRC is not qualified to declare Taiwan's sovereignty." In July 1999, Lee again called for the relations between the ROC and the PRC to be conducted on a special state-to-state basis rather than within the one-China framework.

The CCP made it clear that it adopted a policy of "peaceful reunification" rather than "armed liberation" with respect to Taiwan at the Third Plenum of its Eleventh Central Committee in December 1978. This policy included proposals for consultations and negotiations on an equal footing between the two sides. Since the early 1980s, Beijing proposed the "one country, two systems" plan, which has served as the basis of Beijing's policy of peaceful reunification toward Taiwan. The "one country, two systems" formula includes the co-existence of socialism and capitalism within a unified China. According to the formula, as a special administration region of the PRC, Taiwan would enjoy a high level of autonomy, including independent executive, legislative, and judicial powers, and its own armed forces. Representatives from Taiwan would be allowed to participate in the central government in Beijing, even though the government in Taipei would be a local authority and its existence of autonomy would not conflict with the policies of the central government. Taiwan would be an autonomous political entity, but the PRC would be the sole legitimate representative of China in the international arena. For the time being, Beijing still reserves the right to achieve unification through military force under extreme circumstances including (1) declaration of independence by Taiwan; (2) foreign interference in Taiwan's domestic affairs; (3) occurrence of domestic turmoil on the island; or (4) refusal of negotiation for a long period of time.

In August 1993, Beijing issued a policy white paper entitled "The Taiwan Question and Reunification of China." By this time, the DDP had achieved a breakthrough in its electoral performance and Taipei had begun to promote itself as a political entity on an equal footing with Beijing and to campaign for entry into the United Nations. According to the white paper, the PRC is the only representative of China in the United Nations and its related organizations. Beijing rejected all the formulae proposed by Taipei for Taiwan's participation in international organizations, such as "one country, two equal political entities," "dual recognition," "two Chinas," "one country, two seats," and "one China, one Taiwan." Taiwan's participation, for instance, under the title "Chinese Taipei" in the Asia-Pacific Economic Cooperation forum was the result of an agreement between the PRC and other member states, and this title was not applied to other intergovernmental organizations. Taiwan's participation in non-governmental organizations also required the consent of the PRC (Leng, 1996). Jiang Zemin's eight-point statement on relations with Taiwan has served the basic guidelines for the PRC's peaceful reunification since it was delivered on January 30, 1995. The eight points were: (1) the "one China" policy is the basis of peaceful reunification; (2) under the one China condition, Taiwan can develop cultural and economic relations with other countries; (3) reunification should be realized through negotiations; (4) military force is allowed to be used to protect Taiwan from foreign forces or to be directed at advocates of Taiwan's independence; (5) economic co-operation between the two sides will be promoted without political interferences; (6) China's reunification is based on Chinese culture; (7) Taiwan compatriots' desire for autonomy is fully respected; and (8) China offers an open invitation for Taiwanese leaders to visit China and has willingness to accept an invitation to visit Taiwan.

In the early 1990s, Taiwan experienced a dramatic democratization process and consequently reassessed its mainland policy. President Lee Teng-hui's visit to the United States in June 1995 was perceived by Beijing as Taiwan's denial of international consensus on "one China." In July 1995, Beijing began to attack Lee for "destroying cross-Straits relations." In March 1996, the ROC held its first direct presidential election against the backdrop of unprecedented military coercion from the PRC. Taiwan's presidential candidates campaigned while Chinese missiles landed near the island's two major ports and air and naval forces of the PLA held live-fire exercises in the Taiwan Strait. The US deployed two American aircraft carrier battle groups in the area to deter China during the height of the tensions. President Lee Teng-hui and Premier Lien Chan won the election with 54% of the popular vote. The island was transformed to a full-fledged democracy characterized by universal suffrage, a multi-party system, direct presidential and legislative elections, political accountability characterized by the balance and separation of powers, and an enfranchised civil society. On July 9, 1999, President Lee Teng-hui made public what Beijing called his "two-state" theory. He declared to Germany's Deutsche Welle television news program (*South China Morning Post*, July 11, 1999): "Since the introduction of its (ROC's) constitutional reforms in 1991 has redefined its relationship with Mainland China as being state-to-state relations or at least special state-to-state relations." His statement set off a new confrontation with the PRC. However, Beijing's fierce renunciation of the Taiwanese president was only verbal.

Chapter 4

Education, Science, and Technology

> There being instruction, there will be no distinction of classes.
>
> *Confucius*

Education is profoundly affected by social settings and is attached to a social context. It is one of the most important ways to develop human resources by increasing knowledge, skills, and capacities of people in modern economies. Nothing like the national attitude towards education and scientific knowledge can determine a nation's comparative advantage in globally connected economy. Truly, no epoch like the contemporary one has experienced such a rapid creation of knowledge in so many fields and such an intensive utilization of new knowledge to all aspects of our life. A nation has to continuingly endeavor to improve educational systems, to provide infrastructures for R&D activities to sustain economic national growth and comparative advantage. No nation can sustain economic development without sufficient attention paid to education and science.

Confucius' classification of people has exhibited an enduring impact on Confucian civilization: "Those who are born with the possession of knowledge are the highest class of man. Those who learn, and so, readily, get possession of knowledge, are the next. Those who learn after they meet with difficulties are another class next to these. As to those who meet with difficulties and yet do not learn; they are the lowest of the people." Confucius places people who do not learn even after meeting with difficulties in the lowest category, and placed the people born with knowledge in the highest. Confucius said that he did not meet with any person born with knowledge. Instead of assuming men to be born into different classes, Confucius holds that men are born nearly alike. "By nature, men are nearly alike"; assures Confucius, "by practice, they get to be wide apart." He held that natural talents vary among people, but the most important factor for knowledge accumulation is one's sincerity and efforts. Confucius proposed equal opportunity of education for all. "There being instruction," argues Confucius, "there will be no distinction of classes." In Confucian tradition, man is "classed" according to knowledge, virtue, action, and merit. Both knowledge and virtue are accumulated through education and life experiences. As far as human life is concerned, nothing is so important as to learn and constantly self-improve. In *The Doctrine of the Mean*, Confucius says:

> To be fond of learning is to be near to knowledge. To practice with vigor is to be near to magnanimity. To possess the feeling of shame is to be near to energy. He who knows these three things, knows how to cultivate his own character. Knowing how to cultivate his own character, he knows how to govern other men. Knowing how to govern other men, he knows how to govern the empire with all its States and families. All who have the government of the Empire with its States and families have nine standard rules to follow: the cultivation of their own characters; the honoring of men of virtue and talents; affection towards their relatives; respect towards the great ministers; kind and considerate treatment of the whole body of officers; dealing with the mass of the people as children; encouraging the resort of all classes of artisans; indulgent treatment of men from a distance; and kindly cherishing the princes of the States.

In Confucian tradition, for the mind to be good, it needs to be active, constantly learning and practicing. Men are naturally nearly equal, but not necessarily socially and economically. There is a permanent belief in Confucian tradition that a good society should be hierarchically organized with virtuous and talented men at the top. This structure is not to serve any privileged class or group of people, but to best serve the people. It is held that men are different in talent and society should have an ordered structure. Since different social positions require different talents, it is necessary to employ people according to talent. The foundation of the Confucian hierarchical structure is education and self-cultivation. By putting cultivated and talented men in important positions, society benefits as a whole. To provide an effective social system, the society should provide opportunity for all to rise in the hierarchy. Confucianism is not a religion and there is no final "authority" over truth. Since Confucianism does not fix any authority for truth, it emphasizes individual capacity for judgment according to changeable circumstances. People, if uneducated, can rarely have harmonious interpretations about social and economic situations. Society may not be maintained in a desirable order if masses cannot agree on political and economic issues. In addition, if masses are enriched, they will not be easily motivated to violate social order. In Confucian tradition, the government should first guarantee the livelihood of the people. However, material living conditions are the "initial concerns" of the government in socio-economic processes. As soon as livelihood is secured, the government should spread education. Indeed, the contents of traditional education are different from these of modern education. This implies that even if the government is economically oriented, a modern government should emphasize science and technology for economic purposes because science and technology are basic to economic development.

4.1 Education in the Colonial Time

> To lead an uninstructed people to war is to throw them away.
>
> *Confucius*

It is argued that the Japanese colonial government made positive contributions to Taiwan's economic miracle through constructing infrastructure and spreading primary education. To spread education without class distinction is the basic principle of Confucianism. Since Confucianism had influenced the Japanese educational ideal in modern times, Japanese education could be spread in Taiwan with little cultural resistance. In modern times, the Japanese have been far more effective in applying the Confucian principles than the Chinese (Morishima, 1982; Zhang, 1998). Before explaining education on the island in the colonial time, we explain a little about education before World War II in Japan. The traditional Japanese and the Chinese cultures are similar in many aspects. The two races had used the same language among the educated and officials, had read the same classics of history and philosophy, had enjoyed the same literature, had got inspiration from the same masters in painting and poetry, had practiced calligraphy of the same masters, had shared the same origins of beliefs, had known the same cultural heroes, and had dressed clothes designed from the same principles, for some centuries before they were influenced by the West. Nevertheless, the two cultures had different attitudes toward education when faced with the challenges of the Western powers. To understand this difference, we note that China was under

Manchu control from 1644 to 1911. The introduction of Western technologies and institutions would not give advantages to the Manchus. Such "racial conflicts" did not exist in Japan.

Japan's modernization began with the Meiji Restoration in 1868. The event overthrew the Tokugawa family who had held the reins of central government for over 200 years. In the early years, the Meiji government made innumerable efforts to survey and understand the world's economic systems and technology. From 1868 to 1881, the government was concerned with what to do. The Ministry of Education (*Monbusho*) was established in 1871 before any other government department. In 1872, the new government set up a modern conscript army and laid the foundations for the education system. The school system proclamation of 1872, which "aims to realize, whether for commoners, nobles, *samurai*, farmers, craftsmen, merchants, or women, education for every family in every town and every member of every family," was a declaration of equal-opportunity and compulsory education for all. The plan divided the whole country into eight university districts, each of which was divided into 32 middle school districts, and each of these into 210 primary school districts, with one primary school in each. The primary schools were to be divided into higher and lower, each with a 4-year curriculum. The plan was quite democratic and ambitious. However, the central government could not provide full financial backing and the people in districts carried a heavy burden. The education system was reformed under the Education Order of 1879.

Japan soon started to set up a national and compulsory school system that provided primary education for all children regardless of status, creed, or sex. It was widely agreed among Meiji bureaucrats that the cost of education and training should be granted the same priority in terms of budget allocation as public works. The Meiji regime provided good opportunities for its citizens to use their knowledge. The most fortunate thing that could happen to an individual under the Meiji system was not to be born as the child of a rich family, but rather to be born with a good intellect. Whereas the slogan in the People's Republic of China only two decades ago was "the cheapest thing in China is knowledge," in Japan 100 years ago, a man said "if he is a university graduate, I'll marry my daughter to him." This difference between the Chinese and the Japanese is the key factor for explaining why the Chinese had been globally humiliated and the Chinese people had domestically suffered from economic poverty and political dictatorship in the last century. The Meiji leaders recognized that knowledge and expertise as well as loyalty were necessary qualifications for recruitment into a bureaucracy for industrialization. During the 1880s, recruitment procedures based on examinations and educational qualifications were instituted. The foundations were laid for a state bureaucracy staffed by the elite of a highly competitive national educational system during the Meiji period. The state bureaucracy had been structured to recruit the nation's most highly talented personnel in terms of educational achievements. They were recruited through meritocratic rather than political or personal criteria. Once in government agencies, they typically served in single agencies for the bulk of their professional careers, demonstrating high degrees of loyalty to these agencies and to their profession. They were well paid and were given wide scope in carrying out their duties. To become an official through examination had been the practice in the Confucian China for many centuries. In terms of hiring a man according to talent, Meiji Japan had become more Confucian than Tokugawa Japan. In the early 1880s, government leaders began to feel that the purpose of education should cultivate the virtues of obedience, patriotism, loyalty, and filial piety. Japanese Confucianism was actually used in the service of the new state. Scholars who considered Confucianism as the best moral guide for the young began to exercise strong influences on the Ministry of Education. The liberal idea that education could make people free lost its popularity. The most important Meiji pronouncement on shaping the educational system was drafted under the influence of the emperor's Confucian Lecturer. The Rescript on Education issued in 1890 remained the basic statement of the purpose of education for half a century.

Although the colonial government did provide the same educational opportunity to the Taiwanese in Taiwan as the Japanese government to the Japanese in Japan, the basic vision about education and learning held by the Japanese influenced the educational policy in the colony. The main goal of the colonial education in Taiwan was reflected in a 1941 Japanese teachers' manual: "It is not enough to give them the ability to speak Japanese. The goal is much more: it is to inculcate the Japanese way of thinking and of experiencing emotion and to cultivate the Japanese spirit" (Tsurumi, 1977: 133). By 1913, the colonial government had compiled the first complete set of Japanese language and ethics textbooks, each having 12 volumes for grades 1–6 of pupils in common schools. In 1922 and 1941, they were renewed to cope with the policy changes of the colonial government. After analyzing the contents of textbooks in colonial Taiwan, Tsurumi (1977: 137–44) identifies the following major values that the colonial government wanted to instill in Taiwanese children: (1) loyalty to the Japanese emperor and his agents; (2) the importance of learning and the Japanese language, and the necessity of attending school; (3) unconditional obedience to parents and teachers; (4) hard work to earn a living as well as using one's knowledge and skills for the sake of society; (5) to be a good Japanese citizen meaning to think and to act like an obedient, hardworking Japanese subject; and (6) following social norms in everyday life, such as tidiness, clearness, support for social order, respect, honesty, avoiding annoying others. The above-mentioned values did not change much during the colonial period. The Japanese colonial educational values were not so much different from that of the traditional manifestations of Confucian educational values in China. It is observed that during the colonial period, there were differences between textbooks for the Taiwanese and the Japanese pupils. The Japanese government educated the Japanese pupils in a way similar to that the traditional Chinese educated Chinese pupils, while the colonial government educated Taiwanese pupils in a way similar to that the Tokugawa Japanese educated Japanese pupils. Tsurumi (1977: 45) observed that for the Japanese pupils, the textbooks often included stories of individual ambition and achievements of men and women born into common or poor families; while for Taiwanese pupils, the textbooks tended to include stories about harmony with family and local community and about the same occupation of the father and his sons. Tsurumi (1977: 145) concludes: "Common school Japanese language and ethics textbooks suggest that the common school was definitely meant to assimilate Taiwanese but only at the bottom of the Japanese social order. As individuals or as a group they were not encouraged by the schools to rise to positions of power or decision-making. Their textbooks aimed to make of them faithful Japanese followers, not able Japanese leaders."

The ideal of Japanese education in Taiwan followed that of Meiji Japan, which regarded education as fundamental to the modernization of the country and its people (Ku, 1997: 171). The educational goal was to provide the skills and attitudes required by those living under a great power and to select an elite group for political and economic decision-making. Japanese colonial education in Taiwan also emphasized disciplining Taiwanese to think and behave under the Japanese rule. In 1896, the colonial government told Taiwanese that they were to be "moralized" (i.e. "Japanized"). Japanese scholars came to Taiwan, setting up schools to train teachers in Japanese language education. Since 1898, Japanese colonial education began to be realized in a system of schools, curricula, pupils, teachers, and administrators (Tsurumi, 1977). The colonial government only saw to it that the Taiwanese would get trained for life and work in a new world and educated to be unquestioningly loyal to Japan. Uchida Kakichi (Tsurumi, 1977: 49), the Japanese Civil Chief in the Government-General in Taiwan from August 1910 to November 1915 expressed the colonial government's attitude toward the education of Taiwanese at a conference of local officials in May 1915 as follows: "Education in a colony is not purely for the purpose of advancing education ... Teaching such courses has often done reparable damage ... Virtually all colonial powers pursue a policy of promoting vocational education to provide students with practical skills. The people of Taiwan should be taught practical skills too so they may earn a living and enjoy happiness."

When Taiwan was a colony of Japan (1895–1945), Taiwan instituted a system of universal primary education for grades 1–6. Japanese education in Taiwan was limited to elementary education. The comprehensive schooling system was controlled by the Japanese state. The language of instruction was Japanese. To enable the Taiwanese to speak Japanese, the colonial government set up thousands of Japanese-language classes all over the island to teach Japanese among young people and adults beyond school age. Colonial education in Taiwan was to equip people with basic knowledge and modern skills. The policy was to enable people to effectively serve Japanese economically and to educate the subordinate people to accept the existing social order and Japanese dominance. The colonial government introduced a strict censorship system to check publications and newspapers in Taiwan. Many social groups such as the Woman's Society, the Society of Custom Reform, and the Youth Group were established by the colonial government for assimilating the Taiwanese people. Publications were printed in Japanese. Newspapers had to get permission from the colonial government. The colonial government also strictly controlled other media like radio stations (Ku, 1997: 174). No one could spread any word that might threaten Japanese rule.

The Japanese limited the supply of education to Taiwanese only to elementary level. In 1915, the first Taiwanese middle school was founded, and by 1939, only nine middle schools were available to Taiwanese. Until 1915, Taiwanese had no opportunity to get higher education except in a teachers' college or a medical college. The two colleges enrolled only a few hundred students. The higher educational opportunities for Taiwanese were limited to the study of practical subjects such as agriculture and medicine. Taiwanese students were not allowed to study politics and law. The Taiwanese could move upward through higher education, but the direction of such mobility was limited to technology rather than politics to avoid potential threats to the Japanese rule. Although the educational system in the colonial time was limited in size, it was comprehensive and modern. The Japanese colonialists introduced progressive and scientific education to produce literate clerks and officials for their colonial administration. The literacy rate among Taiwanese, measured by the ability to read or write Japanese raised from 1% in 1905 to 12% in 1930, and reached 27% in 1940. The primary enrollment rate for ages 6–14 was 37% in 1930–1931 and by 1943–1944 it reached 71%. When the Japanese left Taiwan in 1945, Taiwan was one of the most literate populations in Asia (Wo, 1991).

4.2 Education in Taiwan

> The scholar is not cast down, or cut from his root, by poverty and mean conditions; he is not elated or exhausted by riches and noble condition; he feels no disgrace that rulers and kings may try to inflict; he is above the bonds that elders and superior may try to impose; and superior officers cannot distress him.
>
> *Confucius (Li Chi)*

Discipline is highly appreciated in Confucianism. For more than 50 years, Taiwan had been cut off from the mainstream of Chinese culture and pressured to learn the Japanese language and culture. It seems that the Japanese had played a positive role in making the Taiwanese to respect education and discipline during the colonial period. The Japanese held all the managerial and entrepreneurial posts in colonial Taiwan. When the Japanese left Taiwan in 1945, Taiwanese people who obtained no more than an elementary education did not accumulate sufficient human capital for managing a state. During 1946–1950, about two million people moved to the island from the mainland. Among these mainlanders, many were administrators, technicians, and doctors. They were able to fill the places where the Japanese had left. Even during the initial stages of industrialization, Taiwan did not lack administrative personnel. Among the mainlanders who arrived in Taiwan after 1945 were a considerable number of writers, historians, archaeologists, painters, calligraphers, Chinese opera performers, and other intellects. A significant number of the mainlander elite arriving in Taiwan had received advanced degrees in the United States. In addition, the ROC shipped to Taiwan 3000 boxes containing the cream of Chinese art from the Palace Museum in Beijing. In 1965, a National Palace Museum was opened in Taipei where many of mainland's priceless objects were placed on display.

Although the colonial education was limited to the elementary level, it introduced scientific and technological education into Taiwan's school system. After Taiwan was restored to Chinese sovereignty, the government made immense efforts to promote education. Since the KMT's position was quite similar to that of the Japanese in the late 1940s and 1950s, it is reasonable to expect that the KMT would "imitate" the Japanese in developing education in Taiwan. Since the Japanese had already established a sophisticated schooling system, the KMT was able to rapidly spread primary education. By 1950, Taiwan had 1231 elementary schools, 77 vocational schools, six colleges or junior colleges, and one university. It had over one million students attending school at elementary level or above. The ratio of school enrollment to the population of school age in 1950 was 80% for the first level (Wo, 1991). Like the Japanese colonial government, the KMT strictly controlled education in post-war Taiwan. The government established a top–down administrative system in education from central government to local authorities. The Ministry of Education was the top of the hierarchy. The departments of education at local levels were organized to correspond to the structure of the Ministry of Education. The local organizational structure was arranged in such a way that the local authorities could effectively implement the policies of the central government with consideration of local tradition and conditions. The Ministry of Education comprised seven major departments separately in charge of higher education, technological and vocational education, secondary education, elementary education, social education, physical education, and general affairs. Various bureau, offices, and committees were also attached to The Ministry of Education to perform particular functions, such as military training for students, offering guidance on school discipline and moral education, promoting Mandarin as the national language, and compiling and screening textbooks.

In terms of numbers of both schools and students, a major part of schools is state owned in the Taiwanese schooling system. The state sets up a comprehensive state-owned school system from kindergarten to higher education. Although the numbers of schools and students in the private sector tended to increase, their establishment, courses, textbooks, students, teaching hours, and other standards were strictly monitored by the state. The government primarily directed the planning and development of formal education in Taiwan. The Ministry of Education controlled nearly every aspect and stage in the development of the educational system, including both public and private institutions. The government regulated the total number of schools, and their types and levels. It also set the maximum number of students per classroom and per grade level and controlled credential requirements and methods of teacher evaluation for all instructors. The government also regulated school curricula, content, and number of required courses and minimum and maximum credit requirements for every major.

Although the Japanese left Taiwan with one of the most literate populations in Asia, in fact the level of educational attainment was not high, except at the elementary level. It was in the first post-war decade that Taiwan saw the widespread provision of basic education, including rural education. Since the KMT came to Taiwan, strengthening education had been its priority. Article 164 in the Constitution of the Republic of China proclaims that no less than 15% of the national budget shall be appropriated for education, culture, and science; so shall be 20% of the provincial budget and 25% of the county budget. Article 18 of the Second Constitution Amendment in 1993 further outlines the roles of science and technology in national development. As Taiwan accumulated physical wealth, its commitment of resources to human capital accumulation also expanded. As shown in Table 4.1, based on Wo (1991), education expenditure raised from 2.1% of GNP in 1955 to 3.3% in 1965, then increased to 4.2% in 1975, and reached 5.5% in 1985. Education's share of total

Table 4.1 Educational Expenditure (EE) in Taiwan, 1955–1985

	1955	1960	1965	1970	1975	1980	1985
EE as a % of TGE	11.6	15.1	17.8	20.5	18.2	18.1	20.2
EE as a % of GNP	2.1	2.5	3.3	4.6	4.2	4.7	5.5

TGE, total government expenditure; GNP, gross national product.

government expenditure also increased. It increased from 11.6% in 1955 to 20.2% in 1985.

"Let a good man teach the people seven years," advocates Confucius, "and they may then likewise be employed in war." One thing that Chiang Kai-shek understood thoroughly was that no victory could be won if soldiers were not disciplined. Since the KMT came to Taiwan in 1949, it made every effort to ensure the best educational environment for producing engineers and scientists. In the late 1960s, the government reformed the educational system to facilitate industrial development. Originally, junior high schools were divided according to academic and vocational curriculum. By 1968, junior high schools became solely academic because high technical industries required a long period of academic training as the basis for advanced vocational training. The government enforced vocational and technical education in vocational high schools and in 5-year junior colleges. The government shaped education to promote economic growth. In the 1950s, the government concentrated on expanding primary education to build the work force. The KMT government extended free education from 6 to 9 years in 1968. Nine years of free education was made compulsory in 1982 and was extended to 12 years in 1993. From the 10th through the 12th years of free education, vocational and employment-specific education is emphasized. Advanced education in colleges and universities stresses the sciences, engineering, and other kinds of technocratic expertise. By 1997, over 99% of the students graduated from elementary and junior high school; 85% of the graduates of junior high schools attend academic or vocational high schools; and nearly half of the high school students go on to colleges or universities (Stevenson, 1998). In the 1970s, the state encouraged vocational and technical education at the senior middle school level as the economy increasingly demanded for trained workers and technical personnel. In the 1980s, the state emphasized higher education.

Taiwan's education system has three levels — primary, secondary, and higher. The secondary level is made up of 3 years of junior high school and 3 years of senior high school or senior vocation school. The first 9 years of school, 6 years of primary school and 3 years of junior high, are free and compulsory. After junior high school, students wishing to continue education have to take an exam to determine whether they enter a senior high school, a senior vocational school, or a 5-year junior college. Table 4.2 provides school attendance rates (representing the number of students at each level divided by the population in the age group specified, expressed as percentage) by level of schooling during the period 1949–1988. Table 4.2 is based on Hermalin *et al.* (1994: 68). Along with government investments in education, school enrollment rates increased between 1952 and 1973. Primary education was almost universal by 1958. Enrollment at the secondary and tertiary levels increased rapidly from the late 1950s to the late 1970s. The sharp increase at the junior high level was associated with the 9-year compulsory schooling initiated in 1968. There was also a sharp increase in the education of women during the same period. Families would provide daughters education opportunity to enhance their marriage prospects because of the rapid rise in the education of males. Moreover, there was also a dramatic increase in job opportunities for young educated women in the job market. Parents wanted their daughters educated since unmarried daughters usually contribute a significant portion of their earnings to their parents (Hermalin *et al.*, 1994).

Table 4.2 School attendance rates by level of schooling, 1952–1988

	Primary school (ages 6–11)	Junior high school (ages 12–14)	Senior high school (ages 15–17)	College (ages 18–21)
1952	84.0	17.1	7.7	1.5
1958	94.8	36.9	15.6	3.6
1964	96.8	43.5	23.7	8.1
1973	98.1	77.3	47.9	21.3
1979	99.7	86.0	52.8	23.9
1988	99.9	90.6	76.0	30.9

Taiwan has produced a large pool of well-trained university and technical college graduates. The number of science and engineering degree holders increased significantly over years. By the 1990s, over 85% of the students had attended senior high, technical, and vocational schools (Lin, 1998: 189). The KMT had succeeded in creating a skilled and knowledgeable work force. Before the KMT came to Taiwan, only a small percentage of people attended high schools and universities. In 1947, the KMT renamed Taihoku National University founded by the Japanese in 1928 as National Taiwan University. The demand for higher education has been higher since the KMT moved to Taiwan. Many students would spend several years in self-study, preparing for the university exam. Taiwan rapidly produced a well-educated labor force to satisfy labor demand for sustaining a complex industrial and knowledge-based economy.

Knowing that Taiwan was unable to provide higher education, the government encouraged students to go abroad for post-graduate studies. The government set up programs to financially support students to study abroad. Major US universities also offered various scholarships, fellowships, assistantships, and loans to Taiwanese students who could not otherwise afford education in the US. In the 1970s, university graduates tended to go to abroad (usually to the US) for advanced degrees and then made careers there. Over 2000 students left Taiwan each year. In the late 1970s, the number was over 5000. In 1992, more than 33,000 Taiwanese students and scholars were studying in the US. In 1993–1994, the number of Taiwan students enrolled in US colleges and universities was 37,581 (Tsiang, 1999: 251–3). Taiwan's policy of unrestricted emigration yielded outflow of foreign trained scholars and scientists in the 1960s. In 1965, the number of students who returned was 5% of students leaving. After finishing post-graduate studies, many students found jobs abroad. The number returning in a single year did not exceed 1000 until 1982. Since the late 1980s, the figure gradually increased as wage rates in Taiwan became competitive and living conditions were improving. As Taiwan's economy boomed, new employment opportunities for highly trained technical people were created. Taiwan's government made great attempts to recruit back many of its educated professionals into higher education, research institutions, major government programmes, and the private sector. The number of professionals returning in 1994 was 6510 (Gold, 1998: 55). These expatriate scholars have made significant contributions to

Taiwan's industrialization and democratization. After the late 1980s, science education, scientific instrumentation, and general research in universities rapidly expanded. In early 1993, the ROC president, premier, and two-thirds (19) of the cabinet-level appointments had PhDs, with 18 of them, including the president and the premier, obtaining their PhDs from American universities (Chiou, 1994). Now, many businesses, industrial, cultural, and political elites in Taiwan are American educated. Although Taiwan did not outspend many other countries, they performed excellently in international educational comparisons. Students' motivation and cultural preferences for knowledge are considered important factors.

The KMT party-state utilized the education system also for purposes of socialization, political indoctrination, and control. Once the KMT had taken over Taiwan from Japan, the immediate educational goal of the KMT was to clear Japanese influences and to establish the national identity of China. The educational goals of the ROC in Taiwan were defined in Article 158 of the Constitution as follows (Ministry of Education, 1984: 9): "Education and culture shall aim at the development among the citizens of the national spirit, the spirit of self-government, national morality, a healthy physique, scientific knowledge, and the ability to earn a living." In the KMT's early years of ruling, moral education meant to shape pupils' values and behavior into those expected by the KMT and its ruler. Students had to take courses in the thought of Dr Sun Yat-sen, the official ideology. The Ministry of Education had strictly controlled almost all aspects of the curriculum and administration until the late 1980s. Generally, moral education in Taiwan paid much more attention to what the government had done for developing Taiwan than to enabling pupils to think independently. The government claimed that it was the best in the world, but it did not provide proper information to help pupils to compare policies (Ku, 1997: 177–81). The KMT monopolized the role of the normal education system in training teachers for elementary and secondary schools. It required teachers to be proficient in their professional subject and to act as a political model to students. The Training Standards for Students in Normal Schools enforced by the education authority in 1958 required that the teachers must be able to teach military knowledge, to love and contribute to the country, to behave in the way expected by society, and to be loyal to the KMT's ideology and policy against the communists (Lin *et al.*, 1990: 105–6; Ku, 1997: 178). In January 1994, the University

Law was passed, which provided much more autonomy across the board to university faculty, administrations, and students in the direction of shared governance (Gold, 1998: 55).

4.3 Mandarin Versus Taiwanese Language

> In ancient times, men learned with a view to their own improvement. Nowadays, men learn with a view to the approbation of others.
>
> *Confucius*

Languages are important resources in society. There should be psychological, social, and economic laws in creation, acceptance, and utilization of language. Education in multiple languages is costly not only in terms of labor, time, and money, but also tends to cause confusions among people. Moreover, people with few resources accumulating language skills may have difficulties in reconciling different information embodied in different languages with which they are confronted. In less-developed stages of socio-economic development, there may exist multiple languages in a nation and each language is spoken by a small group of people and is important as any other languages in daily life. In such a society, each language may communicate only primary ideas and thought. As society becomes increasingly educated and complicated, problems associated with multiple languages become increasingly serious. Due to forces of communication efficiency and costs of education, there is a tendency for society to utilize a single (dominant) educational and official language. Nevertheless, functional status and sentimental values of multiple languages tend to be in conflict when the society converges towards a single language. Chinese culture was an integration of many cultures with different languages. There has never been any single language commonly spoken among all the regions in China. People write and read the official language in formal education and public activities and speak their own dialects among family members and friends. The national language co-exists with multiple local dialects.

In the early part of the 50 years of Japanese rule, there was not much need for Taiwanese people to master Japanese. As Taiwan's economy was further integrated into Japanese economy and as there was an increasing need for formal education for the Taiwanese, Japanese was gradually spread among the Taiwanese. In the late 1930s, when compulsory 6-year Japanese education was put in effect, Japanese began to rapidly spread among the Taiwanese. However, during the entire colonial period, only a small number of people used Japanese within family (Cheng, 1994: 360). When Taiwan was returned to China in 1945, few Taiwanese spoke Mandarin. The majority of the population spoke either Taiwanese or Hakka (basically dialects of South China) as their first language. A great portion of the population were bilinguals with their first tongue a dialect of South China and Japanese their second language. As a consequence of colonization, many Japanese words were introduced in Taiwanese.

After Taiwan was handed over to the KMT before the KMT moved to Taiwan, the KMT governed the mainland as well as Taiwan. Since Taiwan was a province of China, the ROC government used Mandarin as the national language. Mainlanders who came to Taiwan were from different provinces of China speaking various regional dialects, even though they could communicate in Mandarin. After the KMT moved to the island, it was confronted with new problems with Mandarin as the official language on the island. Since Mandarin speakers were in minority, the government had to take extraordinary steps to maintain the status of Mandarin against the majority to use the "family language" as common language in the public. If the KMT insisted itself as the legitimate government of the whole of China, it had to maintain Mandarin as the national language in Taiwan. The KMT regarded Mandarin as a weapon to speed up economic growth, to foster the national identity of pupils, to shape their minds as Chinese, and to pursue them to reinstate KMT power all over China.

To strengthen its Chinese-oriented unionism and to continue historical links with cultural China, the KMT promoted Mandarin as the educational language at all schools. The KMT government enforced a strict policy of using only Mandarin for official affairs, in schools, on radio, and on television. The KMT strictly controlled the mass media. It intervened in the mass media through legal as well as economic means. For instance, the KMT bought most shares in media companies, monopolized broadcasting channels, established KMT-owned publishers, and helped members of the KMT to become bosses and chief executives. By the late 1980s, all the television stations depended on the state and the KMT for investments, and the chairmen of the boards of these stations were assigned by the government and the KMT (Tien, 1991: 243–4). By 1987, there were 31 newspapers in

Taiwan, of which four were edited and published by the KMT, two by the government, and five by the military (Ku, 1997: 178). The KMT also had strong influences on private newspapers. The opposition had few ways to tell the public its beliefs, values, and policies. Television was first aired in 1962. In the beginning, Taiwanese shows were permitted. However, in 1972, the government ordered that all television stations could not air more than one hour per day of Taiwanese language programs. In 1976, the KMT government made another rule that all television shows had to be in Mandarin and the shows in Taiwanese would be gradually phased out over years (Wachman, 1994: 53). Penalties were imposed on children who used the Taiwanese dialect in school.

A considerable proportion of Taiwanese families positively responded to the language policy. Fluency in Mandarin was generally perceived as a measure of upward social mobility. Many parents encouraged their children to use Mandarin so that they can achieve a higher academic standing at school. Some Taiwanese-speaking parents spoke to their children in Mandarin to help them to get better grades in school. Despite government's efforts, not many Taiwanese could write properly in Chinese. According to Cheng (1994: 366), this low ability to write in Chinese mainly resulted from: (1) difficulties to master the huge number and complexity of Chinese characters; (2) a custom of evaluating one's scholarship by one's own calligraphy (this tradition tended to discourage to write if one had no self-confidence with his calligraphy); (3) lack of a stable norm of modern Chinese; and (4) a general belief among masses that writing was an ornament and a display of learning. According to Cheng (1994), the KMT government "suppressed" linguistic differences in order to reach language unification. Cheng's argument was based on the following observations: (1) Taiwanese was not allowed as a medium of instruction at any level of school, except in the beginning months of instruction of first graders; (2) no instruction on Taiwanese was given at school to help the mainlanders' children communicate with the Taiwanese's children; (3) no instruction on Taiwanese was given to help community members communicate, trust, co-operate, and appreciate each other; (4) no effort was made to teach the linguistic structure of Taiwanese; (5) no attempt was permitted to popularize the vernacular writing in Taiwanese; (6) public use of Taiwanese was officially forbidden in the troops, schools, and government except in legislative organizations; and (7) no effort was made to make the basic scientific knowledge about the structure and history of Taiwanese available to students and the general public.

Restrictions on the use of Taiwanese have been already loosened. It is even fashionable to speak Taiwanese in certain settings. Intermarriages between speech groups and mobility in urban life have blurred the borderlines that once separated speech communities. Moreover, Taiwanese has become important in commerce, political campaigns, and government. As pointed out by Cheng (1994), if one uses the criterion of fluent speaking ability, the percentage of the population who can speak Mandarin might not be very high. Many people can speak Mandarin only in simple conversation. Cheng lists up fours reasons for the low proportion of those who can speak in Mandarin even in small meetings: (1) the Taiwan educational system emphasized writing ability and neglected speaking ability; (2) the system trained students to listen and repeat rather than speak and discuss; (3) most children's ability to express themselves were underdeveloped because they spoke Mandarin at school and the native language at home; and (4) their mother tongue was used in their daily life. Taiwanese speakers spoke among themselves usually only in two situations: (1) in school or the armed forces, where it was forbidden to speak non-Mandarin language; and (2) among children when they played games that they have learned at school.

4.4 Science and Technology (S&T) and the Government Policy

> When I was young, my condition was low, and therefore I acquired my ability in many things. But they were mean matters. Must the superior man have such variety of ability? He does not need variety of ability.
>
> *Confucius*

After having governed the mainland for many years, the KMT understood the significance of S&T for industrialization and had accumulated governmental skills when it came to Taiwan in 1949. The Japanese left a good educational infrastructure to the KMT and in 1949 there was an influx of skilled managers, technicians, and entrepreneurs from the mainland (Wo, 1991: 1030). Over years, the KMT government played an important role in spreading knowledge and technology for economic growth and industrial upgradation in Taiwan. The state was the initiator, facilitator, and supporter of R&D and technological restructuring (Simon, 1998). The government made a development planning that channeled labor through education and training program to meet Taiwan's changing personnel needs.

Taiwan's effort for S&T development was enforced in 1959 when the government approved the "Guidelines for National Long-term Science Development." The guidelines aimed to create an environment for S&T development, which was considered the key factor for Taiwan's modernization in the long term. In 1959, the National Long-term Science Development Council, renamed as the National Science Council (NSC) in 1967, was established. Since then, the NSC, located directly under the Executive Yuan, has served as the top agency on S&T development on the island. All policy proposals and recommendations regarding S&T issues in Taiwan should be passed to the NSC. The NSC has eight divisions and three special subunits. Each organizational unit is responsible for specified S&T areas. It is responsible for "drafting S&T policies and strategies as well as proposing plans and programs for S&T development; promoting both basic research and applied technology pilot research; improving S&T research environment; and cultivating and recruiting S&T personnel" (NSC 1988: 18). All ministries and government agencies can submit policy proposals and recommendations to the NSC. The National Science and Technology Conference held once every 4 years was an important source of recommendations for long-term S&T policies. In the conference, many scientists, engineers both at home and abroad, entrepreneurs, and administrators get together to evaluate the past performance and discuss the future direction of S&T development. The first conference was held in 1978. The results of the Conference were the "Science and Technology Development Program," which was approved by the Executive Yuan in 1979. The program identified four strategic sectors, energy, material, information, and automation. In the second conference held in 1982, four more sectors were added as strategic sectors and training and education of high-quality S&T manpower was emphasized. The "Technical Manpower Cultivation and Recruiting Program" was adopted in 1983. The third conference in 1986 proposed the "Ten-year S&D Development Plan," demanding continuous increase of overall R&D investments toward the next decade and efficient allocation of R&D

funds and adopting several policy measures to encourage private R&D investment.

The KMT government has made great efforts to build up a sophisticated S&T infrastructure for the island's development. These efforts included the establishment of several government-sponsored laboratories, the formation of industry-focused assistance organizations, expansion of graduate-level technical education programs, and establishment of special funds for supporting acquisition of foreign technology and domestic R&D programs. In the 1960s, the government established several research and service organizations to promote technological and managerial upgradation in industry. The government sponsored research institutes for chemicals, mining, energy, glass, textiles, and food processing. For example, the Metal Industries Development Center was established in 1963 to spread improved production and quality control methods. In 1965, the government established the China Data Processing Center to encourage the development of the computer industry in Taiwan. The government had already started to promote the use of computers by the late 1960s. By the mid-1960s, the government had improved domestic infrastructure and made policies that developed the island as an attractive place for foreign investment. Although direct foreign investment began to increase in Taiwan, little direct technology transfer took place. Most foreign companies were involved in simple assembly-type operations where they could take advantage of lower labor costs. The export processing zones operated like foreign enclaves. There were few contacts between the local economy and the foreign market, except that workers moved in and out of the zones according to employment opportunities. Many workers who had been trained to work in the zones started their own companies out of the zones or brought their skills into the local economy. These workers facilitated technology and skills transfer, especially in terms of middle-level management and technical personnel.

Taiwan's attempts to create a capable and responsive R&D infrastructure began to take shape in the early 1970s. Faced with rising wages in domestic market, growing costs of raw materials such as petroleum, and expanding protectionism in many countries at that time, the government recognized the necessity of speeding up S&T development. From the mid-1960s and the 1970s, the number of foreign technical co-operation agreements began to increase. Since foreign firms wanted to employ local talent, it was often cost-effective for foreign firms to help upgrade local capacities. The government sometimes also required foreign assistance in technology transfer and skill training as part of the approval process of the establishment of a foreign-invested factory (Simon, 1992). Taiwan has been greatly dependent on foreign technology. The basic technologies for the development of key export industries such as consumer electronics and industrial petrochemicals and steel were created in the US, Western Europe, or Japan. Taiwan is now a major buyer of technology in the international marketplace. It was observed that the practices of American and Japanese companies differed greatly in technology transfer (Simon, 1996). Japanese firms often made a technical co-operation agreement when forming a joint venture to further increase return from their technology rather than to provide much technology transfer. Technical co-operation tended to be used by Japanese firms as a means to penetrate the Taiwanese economy. Co-operation agreements were frequently used to "enforce" local firms to buy parts, components, or raw materials from the technology supplier. It was observed that US companies tended to provide much more actual technology transfer. By the early 1990s, Taiwan's strategy for technological advance was composed of the following five main components (Simon, 1992: 125–6): (1) the government designed financial and tax policies to encourage firms to adopt new ideas and innovations, and state-led banks and other financial institutions played an important role in supporting the major industrial initiates; (2) the government used both economic policy instruments and financial incentives to encourage the diffusion of existing technology; (3) the government implemented a series of policies to improve imported technology and its utilization, reduced taxes on technology imports, and implemented policies for regulating foreign direct investment so that MNC activities were consistent with Taiwan's overall technological progress; (4) the government made major investments in education and training in the fields of engineering and science; and (5) the government made great efforts to collect and disseminate economic and technical information to enable firms to be aware of changes in global and regional market situations, foreign government policies, and progresses in science and technology in the world. The government sent or sponsored numerous technology missions abroad to scout out potential partners and suppliers of key know-how and equipment.

The government actively promotes technology. State firms are engaged in technological development. Government firms are important suppliers of technological know-how to local firms. The government organizes research with large-scale projects and then transfers the results to the private sector at low cost when commercialization is feasible. For instance, the government was involved in integrated circuit (IC) chip design and manufacturing, automation, and development of liquid crystal display (LCD) technology. Taiwanese firms could rely to some extent on private contacts and public research programs. Most Taiwanese enterprises were small or medium sized. They often found it difficult to engage in R&D activities or to provide adequate specialized training for their employees because of high costs involved. Expenditure on civilian R&D in Taiwan as a proportion of GNP was much lower than in advanced economies like Japan or the US. The state tried to remedy this disparity by organizing R&D in its own science parks. After the mid-1980s, general research in universities greatly increased. The government provided additional funding to academic departments involved in R&D. The government set up a "key research institute" and "center of excellence" at each of the four national universities: National Taiwan, National Tsing-Hua, National Chiao-Tung, and National Cheng-Kung, in the fields of applied mathematics, material science, information technology, and aviation and aerospace technology, respectively. In the 1990s, technical contributions from Taiwan were listed among the 20 top countries in the world (Lin, 1998: 190), even though it is difficult to estimate contributions of education and R&D to Taiwan's economic growth (Young, 1995; Chen, 1997).

In 1973, the Industrial Technology Research Institute (ITRI) was established as part of the Ministry of Economic Affairs. ITRI was placed directly under the Ministry of Communications. It was originally designed to develop applied industrial technologies for key components and capital equipment. However, ITRI soon moved beyond its original task. It deals with tasks such as development of a nation-wide infrastructure, international technology scanning and acquisition, technology transfer from foreign sources to the domestic SMEs sector, and specification of clusters of support industries. The results of research carried out by ITRI were transferred to private firms at the appropriate time through multiple channels. It has 11 divisions, including electronics, opto-electronics, computer and communications, chemicals, energy and resources, mechanical industry, materials, measurement standards, pollution control, industrial safety and health, and aviation and space, according to the strategic sectors to be promoted. Among ITRI's several functionally distinct institutes, the most important one is the Electronic Research Service Organization (ERSO). Although ERSO is officially a part of state bureaucracy because it is located under the Ministry of Communications and its budgets are reviewed by the state, the identity of ERSO as a part of state bureaucracy is blurred because it makes profits through the sales of its products and research contracts with the private sector and these profits are used for further researches. In fields related to ICs and other complex microelectronic components, ERSO has become the premier research institute on the island. To develop electronics technologies in Taiwan, ERSO concentrates on five technology areas: semiconductors, computers and communications, industrial automation, quality and reliability, and thin film technologies. It has provided technical support to many IC manufacturers and wafer makers. It has also trained young engineers, some of whom left the organization to establish their own firms.

In 1978, the total R&D spending was only US$111 million, about 0.48% of the GNP. The government's share was 56%, while the private sector provided about 30% of the total spending. Within the private sector, R&D spending was only 0.12% of the sales for domestic firms, while the corresponding figures in Japan and the US were 2–3%. Taiwan's firms spent far less on R&D than the Japanese and US enterprises. Since then, things began to change, as Taiwan had to upgrade its industries for survival in international markets. The government adopted new strategies to promote high technology through assisting high-technology industries and upgrade education. Recognizing weak incentives for many local firms to invest an appreciable percentage of their revenues in R&D, the government adopted a strategy that essentially sought to build products designed and offered by foreign firms. It was designed to stimulate the diffusion of high technologies to domestic enterprises through linkages with high-technology multinational companies (MNCs). The government has also offered a large number of financial and tax incentives, such as accelerated depreciation allowances, investment tax credits, deferral of income tax payments, and duty-free import of selected machinery and equipment, to local companies to expand their R&D investments (Simon, 1998: 157).

The Science and Technology Advisory Group (STAG) under the Executive Yuan was founded in 1979 to assess global trends in science and technology and formulate relevant policies in conjunction with the National Science Council, the Council for Economic Planning and Development, and the Industrial Bureau of the Ministry of Economic Affairs. In 1979, the government initiated a Science and Technology Development Program with a sizable amount of financial support for R&D. The government initiated another program for promoting strategic industries (such as machinery manufacturing, information, and electronics) with tax holidays, low-interest loans, and subsidies. In 1981, the government established a science-based park. About half of the employees in the park hold university and higher-level degrees. By 1985, the park included 49 companies with a total investment capital of US$46.8 (Hermalin *et al.*, 1994: 80). By this time, national R&D expenditure was 1.0% of the GNP. The percentage continued to grow. From 1983 to 1994, the annual growth rate of R&D spending was about 15%. The number reached 1.65% of the GNP in 1990, and 1.82% of the GNP in 1994. In June 1995, the government published its first White Paper on S&T affairs. It planned to increase R&D spending by 14.2% per year until 2002. The government hoped to attract more young engineers into government-sponsored enterprises. Young engineers may not serve their compulsory military service if they promise to work for at least 6 years within government-sponsored research institutes and think-tanks (Simon, 1992: 139, 1998: 157–8).

During the 1980s, the government encouraged development of the computer industry. In 1980, the government established an industrial park, the Hsinchu Science-based Industrial Park (HSIP). The primary objectives of the HSIP were to create an infrastructure for upgrading R&D capacities and the high-technology industries and to attract as many Chinese graduates educated abroad as possible. In a broad sense, the park symbolizes Taiwan's move into the next stage of economic development, which is characterized by skill- and knowledge-intensive industries and a high share of services in national economic activities. In the early 1980s, the HSIP was planned to attract high-technology companies from abroad. The HSIP was devoted to IC manufacturing and computer design. HSIP offered a large range of fiscal and relative investment incentives, such as low-interest loans, the right to retain earnings of up to 200% of paid-in-capital, a 5-year income tax holiday within the first 9 years of operation, accelerating depreciation of R&D equipment, and low-cost land, to attract qualified investment (Liu, 1993: 306–7). In return, companies that had invested in the park were required to spend a certain proportion of their revenues on R&D and to employ a minimum percentage of scientists and engineers in their workforce. Because the park was located close to ITRI, the Chiang Kai-shek International Airport, and two well-known technology-oriented universities, this helped HSIP to quickly diffuse new technology to Taiwan's computer industry. The park was designed to create opportunity for the private sector to move into high-technology industries that will become Taiwan's future source of competitive advantage. By 1994, the park was home to 165 companies, which have been approved and were already in operation, with total revenues of US$6.7 billion. The park employed 40,600 people, over 50% of whom had college degrees with 12% holding advanced degrees. In 1993, the average ratio between R&D spending and production value among the firms in the park was 5.4%, which was much higher than the 1.0% for firms outside the park (Simon, 1998: 160–1). HSIP's total sales reached US$4.9 billion in 1993 (Hong, 1997: 52). Many of the top executives and engineers of Hsinchu-based companies had worked in the US. There were 73 enterprises in the park that were set up by foreign-returned Chinese in 1994. These local and global networks enabled the companies to rapidly respond to changing technology and international markets (Ernst, 2000). Different from its initial goal to attract firms with the plans and skills to improve products already developed in the industrialized nations, the park has been concerned with attracting the potential for innovation and new products and developing new technologies. The park makes efforts to remain at the forefront of technological innovation and development.

From the late 1980s, a large number of Taiwanese scientists who went abroad for graduate study began to return to Taiwan. The government made great efforts to track these scientists down and entice them back. As salaries in Taiwan for those with PhDs are comparable to those in the US and Taiwan has become an open society with high standards of living, significant numbers have returned. These returned scientists have played a significant role in increasing the technological sophistication of the Taiwanese computer industry. Many returning engineers had contacts with Silicon Valley in California, which helped Taiwanese firms to remain at the forefront of technological development. The National Science

Council statistics showed that between 1990 and 1994 some 23,000 Chinese returned with a PhD or Masters Degree. The reversal of the brain drain has helped Taiwan to speed up development of its high-technology industry. The work experience of these Chinese has become not only the main vehicle for diffusion of foreign technology, but also a main pool for Taiwan's creativity.

4.5 Taiwanese Computer Industry Competes in the Global Market

> Hearing much and selecting what is good and following it, seeing much and keeping it in memory – this is the second style of knowledge.
>
> *Confucius*

The information industry in Taiwan most vividly illustrates the interaction between government policy, labor force quality, technological progress, foreign investment, and changing comparative advantage. Its success is often used as a fine example of how government intervention can lead to the successful development of an industry. The information industry of Taiwan took shape and is one of its most successful industries. The development of the industry started in 1954 when the National Cash Register established its subsidiary in Taiwan. In 1956, International Business Machines (IBM) also set up its subsidiary in Taiwan. In 1965, Taiwan Sugar Corporation, among all the government organizations, was the first to install the IMB 1440 system and to apply computers in business practices. By the early 1970s, computer applications had become well known among business and government organizations. In 1970, the Executive Yuan established the electronic data processing center to help the government agencies and educational institutions to design their own computer application systems. In August 1974, Dr Sun Yun-hsuan, then the Minister of Economic Affairs, visited Dr Pan Wen-yuan, a Chinese-American electronic engineer. After long discussions, they agreed on three points (Hong, 1997: 47): (1) the electronic industry should be selected as the targeted sector in order to upgrade Taiwan's industrial capacity; (2) Taiwan should purchase rather than develop semiconductor technology; and (3) Taiwan should employ overseas Chinese engineers and scientists to prepare and undertake various semiconductor projects.

In September 1974, the ITRI founded the ERSO to carry out R&D related to electronic technologies. ERSO is located in Hsinchu Park and linked with the ITRI. Through collaboration with universities and domestic electronic companies, the organization was responsible for introducing many new technologies in Taiwan (Chang, 1992). ERSO was the island's premier research center in terms of Taiwan's advancements in microelectronics. It often took the lead in developing the crucial technologies and then transferred them to personal computer (PC) enterprises. For instance, ERSO was the driving force in the establishment of a VLSI company (Taiwan Semiconductor Manufacturing Corporation) in which Philips and National Chaiotung University were also involved (Simon, 1992). Many scientists and engineers acquired technical expertise and experience in ERSO and then started their own ventures in the PC industry. This speeded up the diffusion of technology into the PC industry. In 1979, the Institute for Information Industry was founded with the financial assistance of the government and the private sector. The institute was responsible for software development, assistance in computerization, collection, analyses, and dissemination of technical and marketing information. In 1980, the Council for Economic Planning and Development introduced the Ten-Year Development Plan for the Information Industry of Taiwan, 1980–1990. In September 1982, the industry was chosen as a strategic industry. The industry received several kinds of financial aid, such as low-interest loans, favorable tariff rates for imported components, investment tax credits, and accelerated depreciation for capital expenditures. These incentives eased the financial burden of small and vulnerable PC firms.

It was observed that Taiwan's labor advantages and future policy priorities matched well with the typical characteristics of this branch of industry (Hoesel, 1996). The labor market in Taiwan was characterized by shortage of low-cost labor and abundance of well-trained personnel. Taiwan's labor force could well serve the knowledge- and capital-intensive information industry. Moreover, Taiwan does not have energy resources and the information industry requires little energy. The information industry could serve Taiwan's intentions to shift from low-value-added to high-value-added production operations. Since 1980, the information industry has grown rapidly and contributed greatly to Taiwan's economic growth. In the first half of the 1980s, foreign companies such as Atari,

Digital, Philips, and Wang established offshore production facilities in Taiwan. These MNEs transferred technology to Taiwan in various ways, such as training personnel. By 1985, Taiwan's information industry was characterized by offshore and original equipment manufacturing, which represented 58% and 37% of total information production, respectively (Hoesel, 1996). By 1987, the world market share of Taiwan's information industry was 3.1%, and was ranked sixth, after the United States, Japan, West Germany, the United Kingdom, and France. Following electronics and textiles, it became the third-largest export industry in Taiwan.

Among all of the products in the information industry, PC is the most important one. Even by the early 1990s, Taiwan had become one of the largest PC exporters in the world. Table 4.3, which is based on Hong (1997: 3), shows the island's world market share in PC-related products in 1994.

Its annual export amounted to more than US$1.5 billion. The capacity of some large PC companies in developing new products and technology had not lagged far behind the leading global giants by the early 1990s (Chang, 1992). A turning point for the PC industry came in March 1982 when the government banned manufacturing of video game machines. This policy change made many small-scale firms to produce PCs. These firms could only make imitations of uncomplicated designs. In 1983, ITRI, in co-operation with several local firms, accomplished a project for developing IBM-compatible PCs. In the 1980s, the PC companies exported their products mainly via original equipment manufacturing. Because of this "middle-man" strategy, they did not have to spend money on establishing distributional networks or on consumer-oriented promotion to develop brand preference. They did not have to spend money on

Table 4.3 Taiwan's world market share in PC-related products in 1994, in percentage

Products	Share	Products	Share	Products	Share
Motherboard	80	Network interface card	34	Terminal	22
Mouse	80	Graphic card	32	Network hub	18
Scanner	61	Switching power supply	31	Audio card	11
Monitor	56	Notebook PC	28	Desktop PC	8
Keyboard	52	Video card	24		

R&D. PC companies gradually developed their own brands and began to directly penetrate the consumer market.

Most of the PC companies in Taiwan were small or medium sized. It is commonly held that only large, diversified multinational enterprises can internationally compete in high-knowledge-intensive industries. It is argued that small firms have limited resources and capacities for knowledge creation. They do not have sufficient capacity to influence pricing, development of markets, formation of market structure, and technological change. This is especially true for small enterprises from the island. Taiwan does not provide a large domestic market for its small enterprises not to suffer from heavy fluctuations in international demand. Taiwan's limited domestic market limits the scope for technological spillovers. Irrespective of these possible disadvantages, SMEs could enjoy some advantages. The small PC companies of Taiwan avoided costly marketing, manufacturing, and R&D investments. Although these companies did not benefit from economies of scales, product life cycle of the PCs lessened their possible benefits. Moreover, the entrepreneurs in the small PC firms who were usually the founders tended to be strongly motivated for economic success and they were able to monitor their businesses closely without being involved in complicated managerial problems. They were able to quickly respond to changes in market conditions. Although Taiwan's PC firms were not true innovators, they could immediately imitate and even improve new designs or radical innovation introduced into the market. PC companies in Taiwan could meet the challenge of innovations in the international markets earlier than their international rivals. They were often quick to "improve" original innovations and then sell the modified products at a much lower price. Taiwan's SMEs proved able to compete in the knowledge-intensive and highly globalized computer industry. They were the main carriers of rapid development of Taiwan's computer industry, which was the most broad-based industry in Asia outside of Japan. Taiwan's computer industry has many world-class suppliers for a variety of computer-related products, key components, and knowledge-intensive services. Taiwan was the world's largest supplier of computer monitors, motherboards, switching power suppliers, mouse devices, keyboards, scanners, and a variety of add-on cards. Since 1994, Taiwan has become the world's largest manufacturer of notebook PCs (Hung, 2000).

Ernst (2000) focused on inter-organizational knowledge linkages with other firms and organizations. It is argued that Taiwanese computer companies benefited from their strong ties with large Taiwanese business groups and public institutions for learning and knowledge creation. These SMEs can compete globally also because they properly utilize international knowledge linkages to overcome their size-related disadvantages. Policy and institutional innovations also helped SMEs to establish inter-organizational and international knowledge linkages. Ernst identified the following five main characteristics in Taiwan's industrial development policies: (1) Taiwan did not restrict the number of firms within each industry group, except a few mining and utility industries, and allowed any domestic firm to invest, subject to the same tax and other conditions. This policy encouraged domestic competition and diversification of industry structure. (2) The government assisted SMEs' modernization in many aspects, such as market promotion, management rationalization, co-operation and promoting strategic alliances, loans, upgrading technology, and labor training. (3) There was no discrimination against any firm within the SME category. This neutral policy guaranteed conditions for fair competition among SMEs. (4) With a few exceptions, domestic and foreign investments were equally treated. (5) At least until the early 1980s, directed credit did not play a significant role in Taiwan's industrial policies. Taiwan's industrial policies also evolve as industry has become more complicated and international environment is changed. As pointed by Ernst, FDI into Taiwan played a catalytic role for knowledge creation throughout the development of Taiwan's computer industry. Through "learning by observing" operations and management of foreign companies, Taiwanese workers and managers learned about advanced organizational techniques and noticed the inefficiency associated with traditional Chinese management practices in modern industries.

4.6 Taiwan's Economic Growth and Human Capital Growth

> When the man of high station is well instructed, he loves men; when the man of low station is well instructed, he is easily ruled.
>
> *Confucius*

The industrial regions in East Asia have given enthusiastic allegiance to the so-called Confucian values of education, frugality, and hard work.

There is a great similarity in education among these regions (Morishima, 1982; Lee, 1991; Low *et al.*, 1991; Tu, 1991, 1994; Deuchler, 1992; Lim, 1992; Morris and Sweeting, 1995; Hall, 1997). In traditional Confucian education, homogeneity is emphasized in order to maintain an ordered society. Through education, homogeneity is perpetuated and reinforced by fixing in the child, from the beginning, the essential similarities that collective life demands. It has been argued that these values have played a positive role for rapid industrialization and widespread education in these regions. The education style in the Confucian regions has often been "criticized" for not allowing students to have any time for playing. Boys and girls study hard with little time left for playing. It has been pointed out that the Confucian education systems do not stimulate creativity and curiosity in children. The requirements of uniformity and learning are emphasized. This results in the fact that Confucian cultures emphasize the discipline to follow up brilliant new ideas with down-to-earth applications. To learn hard and to recognize the primary importance of education are the basic factors for the economic successes of the Eastern Asian economic miracles. Without overworked children and over-conformist adults, the industrialization might not have been so rapid. It is generally held that the traditional way of education has made positive contribution to the rapid industrialization of the regions. The economic history of these regions show that education without little playing is perhaps a very effective way to making take-offs from a poor and less-educated stage to a rich and well-educated stage in their economic evolution. However, there are few theoretical studies about the role of playfulness on human capital accumulation and economic development.

We now provide some theoretical insights into the dynamics of Taiwan's human capital policy, based on Zhang (2001b). As mentioned before, Taiwan has emphasized education, skill, and creativity differently in different times. As Marshall (1890) argued: "The growth of mankind in number, in health and strength, in knowledge, ability, and in richness of character is the end of all our studies ... We cannot avoid taking account of the direct agency of man in production, and of the conditions which govern his efficiency as a producer." We observe that human capital may be accumulated through different kinds of human activities and different societies demand different structures of human capital. It is observed that the ways in which human capital is accumulated are dependent on stages of social and economic development (Durkheim, 1956; Reilly, 1974; Kraus, 1990; Cohn and Johnes, 1994; Keeves, 1997). Each type of civilization requires specified form of human capital. In traditional China and the cities of Greece and Rome, education trained the individual to subordinate himself to the collectivity and to become a "fixed" element rather than an autonomous personality of society. The Athenian education tried to produce cultivated souls, capable of enjoying beauty and the joys of pure speculation. Rome's educational purpose was to make children become men of action, devoted to military glory, indifferent to letters and the arts. In the Middle Ages, education was all Christian. In modern times, sciences assume the key places in education. It is argued that at each stage of economic development there may be correspondingly effective ways of human capital accumulation. For instance, if Japan, Korea, Taiwan, Singapore, and Hong Kong had been infused with individualism comparable to European and American individualism in their educational systems in their initial periods of industrialization, East Asia might not have been able to achieve any economic miracle. On the other hand, if these same countries do not adapt their educational systems in order to meet with the need of knowledge-based globalizing economies, development of these economies might not be sustainable. We theoretically show that when an economy is industrializing (taking-off from poverty), "playfulness" may harm economic growth; when the same economy has become highly industrialized, a "proper" increase in playfulness may benefit the national economy. Our analysis show that it might be reasonable for newly industrialized economies like Singapore, Korea, Taiwan, and Hong Kong to increase playfulness in order to sustain economic development. On the contrary, for undeveloped economies such as Mainland China (in which "playfulness" may not effectively grow human capital), increases in time and natural resources on education may speed up economic growth.

We hold that as the Taiwanese have become rich and educated and Taiwan is entering into a knowledge-based economy, leisure is playing an increasingly important role in economic development. To increase "playfulness" is not only for enjoying life but also for making the labor force to have the following requisite qualities described by Marshall (1890): "To be able to bear in mind many things at a time, to have everything ready when wanted, to act promptly and show resource when anything goes wrong, to accommodate oneself quickly to changes in detail of the work done, to be ready and trustworthy, to have always a reserve of force which will come out in emergency, these are the qualities which make a great industrial people. They are not peculiar to any occupations, but are wanted in all." We hold that leisure enables people to accumulate (some aspects of) human capital. In fact, leisure has never been so socially justified in human history like in contemporary industrialized economies. Irrespective of the claimed decline in the so-called Protestant ethic, the Western world is economically effective and rich. In the pursuit of self-actualization, people have come to see playfulness and leisure as an opportunity for personal creative enrichment and for developing a new, more open, and human society. Faced with such unprecedented phenomena, we ask how contemporary post-industrial economies can be created and maintained by men and women who spend great energies and a lot of money and time on playing. What is the relationship between economic development and leisure? Will the so-called traditional Asian (Confucian, for instance) values decline in a similar way as the Protestant ethic when East Asian industrial economies enter into knowledge-based economies?

An original feature of the model by Zhang (2001) is that three sources of human capital accumulation, learning by producing, learning by education, and learning by leisure are taken into account within a single theoretical framework. It is argued that producing, education, and playing may play varied roles in human capital accumulation in different stages of economic development. Although an action of playing may be conducted not for economic purposes (because playing has its own purposes or values), high playfulness can hardly be sustainable in the long term if it has only negative impact on economic development. Technology has constantly expanded the vistas of what leisure can offer to us by creating new products and recreational opportunities. Modern technological society has provided more informal learning opportunities with its abundance of complex commodities and services. One has to constantly update one's knowledge to be a part of sophisticated and complex human networks and to constantly improve ability to handle complex machines. Moreover, rapid industrialization has broadened the roles of leisure, making its utilization more central to self-concept, health, learning, economic and spiritual well-being. The pursuit of a modern rationalizing life requires an approach to life that fully integrates work, learning, and playing. Here, we refer "education" only to "formal education," such as in schools, universities, and other educational institutions. We use the words play, recreation, and leisure interchangeably, even though they may have distinctly different meanings (Kraus, 1990). In our approach, playing is mainly referred to leisure activities of individuals. Leisure may include a variety of activities such as sports, games, travel, cultural entertainment, or participation in arts, hobbies, membership in social clubs or interest groups, nature-related activities such as camping or hunting and fishing, attendance at parties or other special events, or fitness activities. Leisure activity may be enjoyed along with thousands of other participants or spectators, or may be an intensely solitary experience. In traditional societies, learning is usually conducted through education or training in formal or informal institutions. As societies have increasingly become economically enriched and socially complicated and playing of "sophisticated games" is no more a luxury limited to few but has become available to an increasing number of people, learning by playing may become far more important for modern men's social and economic survival than commonly recognized.

We will not explain Zhang's model in detail because of its technical complexity. We now discuss some of the highlights of the model. The theoretical model shows that in the initial stage of industrialization when learning by producing tends to be effective for human capital accumulation, the government investment in human capital (except in providing elementary education to every citizen) may not be economically desirable. When the economy has become industrialized and the efficiency of human capital accumulation by education is much higher than that through learning by producing, it might be effective for the government to increase investment in (high) education in order to speed up economic growth. It may be argued that the main concern of the governments of East Asian economies such as Singapore, Korea, Taiwan, Hong Kong, and China is related to economic growth rates, at least during initial stages of their rapid industrialization. In order to explain human capital policy in a given stage of industrialization, it is necessary to examine possible relationships between growth rates and education policy. It can be shown that when the government increases the tax rate in order to enlarge the education sector, the growth rate may be either increased or reduced due to trade-offs between the effects on the output, learning by producing, the performance of the education sector, and learning through playing. When the government increases the tax rate, the labor and capital employed by the production sector will be reduced. Hence, the output is reduced. This means that the contribution to human capital growth due to saving is reduced. Hence, the growth rate tends to be reduced due to the reduced output. The reduction of the output also reduces the contribution to growth through learning by producing. Since the education sector has more money, it employs more teachers and has more classrooms, computers, and books. The education sector tends to speed up economic growth. Moreover, the growth rate tends to be reduced since the contribution to economic growth through learning by playing is reduced. The growth rate may be either increased or decreased when the government spends more money in education.

If we are concerned with an economy at the stage of initial industrialization, it might be reasonable to assume that human capital accumulation through learning by leisure is negligible. In this case, the growth rate is due to physical capital accumulation, human capital accumulation through learning by producing and learning by education. It is proved that if the economy's education system is not effective and the labor learns effectively by producing at the initial stage of industrialization when the economy has little physical capital, its growth rate is high if the government does not make heavy investment in education. We may thus argue that if a growth-oriented economy does not have an effective educational system at the initial stage of industrialization and is relatively effective in learning by producing, the economy reaches fast growth if the government invests in education as little as possible. As industrialization is advanced and the education sector's efficiency is improved (for instance, due to the influence of returned students from foreign advanced countries), the growth rate is speeded up if the government increases investment in education. We apply these conclusions to discuss Taiwan's manpower policy in its initial stage of industrialization. It seems acceptable to assume that Taiwan's government had made its education policy mainly to maximize the economic growth rate. In order to respond to the social and economic development, the education system was required to develop to produce a literate and disciplined work force. In the 1950s, basic education was strongly emphasized and technical education was in its infancy. When Taiwan came under KMT control, it did not have any sufficient supply of sophisticated teachers and its economic conditions were not good. Our analysis shows that that it might reasonable for the government to relatively neglect higher education in the early years of industrialization in order to maximize the growth rate. Our analysis also forecasts that the growth-oriented government should be concerned with skill upgrading as soon as the economy accumulates sufficient physical capital and the education sector's efficiency is improved. In the 1980s, Taiwan was losing its competitiveness to other lower-cost countries. The KMT government began to be concerned with issues of economic upgrading. The government recognized that if economic growth was to be sustained, it had to take action to create the requisite human resources. The industrial policy for Taiwan's economy was to develop a Taiwanese industrial economy based on skills, science, technology, and knowledge.

As Taiwan's economy has become more knowledge-oriented and flexible, it is necessary to further improve and transform human capital structures of labor in order to meet the need of a knowledge-based global economy. However, human capital improvement is not necessarily through spending more time on formal education. Human capital may be increased though playfulness and communications. It can be shown that under certain circumstances, it may not benefit the economy if people spend more resources on formal education. In fact, it is possible to show that if the dynamic system is unstable and the "weighted reduction" per unit of education time to human capital growth due to the reduction in education time is less (more) than the weighted increase per unit of leisure time to human capital growth due to the increase in leisure time, then an increase in leisure would harm (benefit) the long-run equilibrium. Since the equilibrium is unstable, we see that it is difficult to forecast actual paths when the system leaves off its long-run path. On the other hand, if the dynamic system is stable and the "weighted reduction" per unit of education time to human capital growth due to the reduction in education time is less (more) than the weighted increase per unit of leisure time to human capital growth due to the increase in leisure time, then an increase in leisure would benefit (harm) the long-run economic growth. This means that if no human activity exhibits increasing returns to scale and if students have been heavily occupied with education (or they have little leisure time), it would benefit individuals as well as the national economy if students have more leisure time. We conclude that when the economy is highly industrialized (which makes people more effective in accumulating human capital through playing) and there is no activity that can drive the system dramatically to change, then people in the industrial regions like Singapore and Taiwan may benefit from increasing leisure time. We thus see that it is possible for the economic system to perform better by increasing leisure time and reducing formal education time.

We hold that it is due to the need of new types of workers (as well as consumers) that leisure is playing an increasing role in sustainable economic development. As people in Taiwan have become rich and highly educated, their leisure times tend to be spent on healthy and more knowledge-related activities. This means that their leisure activities might play an increasingly positive role in human capital accumulation. This further implies that increases in knowledge through playing would reduce (relatively) the importance of formal education. Moreover, as formal education has become more expensive, the relative return from education tends to decline (with other factors fixed). It might thus economically benefit the Taiwanese economy if some of education time is switched to leisure time. Our model includes this case. Jung (1989: 63) assures:

> Not the artist alone, but every creative individual whatsoever owes all that is greatest in his life to fantasy. The dynamic principle of fantasy is play, a characteristic also of the child, and as such it appears inconsistent with the principle of serious work. But without this playing with fantasy no creative work has every yet come to birth. ... It is therefore short-sighted to treat fantasy, on account of risky or unacceptable nature, as a thing of little worth. It must not be forgotten that it is just in the imagination that a man's highest value may lie. I say "may" advisedly, because on the other hand fantasies are also valueless, since in the form of raw material they possess no realizable worth. In order to unearth the treasures they contain they must be developed a stage further. But this development is not achieved by a simple analysis of the fantasy material; a synthesis is also needed by means of a constructive method.

For the young generation of Taiwanese, "play" is necessary for Taiwan to fully join high civilization. It is worthwhile to notice that a "fantasy-focused" culture may be unable to create any realizable worth.

Chapter 5

The Economic Miracle

> If your Majesty loves wealth, let the people be able to gratify the same feeling, and what difficulty will there be in your attaining the Imperial sway?
>
> *Mencius*

Rapid and sustainable industrialization of the Confucian regions was an unexpected phenomenon. During the first half of the twentieth century, Taiwan achieved little growth, at least in per capita terms. Even by the early 1960s, economic conditions and levels of income were not very different from those in African countries (Maddison, 1989: 15). In the 1960s, economists predicted that India, Pakistan, and Sri Lanka as well as Argentina, Brazil, and Colombia would achieve outstanding rates of economic growth (Farnie, 2000). They did not expect that the four Confucian regions, Taiwan, Hong Kong, Singapore, and Korea, would undergo any comparable development to that attained in South Asia or in South America. However, the economic achievements of these East Asian regions far surpassed those of the other regions.

The recent history of Taiwan's economic development is remarkable. Since 1950, the island has been transformed from an agricultural backwater into an industrialized economy. Its high growth rate was maintained through the 1970s and beyond. From very small beginnings, it has become the world's most dynamic exporters of manufactured goods. Moreover, its spectacular growth has been brought about largely through increased factor inputs. All this has been achieved with relatively modest rates of inflation and with a remarkable equitable distribution of income. Its educational record has been exemplary. Taiwan maintained the faith in education when Western nations and many developing countries were becoming increasingly disenchanted with it (Aldcroft, 1998). Like other industrialized Confucian regions, Taiwan lacks natural resources. Small family businesses and refugees from the mainland, especially from Shanghai, played the predominant role in Taiwan's industrialization.

The rapid economic growth of the Confucian regions is a new phenomenon in world economic development (e.g. Francks, 1992; Findlay and Wellisz, 1993; So and Chiu, 1995; Howe, 1996; Latham and Kawakatsu, 2000). No previous economic growth has been so fast with so many people involved, recently or historically. Japan was the first non-Western country to become industrialized. Japan's economic position in the world has dramatically changed since the end of World War II. Its economic success was called a miracle in the 1960s and 1970s. As discussed in Morishima (1982) and Zhang (1998), Japan's dynamic path of modernization is much influenced by the combination of multiple factors such as Tokugawa Confucianism, the opportunity offered by the West, and the domestic political and economic timing for modernization. Other Confucian cultural areas that happened to be under the positive influences of Western civilization have repeated Japan's pattern of economic development. The Japanese miracle was soon followed by other economic miracles in the Confucian regions. The four Confucian areas, Hong Kong, Singapore, Taiwan, and Korea, have succeeded in rapid industrialization after World War II. The common feature of these four regions is that they were colonized before the War. The Japanese brought mass education to Taiwan and Korea, while the British brought free trade and law to Hong Kong and Singapore. After independence, Taiwan, South Korea, Hong Kong, and Singapore displayed high growth rates in the 1970s and 1980s. It should be remarked that the Chinese could have peacefully lived under "foreign" control if foreign power holders had provided people a peaceful and prosperous environment. A main reason for this attitude is due to the Confucian belief that man is classified by virtue and knowledge. Since states' purpose is to make the people prosperous, educated, and happy, according to Confucianism any person is justified to be a national leader if he performs the duties associated with the position. To obey capable and "benevolent" foreign leaders is not only due to the so-called pragmatism but also due to the conception of being human in Confucian tradition. For the Confucian mind, leadership is a meaningless symbol if it does not stand up to the duty associated with the position.

It has become clear that a main reason for the economic miracles is that they have followed the Confucian principles. Nevertheless, a popular viewpoint about Confucianism is that it neglects economic welfare of people and over-emphasizes obedience to authority. This is perhaps because what is popularly known about Confucianism is based on the interpretations of Confucianism by scholars of the Sung dynasty. A typical character among "gentlemen-scholars" of the Sung dynasty is that they did not approve even talking about profits and economic development. Chen (1911) illustrated the common attitude as follows: "Neither Confucius, nor Mencius, nor Tung Chung-shu, nor any great Confucian before the Sung dynasty, has ever said that the common people should not talk about profits. Moreover, the Confucians of the Sung dynasty did not distinguish the public profits from private profits, and left them both out of consideration. This has been a great obstacle to the economic development of China." When China under the Manchu control began to communicate with the West, Confucianism had been distorted to such a degree that it only meant to memorize the classics without understanding and to blindly obey authorities.

5.1 The Economic Miracle

> The hungry are easily supplied with food, and the thirsty are easily supplied with drink. Confucius said: "The flowing progress of virtue is more rapid than the transmission of imperial orders by stages and couriers." At the present ... let benevolent government be put in practice, and the people will be delighted with it, as if they were relieved from hanging by the heels. With half the merit of the ancients, double their achievements is sure to be realized. It is only at this point that such could be the case.
>
> *Mencius*

Over the four decades from the mid-1950s, the Taiwanese economy had experienced rapid growth, stable prices, low employment rate, and relatively equitable income distribution. In the early 1960s, Taiwan was an agricultural economy, making rapid strides towards industrialization primarily in the processing of agricultural products. In the early stages of its economic development, Taiwan faced problems of capital shortages, insufficient production, high inflation, an international trade deficit, and underemployment (Marsh, 1996). From 1952 through 1994, the real GNP grew at an average rate of 8.6% per annum, and the real per capita GNP grew at 6.3%. Per capita GNP in Taiwan increased from about US$100 in

1952 to US$12,872 in 1996 (Kuo, 1999; Ku, 2000). The annual inflation rate was 4.3%, and the unemployment rate was below 3% from 1971 to 1994 (Kuo, 1994, 1999). By 1991, nearly 80% of the families in Taiwan owned their own homes in a country with a population density of nearly 600 people per square kilometer. In 1991, there were 98 color television sets for every 100 homes, 98 refrigerators, and 166 telephones. From 1952 to 1962, the average annual inflation rate was 8.9%; from 1963 to 1980, the rate was 7.48%, and from 1981 to 1995, the average annual inflation rate was 3.32%. From 1952 to 1962, the average annual unemployment rate was 3.95%, while during the period 1963–1980, the rate declined to 1.93%. Since 1981–1995, Taiwan experienced a shortage of labor and its foreign reserve was on par with, and sometimes surpassed that of Japan. Instead of foreign debts, Taiwan accumulated one of the world's largest foreign exchange reserves. Taiwan's economic growth was characterized by a balanced budget and relatively even income distribution. From 1952 to 1995, the ROC government maintained a sound public finance system (Yu, 1999: 144). During the period 1951–1960, the share of gross domestic savings in GNP was 14.9%; during the period 1961–1970, the share rose to 21.0%; during the period 1971–1980, the share increased to 31.9%; and during the period 1981–1990, the share reached 33.2%. During the period 1951–1960, the share of gross domestic investment in GNP was 16.1%; during the period 1961–1970, the share rose to 21.9%; during the period 1971–1980, the share reached 30.5%; and during the period 1981–1990, the share dropped to 22.4% (Chu, 1995: 182).

Taiwan's economy experienced structural changes through the stages of import substitution, export promotion, and rapid technological upgradation. Taiwan has shown its ability to re-invent and re-engineer itself to respond to the changing demand and supply conditions of the domestic and international economies. Starting from the ravaged state of the Taiwan economy after the end of the colonial period, the government has been able to guard a number of critical transitions in economic orientation and emphasis. In the 1950s, with the US aid the government adopted successfully a policy of import substitution and launched a series of construction projects for economic infrastructure. The government rapidly integrated the economy with roads, ports, power plants, and communications. In the 1960s and the 1970s, the government adopted the economic policy of export promotion. This helped Taiwanese enterprises to upgrade and improve product quality and provided an attractive investment environment for foreign capital.

Over the five decades, the economic structural gravity shifted from agriculture to labor-intensive light manufacturing industry, and then to capital- and skill-intensive manufacturing industry and services. From 1952 to 1962, Taiwan's economy was dominated by the agricultural sector, and average growth rate of the Gross Domestic Product (GDP) was 7.93%. The rapid economic growth was partly owing to the expansion of the export of agricultural products, processed agricultural products, and textiles. From 1963 to 1980, the annual growth rate of the GDP was 10%. During this period, agricultural product exports decreased, while manufactured product exports increased. Maintaining a GNP growth rate of 8–9% from the 1950s through the 1980s, its economic structure and standard of living were transformed within the space of 30 years. From a less-developed country, heavily agricultural and dependent on primary-product exports in the 1950s, it had become by the 1980s a major industrial exporter with an income per capita equivalent to that found in the lower ranks of developed economies. From 1981 to 1995, the annual growth rate of the GDP was 7.52 (Yu, 1999: 142). With exports of US$111.7 billion and imports of US$103.6 billion in 1995, the ROC was the 14th largest country in the world. Along with rapid economic growth, Taiwan also experienced rapid improvements in living standards in terms of education, housing, sanitation, and transportation and communications. Real domestic wages more than doubled during the 1980s, and increases in real wages of unskilled labor exceeded those of skilled labor. Its income distribution remained one of the less unequal in the world. Life expectancy increased from 58.6 years in 1945 to 74.5 years in 1995. In 1945, 28.3% of adolescents attended high school, while in 1995, 94.4% did. In 1945, 11.3% young children attended colleges and universities, while in 1995, 45.3% did (Kuo, 1999: 43). Table 5.1, which is based on TSDB

Table 5.1 Demographic profile of Taiwan

	Population (1000)	Increase rate (%)	Life expectancy at birth		Age structure (%)	
			Men	Women	Under 15	65 and over
1952	8128	3.67	—	—	42.3	2.5
1965	12,628	2.72	65.1	69.8	44.9	2.6
1975	16,150	1.83	68.3	73.4	35.3	3.5
1985	19,258	1.32	70.8	75.8	29.6	5.1
1990	20,353	1.13	71.3	76.8	27.1	6.2
1994	21,126	0.99	71.8	77.7	24.4	7.4

(1995), summarizes the demographic changes in Taiwan during the period 1952–1994. The changing age structure and the increased life expectancy indicate the aging of the population as well as improved living and health-care conditions over time.

5.2 Economic Growth with Government Intervention

> To rule a country of a thousand chariots, there must be reverent attention to business, and sincerity; economy in expenditure, and love for men; and the employment of the people at the proper seasons.
>
> *Confucius*

A Shanghai banker explained the KMT's failure in the mainland as follows (Chang, 1958: 366–7): "This leadership, failing to understand the nature of the economic forces with which it dealt, chose to ignore them. The government could find no alternative with which to finance itself. Inflation was to run its course, and the ultimate fate of the government was sealed. Economic instability finally led to a general loss of confidence in the Nationalist government, and total collapse of political and social morals followed. Into this chaos and political and moral vacuum almost any militant group promising a clean sweep could have moved without strong opposition; and the Communists were there to take full advantage of the situation." Taiwan's economic miracle occurred under the same party that had failed to modernize the mainland.

Adam Smith argued that economic order and prosperity could be achieved through the so-called invisible hand, that is, with minimum intervention from the government. Hayek (1944, 1990) is well known for his negative attitude towards government intervention in economic activities. He argued that the free market constitutes a spontaneous order that has been brought about by the decentralized actions of numerous agents, where the market contains much more information than an individual could even possibly absorb. Through the market the actions and goals of the multiple agents are linked together to form an ordered whole. It is through the market that knowledge is created and applied and the complexity of knowledge economy is kept in order. The knowledge and skills of all the agents in the society can best be utilized if their freedom of action is not restricted and they are not subjected to central control designed to guide social evolution by a centralized authority. The efficiency of the spontaneously created complex order will be destroyed by governmental intervention. Moreover, the behavior of this dynamic system cannot be predicted because of the complexity of the dynamics of knowledge. Although it is obvious that central planning cannot effectively handle a modern system with social and economic complexity and a large population, this does not imply that the state should not intervene. The central and the most difficult aspect of the role of a democratic government lies in determining in what aspects and to what degree the state should intervene in human activities. As mentioned before, Confucian tradition believes that in the most desirable state, the government should make minimal intervention in people's affairs. Nevertheless, when it is poor and faced with threats from neighbors and its population is lowly educated, it is far from the most desirable state. In such situations, intervention by a well-behaved government is not to waste social energies and resources, but to economize utilization of limited human resources and wealth to lead the country towards desirable directions. The KMT government held that if the economic system and the government did not work closely together under the guidance of a rigorously selected and well-trained elite, Taiwan's socio-economic development and democratization could not be effectively carried out. Some justification for this belief is also referred to by Lipset (1959), Huntington (1968), and Huntington and Nelson (1976). It is held that authoritarianism was not to waste social resources but to effectively utilize resources. The KMT government heavily intervened in the economic systems.

During the Japanese colonial period, Taiwan served mainly as an agricultural base. Although the Japanese attempted to construct some manufacturing facilities near the end of its colonial rule, no major Japanese company group set up businesses in Taiwan. Before 1924, the Japanese did not allow the Taiwanese to incorporate a company without Japanese participation. Even when permits were issued, Taiwanese were restricted to small-scale industry, commerce, and land development (Haggard, 1990: 79). Among the Taiwanese, there were no local capitalists or financial upper class that owned disproportionate wealth at the end of World War II (Gold, 1986). When the KMT came to Taiwan, it prohibited the purchase of the confiscated Japanese assets by Taiwanese capitalists. The KMT government owned the assets formerly owned by the Japanese. The KMT owned and controlled large-scale enterprises to spearhead Taiwan's economic development (Wei and Christodoulou, 1998: 240). The state-owned enterprises were designed to control key industries such as steel and shipbuilding. Another role they played was upstream suppliers of raw materials and components to downstream SMEs. By having an independent source of financing political funds through the ownership of the Japanese confiscated assets and wealth brought from the mainland, the KMT government could maintain a relatively independent relationship with society. The KMT government also tried to operate public firms so that it could have a relatively free hand in directing Taiwan's economic development. When Taiwan attempted a take-off in the late 1950s, there was a division of labor between politics by the KMT state (the mainlanders) and economics by the market (the Taiwanese), with the firm control of the state over the key industries. As observed by Bullard (1997), Taiwan's armed forces were also involved in almost all aspects of the modernization process in Taiwan.

The economic evolution that took shape was mainly directed and fueled by government intervention. In Taiwan, intellectuals played a significant role in policy formation and implementation. There was effective communication between government and intellectuals partially because the educational level of senior government officials was high. An important factor for the effective co-operation between officials and intellectuals was the high proportion of officials and intellectuals with an engineering background. They were interested in problem-solving rather than abstract speculation or advocacy of particular causes. According to Wade (1990), the KMT government's intervention of a leadership kind focuses on industries or projects, which are capital intensive (e.g. steel and petrochemicals), or which use technology that must be imported from a small number of potential suppliers (e.g. semiconductor). Leadership tended to be concentrated on industries expected to become internationally competitive but have not yet become so, and on industries that were considered important for the economy's future growth. The government let industries without these various characteristics (e.g. wigs, wallets, and most non-durable consumer goods) to self-evolve in the market. Within high-intervention (or targeted) industries, the government was mainly involved at the stage of creating distinctly new capacities of new or existing industries. In any one industry, and in the industrial sector as a whole, it is possible to distinguish episodes of leadership, followership, and laissez-faire. It is observed that the governmental role in Taiwan sometimes began with leadership and then moved to followership; sometimes began with laissez-faire or followership and then came to leadership.

The first plan on Taiwan was the Plan for Economic Rehabilitation 1953–1956. The plan emphasized the necessity for rapid expansion of agricultural and industrial production due to increased population and for stabilizing prices. The government was also concerned with its balance of payments that was heavily dependent on US aid at a time when foreign exchange reserves were low. The plan emphasized the allocation of public expenditure to agriculture, fertilizers, and textiles. The second medium term plan (1957–1960) specified targets for the growth of national income and investment. The plan justified government intervention by arguing that the market would be unable to meet investment needs. The plan was to increase agricultural production and emphasized export expansion based on processed agricultural goods. In the third plan (1961–1964), the focus was on economic growth and stability. Since US aid was to end, the government attempted to further improve the investment environment to encourage foreign companies to come to invest in Taiwan. The plan also suggested further development of heavy industries including petrochemicals, steels, and specific markets in electronics. During the fourth plan period (1965–1968), US aid ended but Taiwan's economy already began to develop industries that were relatively sophisticated. The fifth medium-term plan (1969–1972) stressed development of infrastructure and price stability. The plan also encouraged exports. The sixth plan (1973–1976) encouraged the development of petrochemicals, electrical machinery, and the nascent computer industry. A number of targets in the plan were thrown off because of the oil crisis in 1973. During the seventh plan period (1976–1981), the government planned to upgrade human resource factors and made manpower planning to secure Taiwan's comparative advantage. The plan promoted a range of energy conservation measures and specified the need to complete the 10 major development projects. The eighth medium-term plan (1982–1985) emphasized a more equitable distribution of income and development of different regions. In the ninth medium-term plan (1986–1989), the government promoted economic liberalization. Environmental issues became an important part in the plan. In the tenth medium-term plan (1990–1993), the government decided to

Table 5.2 Distribution of industry by private and public ownership (based on 1981 prices, in %)

	1950	1955	1960	1965	1971	1977	1980	1986	1989	1992
Private	43.4	48.9	52.1	58.3	77.1	77.2	79.1	82.5	81.5	82.0
Public	56.5	51.1	47.9	41.3	22.9	22.8	20.9	17.5	18.5	18.0

Source: Taiwan Statistical Data Book 1993 (Taipei: Council for Economic Planning and Development, 1993: 84).

expand public expenditure to improve infrastructure and environment. The tenth medium-term plan was followed by the Six-Year National Development Plan (1991–1996). The plan included a number of major infrastructure projects to raise the national income level, to upgrade the quality of life, and to sustain Taiwan's economic growth for the twenty-first century.

The government has guided economic development. Government intervention has been a mixture of fundamental intervention (including the encouragement of macro-economic stability, investment in human capital, stable and secure financial systems, limited price distortion, and receptiveness to foreign technology) and selective intervention (such as trade policies, industrial promotion of targeted sectors, and directed credit). The economic miracle resulted from a combination of private sector vitality and state policy interventions. Although the state-owned sector dominated the economy in 1950, Taiwan's private firms also burgeoned at this time. As shown in Table 5.2, by the early 1960s, the private industrial sector already overtook the public sector in terms of ownership. The rapid growth of the private sector in the 1950s and 1960s was mainly owing to the state policy of free economy with proper intervention and economic efficiency of the private sector.

5.2.1 Import substitution, 1950–1960

The defeated Japanese had left Taiwan's economy in shambles. Resources were depleted during the war. Heavy US bombing destroyed three-fourths of the industrial base, two-thirds of the utilities, and one-half of the transportation network in Taiwan (Ranis, 1979). At the beginning of the post-war period, Taiwan was faced with difficulties that resulted from the destruction of war, the loss of the Japanese and Chinese markets, and the influx of people from China. In 1949, when the KMT government was forced to abandon the mainland, about one and a half million people fled to Taiwan. The local population was about seven million, and so mainlanders accounted for nearly one-fifth of the total population in Taiwan. In 1949, the first organizational body responsible for stabilizing Taiwanese economy, the Taiwan Production Board, was established. It was chaired and supported by able technocrats and got advice from some of the most senior Chinese economists at the top American universities (Gold, 1986).

The government carried out a successful and extensive land reform program in the 1950s. A considerable number of Taiwanese landlords accumulated their wealth by collaborating with the Japanese during the colonial period. The mainlanders did not own private land in Taiwan. The KMT carried out its land reform policy in three stages with a 37.5% rent reduction program in 1949, the sale of public lands, and the Land-to-the-Tiller Act of 1953. The reduction program in 1949 legally limited the amount of farm rent on private tenanted land to 37.5% of the harvest, down from the original 50%. The land bought by tenants through the two programs implemented in 1953 amounted to 71% of the total area of public and tenanted land. The land reform transferred ownership of farmland from large landlords to the farmers actually tilling the land. Changes in tenancy conditions provided a strong incentive for production increases and improved efficiency of land utilization. The reform shifted much capital investment from agriculture to industry. A large portion of the stocks and bonds received by the landlords in payment for their land was invested in industry and business. The reform helped Taiwan to avoid the already limited economic resources being monopolized by the traditional rural dominant class (landowners) and the economy being dominated by a rent-seeking capitalist class. The reform policy also enforced a sizeable number of potential land-based petty bourgeoisie to be more responsive to city-based opportunities open to them. The land reform significantly improved income distribution in rural areas.

The restoration of agriculture production was the first economic priority of the ROC during its early period of rule in Taiwan. By balancing development of agriculture and industry, the ROC created a sound economic base from which to industrialize later. As the agricultural sector's productivity was improved, the economic center of gravity gradually shifted from agriculture to industry. In this period, political and economic resources were monopolized by the state. The state provided a protected domestic market for big enterprises and received political support in return. In the 1950s, the government attempted to modernize agriculture and to enlarge the non-agricultural sector through import substitution. The state shifted agriculture supporting industrial development to an import substitution policy in the 1950s in which labor-intensive light industry supplied domestic needs. The purpose of the import substitution strategy was to divert a part of foreign exchange earned by primary product export away from the import of manufactured consumer goods and toward the import of producer goods in order to establish the domestic import substituting industries. The product of the domestic import substituting industries would replace the previous imports in the domestic commodity market. Taiwan employed the policy package of tariffs, import controls, and multiple exchange rates to promote import substitution. Foreign exchange was limited. Taiwan had to import raw materials and equipment, which led to continuous trade deficit. The major exports were agricultural goods. As agricultural productivity increased, surplus farm labor became available. The government relocated this labor pool into light, labor-intensive industries such as wood products, textiles, plastic products, papers, and electrical appliances. These industries did not require many capital inputs or skilled labor, but provided a quick return in profits. Between 1948 and 1955, the average nominal tariff for all imports more than doubled, rising from 20 to nearly 45% (Tao, 1969: 175–8). It was estimated that effective tariff rates were much higher than the nominal rates. Taiwan protected domestic markets for nondurable consumer goods more strongly than domestic markets for intermediate and capital goods. The government adopted exchange and trade controls to seal off many of Taiwan's consumer goods markets from foreign competition and to conserve foreign exchange for capital and raw materials imports. The government's measures were largely successful. During 1952–1960, the share of capital imports in total imports was 23%, the share of raw material imports 67%, and the share of consumer good imports only 10% (Ho, 1978: 193). Taiwan's manufacturing sector expanded rapidly. By 1958, manufacturing production was double that of 1950 (Balassa, 1991: 97). New firms were able to supply the domestic market free from import competition and from foreign-owned competitors. Although the import substitution policy promoted industrialization, it failed to solve balance-of-payments problems. Moreover, overvalued NT$ discouraged development of export industries. By the late 1950s, import substitution in goods such as beverage, tobacco, textiles and clothing, paper, and cement was complete. The small size of Taiwan's domestic market became a constraint and the high manufacturing growth rate of the previous few years began to decline. During the early phase of import substitution, the approach proved effective. However, by the late 1950s, the economy grew sluggishly. The government changed its policy from import substitution to an industrialization strategy that relied heavily on export. Between 1958 and 1963, the government reformed its import substitution policy and introduced numerous programs to stimulate export. The government reduced the level of protection on a large number of nondurable consumer goods. Mainly owing to changed domestic conditions, Taiwan began to move towards the outward-oriented development strategy. This resulted in a rapid expansion of industrial export and production from the mid-1960s to the 1970s.

From 1952 to the late 1960s, agricultural growth was vigorous. From the early 1950s to the early 1970s, manufacturing emerged as the leading growth sector. In the 1950s, relative little housing and infrastructure were constructed. After the late 1950s, there was an increasing demand for housing and infrastructure. The growth of construction accelerated. During the period 1953–1973, the annual growth rate of GNP was 8.6% and the annual population growth rate was 2.8%. The real per capita GNP increased at 5.7% per year. For the period 1953–1973, agriculture production increased at an annual rate of 4.6% and the industrial production at 15% per year. Industrial output increased at an annual rate of 11.5% during the period 1953–1963 and 19.7% from 1964 to 1973 (Ho, 1978: 123). In the 1950s, the private trade sector grew only modestly. Most external trades were controlled and managed by government agencies. The most important manufactures in Taiwan were government enterprises and they exported their products through government channels. The government channeled and partly distributed US aid imports. The government controlled and operated the distribution of key raw materials. In 1951–1953, the ratio of foreign trade to GNP was 23%. In subsequent years, the ratio of foreign trade to GNP increased steadily until it reached 81% in 1971–1973.

5.2.2 Export substitution, 1960–1973

For a short period, the import substitution approach to industrialization was successful. However, because of its limited domestic market, the easy phase of substituting domestic production for the import of consumer nondurables was soon ended. From the late 1950s, the government relaxed some of the controls adopted as part of its import substitution strategy and introduced programs to promote export. As economic growth was slowing, the resource-poor island was highly dependent on US aid, and as population was growing fast, the government switched from import substitution to export-led strategy to promote economic growth. The KMT government adopted the policy irrespective of the fact that the academic economists advocated industrialization through protection of infant industries at that time. The government also encouraged foreign and domestic investors to invest in Taiwan, by providing favorable conditions, such as tax holidays, accelerated depreciation, a ceiling on the corporate income tax rate, and a tax regime favorable to enterprises. Foreign manufacturers were attracted to Taiwan also by freedom to repatriate profit and the option of full ownership and managerial control. The government allowed foreign entry into targeted sectors and discouraged foreign entry participation in other sectors. The Industrial Commission handled all applications on a case-by-case basis. Moreover, the government employed a complicated system of domestic tax rebates so that exporters could afford to buy from domestic producers rather than from foreign sources and domestic producers of inputs were still protected despite selling to local buyers at world prices (Robins, 1998: 56–7). In the 1960s, the government further liberalized the economy and established export processing zones (EPZs) and bonded factories. By 1970, Taiwan was almost free of export trade controls.

By 1960, Taiwan's domestic market was saturated with light consumer goods. After 1960, more emphasis was placed on higher capital-intensive industries such as refrigerators, washing machines, televisions, and motorcycles. In the 1960s, the state adopted export-oriented industrialization with labor-intensive export processing industries. Then, the economic policy focused on durable consumer goods and secondary import substitution, including products of the capital- and technology-intensive heavy chemical industry. Savings, investment, and exports increased rapidly. As labor productivity increased and unit labor costs fell, Taiwan's export obtained comparative advantage. Taiwan experienced sustained economic growth along with increasing demands for Taiwan's exports. By the late 1960s, the government began to encourage the development of heavy and chemical industries. By the end of the 1960s, manufactured goods had replaced agricultural products as Taiwan's chief export. Taiwan had experienced a sustained rate of high economic growth, averaging 9–10% annually throughout the 1960s and 1970s. Taiwan's manufacturing sector had the spectacular performance record of annual growth rate 17.6% from 1949 to 1973. It greatly increased exports in clothing, textiles, light electrical machinery, radio and television, electronic components, and shoes. From 1963 to 1973, the value of industrial exports rose from US$136 million to US$3794 million with an average annual rate of about 40%. From 1963 to 1973, gross national savings doubled to 33% of the GNP and gross private savings rose at 22.6% annually. In the early 1970s, the manufacturing sector had become the leading sector of economic growth. In 1973, it produced 31% of Taiwan's GDP, accounted for over 90% of the exports, and employed more than one-fourth of the labor force. Its export-oriented development strategy brought increased international trade and recurring trade surpluses in almost every year in the 1970s and 1980s. During the periods of easy import substitution (1949–1954), difficult import substitution and transition to export promotion (1955–1962), and export diversification (1963–1973), the average annual growth rates of industrial production were, respectively, 22%, 10.8%, and 20.1% (Ho, 1978: 187–8). As Taiwan's economy had experienced rapid expansion, by the mid-1960s the existing infrastructures were becoming inadequate for economic growth. The government carried out many public construction projects to improve the island's transportation, communication, and port facilities. Power generation from hydro, thermal, and nuclear sources also increased (Marsh, 1996).

5.2.3 Secondary import substitution, 1973–1981

The quadrupling of oil price in 1973 exacted a heavy toll on the island. In 1974, the economy was severely affected by the world oil crisis and Taiwan experienced high inflation in almost all categories. In 1974, the island experienced the lowest output growth (1.1% in real terms) of the modern period. Observing the global recession and the turnaround of the economic situation, the government revised the Statute for the Encouragement of

Investment with significant changes. The government further cut tax to encourage domestic and foreign investment. After the first oil shock in 1973, the government redirected industry by launching the Ten Major Development Projects, which included heavy industrial facilities such as a steel mill and a shipbuilding and petrochemical plant. The government also made sizable investments in infrastructure, such as nuclear power stations and transportation facilities. Major infrastructure developments, such as the North-South Expressway, the new Taipei airport, harbor development, and the East Coast railway, yielded productivity gains to the entire economy. The program accounted for 30% of Taiwan's total fixed capital formation between 1973 and 1979 (Hermalin *et al.*, 1994: 79). These projects pumped billions of dollars into the domestic economy. The 10 major projects were completed on time, encouraging the development of several new heavy industries (Schive, 1992: 103). The government's policies compensated for falling exports and shrinking private investments. In 1977, the Statute was revised again (1) to speed up the development of capital- and technology-intensive industries; (2) to encourage the spread of stock share ownership and capital resources; (3) to encourage the merging of industries; (4) to promote R&D; and (5) to increase retained earnings of industries. In 1978, the Statute was revised to change tax paid by foreign investors so that a likely inequity due to long-term resident foreign investors would be eliminated (Schive, 1999).

In the fifth 4-year economic plan in 1969, the Council for International Economic Cooperation and Development (CIECD) made promotion of heavy and precision industries the main object of industrial development for period of 1969–1972. The government promoted heavy industries for the purpose of import substitution. The petrochemical industry was considered the primary target of import substitution, and machinery, shipbuilding, and iron and steel industries as the secondary targets. The plan also encouraged further development of export products characterized by high-income elasticity and called for identification of import substitution industries, which can be quickly transformed into export industries. State-owned companies were at the core of this substitution drive. In the following economic planning period, 1973–1976, the CIECD [which was renamed the Economic Planning Council (EPC) in 1973] further promoted capital-intensive industries. The EPC set the priorities to establish an integrated steel mill, to develop the machinery industry, and to promote the petrochemical industry (Chen and Ku, 1999). In 1976, the government extended its regular economic planning period from 4 to 6 years. In the first 6-year plan (1976–1981), the EPC still encouraged the strengthening of the petrochemical, basic metal, machinery, and electric machinery industries to develop an industrial capacity for self-sustained growth. The plan called for increasing the share of capital- and technology-intensive industries in the manufacturing sector from 36.7% estimated for in 1975 to 44.7% in 1981. Since the export drive was based on labor-intensive manufactured goods, its rapid growth brought about a labor shortage accompanied by a rapid increase in the wage rate. During the period 1968–1981, the government not only summoned state-owned enterprises to take charge of the import substitution drive, but also restricted the entry of private firms to guarantee the market share for the targeted enterprises. To protect domestic monopolies of the state-owned enterprises, the government maintained strict licensing control on imports (Chen and Ku, 1999). Priority industries in the import substitution stage were under licensing control, irrespective of Taiwan's trade liberalization in 1973. Moreover, these industries were eligible for tax holidays and accelerated depreciation allowances under the auspices of the Statute for the Encouragement of Investment (Li, 1988). However, imports of these industrial goods were not totally shut out partially because domestic supply of steel and petrochemical raw materials were often unable to meet domestic demand. Although imports were restricted qualitatively, imports of foreign products exerted competitive pressure on domestic producers. Domestic supplies actually could not abuse their monopoly power under the threat of imports.

5.2.4 High technology and innovation since 1980

Having experienced the successful export-driven growth in the 1970s, the entrepreneurs of Taiwan gained confidence that they could be successful in international competition. In the early 1980s, in terms of the multiplicity of commodities and the interdependence of the input–output relation, the production structure of Taiwan had become complicated. After 1980, Taiwan's economic growth has been primarily driven by the exploration of science and technology. In the early 1980s, Taiwan began to speed up economic liberalization with less government intervention in the economy and internationalization with knowledge-intensive exports. The second-stage import substitution as the central focus of economic policy officially ended in 1982. In this year, the government announced its strategic industry development plan that tried to promote industries characterized by the following traits: (1) large backward or forward linkages; (2) large market potentials; (3) high technology intensity; (4) high value added; (5) low energy consumption; and (6) low pollution content. The machinery, transport equipment, electric machinery, and information and electronic industries were selected as four strategic industries. The major policy tools for promoting these strategic industries were tax incentives, low-interest loans, and technical assistance through government institutions rather than trade protection. Changes in the size and character of the labor force affected the government to change its industrial policy. Since the 1960s, the birthrates began to decline in Taiwan. This tendency resulted in a slow growth in the age group 15–24, from 5% per year in 1961–1973 to only 1.2% per year between 1973 and 1985. The growth rate of the total labor force declined from 3.8% per year between 1961 and 1973 to 2.9% between 1973 and 1985. Taiwan experienced labor shortages in the 1980s. Owing to the increase in school attendance rates between 1973 and 1986 at all levels of schooling, the labor force was more highly educated than in the 1970s on average. The decline in the growth rates of total labor force made it imperative to restructure labor-intensive industries. The labor force with high levels of schooling made it economical to establish knowledge-intensive industries (Hermalin et al., 1994).

The demand for revaluation of the NT dollar came at the end of 1985. From 1985 to 1987, the NT$:US$ exchange rate increased from 39.82:1 to 28.5:1. By 1992, the rate reached 25.40:1 (Chu, 1995: 178). A key factor in the rapid appreciation of the NT dollar was due to the consistent trade surplus with the US. Taiwan began to have trade surplus with the US since the early 1970s. In the early 1980s, to reduce its trade deficit with Taiwan the US began to force Taiwan to open its domestic market. As the domestic wage rate and value of the Taiwanese currency skyrocketed at the same time, Taiwan began to exhaust both its labor-intensive comparative advantage and some of the benefits of the regulated and protective institutional structure. In 1987, the trade surplus reached its highest historical level with the US. Before 1987, the government's foreign exchange controls limited Taiwanese businessmen to pursue business opportunities abroad.

In May 1987, the government relaxed its controls on foreign exchange. Individuals were allowed to take abroad up to US$5 million per year. The government also began to carry out financial reform. Both domestic consumption and domestic investment fell behind production, leaving savings very large. Taiwanese businessmen transferred large sums of money abroad. In particular, Taiwan made huge investment in Southeast Asia from 1986 to 1992. Taiwanese investment in Southeast Asia was mainly concentrated in areas such as shoe-making, timber processing, textiles, garments, electrical, computers, agricultural plants, and restaurants. Chen (1994) provided the reasons for Taiwan's investment in Southeast Asia as follows: (1) When Taiwan's economy was booming, people accumulated capital rapidly over the last period. As land prices and wage rates were increased, new investors found it difficult to make profitable investment. The incentives to invest in Taiwan were weak. (2) Pollution had become a serious problem in Taiwan. Polluting firms had to pay a large amount of money for compensation. Manufacturers were forced to move somewhere to avoid the high environmental costs. (3) Small to medium labor-intensive enterprises had to upgrade their productivity with improved technology in order to survive in Taiwan. They would rather shift off-shore to a country with cheaper labor. (4) During this period, the Southeast Asian countries offered incentives, such as cheaper land, liberal rules on remitting profits, and preferential taxes, to attract foreign investment. (5) Taiwan no longer enjoyed the Generalized System of Preferences in the US in 1989. By setting up business in Southeast Asia, Taiwanese firms could gain access to the export quota privileges in the US and Western Europe given to these Southeast Asian countries. (6) Southeast Asia had rich raw materials and cheap labor. These conditions were attractive to Taiwanese labor-intensive firms.

In addition to their manufacturing profits from the domestic markets, big enterprises accumulated capital through the booming stock and real estate markets in the mid-1980s. Big enterprises were more closely interlinked through intermarriage and inter-investment. The government allowed the establishment of new private banks. The new Banking Law set the minimum capital requirement for a new bank at NT$10 billion (US$400 million), while the maximum investment for an individual enterprise was NT$5 billion (US$200 million). The policy led to the merger of big enterprises around the banks. By the end of the 1980s, Taiwan's

Table 5.3 Economic growth during the period 1980–1992

	1980	1982	1984	1986	1988	1990	1992
Economic growth rate (%)	7.1	4.1	11.6	12.6	7.8	5.0	6.0
Per capita GNP (US$)	2344	2653	3167	3994	6333	7954	10,202

100 enterprise groups accounted for 34% of Taiwan's GNP and about 70% of them were owned by native Taiwanese (Leng, 1996: 84–5). This was different in the 1960s when the state and mainland capitalists controlled most of the big enterprises. Taiwan's GNP in 1991 was US$181.1 billion, the 21st largest in the world. Per capita income was US$8810, ranking number 13 in the world. Table 5.3 (based on Chu, 1995: 178) shows economic growth rates and per capita GNP of the selected years during the period 1980–1992.

Its foreign exchange reserves by the end of 1991 were over US$82 billion, the largest in the world. Its export totaled US$76 billion in 1991 and accounted for 42% of the GNP. About 30% of these exports were purchased by the US. Total foreign investment in Taiwan from 1951 to 1991 was US$18 billion, of which the US's share was 28%. The total trade was US$139 billion, the world's 15th largest (Lasater, 1993). In 1991, Taiwan also experienced a growth rate of 7.2%. To stimulate economic growth, the government made heavy public investment in large infrastructure and encouraged domestic investment and domestic demand for locally produced goods. It is in the goods trade that Taiwan had experienced the fastest pace in economic liberalization. The average nominal tariff rate had been decreased from 22.83% in 1986 to 9.65% in 1990.

5.3 Small- and Medium-Sized Enterprises (SMEs)

Taiwan's economy was made up of a large number of independent SMEs. In 1995, the share of SMEs in the total numbers of all firms (991,615) in Taiwan was 98% and employment in SMEs was 80% of the total national employment (Wei and Christodoulou, 1998). Social and economic relations are characterized by intensive government–business relationships. Individuals and organizations are often interwoven by various types of long-term relationships called "ties" or "linkages." It is important to examine these human linkages as they are closely related to the nature of social and economic competition and co-operation, political and economic organizations, and social and economic performance. As mentioned in Wang (1998: 3), the loose and dividing structure of Chinese business groups in modern times has often been attributed to the "disloyal," "uncommitted," "selfish," and "family-centred" characters of the South Chinese culture. It has been observed that Taiwanese tend to urge to control and to be their own bosses. Under the Japanese colonialist policy and the ethnic suspicious between the KMT and the native Taiwanese, Taiwanese people strengthened the Southern Chinese preference: "it is better to be a chicken head than an ox's tail." From contemporary Western viewpoints of economic rationalism, Chinese human networks based on family-ties seem irrational.

The organizational behavior and values in Confucian regions are said to be fundamentally different from Western norms and business logic. A reason for this cultural interpretation is mainly due to fact that there is no general or universal theory of economic management and business.

Most theories are not robust enough to take account of "special circumstances" because they have been built on the assumptions that are only valid for special cultures under special historical environments. According to Adam Smith, family-centered human networks in Taiwan are rational, but fitting for low societies. Smith (TMS: 222–3) described the evolution of human networks as

> In pastoral countries, and in all countries where the authority of law is not alone sufficient to give perfect security to every member of the state, all the different branches of the same family commonly choose to live in the neighbourhood of one another. Their association is frequently necessary for their common defence. They are all, from the highest to the lowest, of more or less importance to one another… In commercial countries, where the authority of law is always perfectly sufficient to protect the meanest man in the state, the descendants of the same family, having no such motive for keeping together, naturally separate and disperse, as interest or inclination may direct. They soon cease to be of importance to one another; and, in a few generations, not only lose all care about one another, but all remembrance of their common origin, and of the connection which took place among their ancestors.

Taiwanese economy mainly consists of small enterprises. Although the economic planners in Taiwan in the past attempted to support the development of large companies (similar to Japanese conglomerates), these large trading companies never really took off. In Taiwan, large trading companies got little support from local business groups. After the KMT came to Taiwan, its focus against excessive state involvement and emphasized the vital role of free enterprise (Woronoff, 1986: 70). Private sector economic power rested almost entirely in the hands of the Taiwanese who composed about 85% of the population. Most firms in Taiwanese business groups are closely owned and controlled by the founders' family members. As mentioned by Wang (1998), family ties such as father–son and brother–brother ties are connectors among core leaders of business groups in Taiwan. The vast majority of Taiwanese firms are family-owned and managed. On a certain scale and under certain circumstances, owner-management can be an advantage. It may create strong cohesion among employees in a cultural environment that practice of law is not trustful. Taiwanese family businesses are typically very specialized in scope. They tend to focus on one market or one product only. They are characterized by a high degree of "centralization".

It is observed that external relations of the enterprises are governed by personal relations rather than by formal arrangements. Personal direction may have advantages in flexibility and adaptability. The organization can make decision rapidly and keep a high degree of confidentiality in business information. However, in such enterprises, family relations tend to be more important for promotion than expert knowledge. The position of the middle management tends to be frustrating. According to Redding (1993), organizations with these restrictions cannot divisionalize, but stay small or continue to grow with the same organizational structure. Fukuyama (1995) argued that Chinese family businesses are non-permanent structures and tend to break up in the third generation. Growth in size and sophistication of organization tends to evolve from centralization to structuralization. Division of labor between the persons and organizational departments tend to become more specified and refined. Standardization such as formal job descriptions and formation of work procedures tends to be strengthened. It does not seem that Taiwanese family businesses would be economically effectively evolved towards formally well-organized enterprises. The new global economic environment is strongly challenging Taiwanese business practice. As Taiwanese companies increase in scale, family management can bring in risks, such as uncontrolled management decisions by owners, the placing of personal interest above the company, and inside trading. Talent cultivation may be limited. Companies have to incorporate skills and knowledge from outside the family in order to produce sophisticated commodities and get comparative advantages in global markets. It is observed that the typical Chinese family enterprise has some advantages but diminish in the present world economic environment (Chen, 1995; Redding, 1995; Bass, 2000).

During the period 1949–1952, Taiwan's GNP per capita was about US$141 and the wholesale price increased at an annual rate of 62%. The capital input to industry and commerce by private business was limited. In the 1950s, many potential entrepreneurs started their own businesses. Woronoff (1986: 71) described the situation as "numerous firms, the majority of them unincorporated, were launched because people thought they saw possibilities in some commercial opening and had to do something to pull themselves out of the morass of chaos and poverty." In the 1960s, the SMEs grew rapidly as Taiwan experienced the economic structural change of labor-intensive products replacing traditional agricultural products as the major export item. Taiwanese SMEs have developed under encouragement of different government policies. In the 1960s and 1970s, under pressure from state monopolies and big firms supported by high import tariffs, small enterprises could not survive in the domestic market. They were forced to concentrate on the international market. They eventually accounted for more than 80% of Taiwan's total exports. Since the mid-1980s, the competitiveness of Taiwan's SMEs was greatly undermined by rising wages coupled with an appreciating currency at home. Moreover, domestic markets in Taiwan were dominated by LSEs. This trend, in addition to government encouragement of exports, resulted in that SMEs were mainly international.

Taiwan's SMEs were international, but not so "global" in the sense that they tended to go to those places where the Chinese had been there. They had become a major force in foreign direct investment (FDI) in Southeast Asia. Taiwanese transnational firms are small and short of managerial and technological resources. They are free from parent company control. Before 1986, Taiwanese firms made a small amount of FDI. The total investment abroad made by Taiwanese firms from 1959 to 1985 was only US$214.9 million. Of these investments 54.4% was located in the US. Since 1986, many Taiwanese firms moved to lower wage countries, mainly Southeast Asian countries and China. Taiwanese firms' FDI mainly flowed to places with low-cost labor. These firms engage in small-scale and flexible production. They form a complicated production network composed of a large number of small and loosely connected specialty producers. High efficiency is achieved through division of labor within the network and flexibility comes from variations and small sizes of firms. The SMEs were successful in "foreign" countries partly because they saved transactional costs by establishing a Chinese business environment. Each of these firms does not belong to any "boss" and can freely co-operate with anyone who seems to bring in profits. When operating abroad, Taiwanese firms co-operate with local firms from different backgrounds with little discrimination. The small dynamic enterprises have formed the vanguard of Taiwan's penetration into the Chinese market. Their business is often conducted out of Taiwan's legal restrictions. Their investments in China are driven by the profit opportunities. They transfer their labor-intensive plants to China's booming coastal provinces. Small private firms tend to move faster than state agents since the latter are slow to reach a consensus on the regulation of cross-Straits economic ties.

SMEs in Taiwan gain access to international markets through networking. Their managerial resources and capital are limited. Chinese style of management makes co-ordination and communication across national borders and different policy regimes difficult. The proprietary assets of family-owned firms are personalized. Applications of these personalized knowledge and skills often require migration of owners and/or other technical experts with their plants. These firms tend to lose home basis once they operate in foreign countries. To illustrate the evolution of SME networks in Taiwan, we discuss Taiwan's fashion shoe networks. In the 1960s, the Taiwanese shoe industry began to be involved in the world market owing to the decision of Mitsubishi, the leading Japanese trading firm dealing in footwear, to shift the manufacture of plastic sandals for the US market from Japan to Taiwan. The Taiwanese fashion shoe industry has been successful in the time–price-based global competition since the early 1970s. Between the mid-1970s and mid-1980s, Taiwan was the world's largest exporter of shoes. Shoe exports rose from US$10 million in 1969 to US$2.3 billion in 1985. About 60% of the shoes were made in factories with fewer than 100 workers and fewer than 4% of the companies employed more than 500 workers. Taiwanese shoe manufacturers have offered a highly diversified product portfolio to the world market.

Making shoes for export was a popular trade in the 1970s. The shoe sector offered salaries 20% higher than other sectors and the low entry threshold of the industry enabled workers to become factor owners. Taiwan's shoe exports reached their peak in the mid-1980s. As the New Taiwan dollar appreciated more than 30% between 1985 and 1990 against the US dollar and labor costs rose by 84% between 1984 and 1988, one-fourth of Taiwan's 1200 shoe manufacturing companies shut down or discontinued operations. Many companies were relocated in the mainland. By 1992, more than 80% of the island's shoe manufacturers had already relocated to the mainland (Hsing, 1999).

The Taiwanese shoe industry is characterized by well-connected and flexible production and marketing networks with co-ordination at both local and global levels by Taiwanese trading companies. Through trading companies' effective co-ordination, Taiwanese fashion shoe companies were able to accommodate the rapidly changing fashion trends and small orders in the world market. Trading companies succeeded in co-ordination through controlling and managing information flows at both domestic and global levels. They accumulated information about individual manufacturers, collected world market information, and negotiated with foreign buyers. Although the Taiwanese shoe industry was highly decentralized, the manufacturer could behave as a coherent production unit and achieve collective scale and scope economies owing to the effective co-ordination of the trading companies. Manufacturers obtained benefits from scale economies through specification and division of labor among manufacturers, where achieved by specified manufacturers, trading companies profited from scope economies through running the orders in the networks of firms. Trading companies were well connected to networks of local manufacturers. A typical shoe trading company had 12–15 partner manufacturers and each company (with an average of seven employees) was highly specified in the sense that it co-ordinated and allocated orders according to the specialty of individual factories (Levy, 1991; Hsing, 1999). These trading companies served as a hub of information regarding the managerial and financial conditions of factories and provided information about foreign markets to partner manufacturers. Since owners of small- and medium-sized shoe manufacturing companies usually played multiple roles such as management, financing, accounting, and marketing, they had little energy and time left for collecting and analyzing information about the export market. Due to lack of linguistic skills, they often could not effectively negotiate with foreign buyers. Shoe manufacturers would sell their products through trading companies. Some Taiwanese trading companies set up branch offices or affiliated firms in foreign countries to gather market information and explore new markets. Through contacting with manufacturers and foreign markets, trading companies were exposed to new trends in fashion design, new technologies, and new materials. Their knowledge about markets enabled them to introduce new production techniques and materials to manufacturers.

In the 1970s, many ambitious entrepreneurs and workers were attracted to the export fashion shoe industry because of the industry's high profits and high wages. When Taiwan began to export shoes, Taichung City soon become the center of the industry as manufacturers, subcontractors, master shoemakers, traders, factor managers, technicians, machine builders, material suppliers, as well as experienced workers were concentrated in the city. Many of these stayed in the shoe business and lived in the Taichung area for many years. A distinctive shoe community was formed in the area. Factories were located in the suburban area; and trading companies, sample production shops, leather and fabric display rooms, and decorative component stores for product development were attracted to the commercial district of the city. Relatively weak links between employers and employees in most small- and medium-sized firms and spatial proximity of these companies led to frequent job hopping in the industry. Perfect competition in the labor market resulted in closer interpersonal relationships in the industry as a whole.

5.4 Economic Structural Transformation

Taiwan's economic growth has been accompanied by economic structural change. The economic structural change during 1952 and 1995 is illustrated in Table 5.4, which is based on Chen (1999: 233–4). Agriculture's share of output declined from 32.2% in 1952 to 3.5% in 1995. The share of industries (which include manufacturing, construction, electricity, gas, and water) was about 20% in 1952, reached 47% in 1987, and then declined to 36% in 1995. The share of services (which include commerce, transport, storage, communication, government services, finance insurance, and business service) is now the largest sector and rising rapidly.

Table 5.4 Economic structural change in terms of GDP, in percentage

	1952	1957	1962	1967	1972	1977	1982	1987	1992	1995
Agriculture	32.2	27.3	25.0	20.6	12.2	10.6	7.7	5.3	3.6	3.5
Industries	19.7	25.3	28.2	33.0	41.6	44.0	44.3	46.7	39.9	36.3
Services	48.1	47.4	46.8	46.4	46.2	45.4	47.9	48.0	56.6	62.1

According to Fu and Shei (1999), the role of agriculture of the post-colonial Taiwanese economy was divided into two stages. The first stage lasted from 1945 to 1973, during which the agricultural sector experienced rapid growth and provided important resources to the rest of the economy. In the second stage, 1973–1995, agriculture became a dependent and protected sector, obtaining resources from the rest of the economy. Thorbecke (1979) identified the following five elements of the Taiwanese rural development strategy that were important for the success of the agricultural sector: (1) land reform; (2) integrated functions of the Joint Commission on Rural Reconstruction; (3) policies to squeeze agricultural surplus; (4) choice of labor-intensive technology in agriculture and manufacturing; and (5) spatial decentralization of industrial development to absorb rural labor. Except making many decisions in designing and implementing these five elements, the government also decided not to interfere in the operation of agricultural agents, where the market mechanism worked efficiently. Since 1973, the government changed its agricultural policy from taxing agriculture to supporting it. This was mainly due to the decline of agricultural production growth since the late 1960s and the relative decline of farmers' income to non-farmers' income, and high market prices after energy crisis in 1973 (Fu and Shei, 1999). These farmers support programs including, for instance, public investment in infrastructure, price supports for outputs, subsidies on inputs and on farmer's welfare, and import regulations. In 1973, the government promulgated the Agricultural Development Statute, which was the first time in Taiwan's history that the government's support for and protection of agriculture was guaranteed by law. The Statute provided some favorable conditions to the agricultural sector such as (Mao, 1991): (1) the farmland that continued to be used as farmland after inheritance was exempted from farmland tax and inheritance tax; (2) the farmland that was sold to another farmer for cultivation was exempted from the land value increment tax; (3) the government would increase public expenditure to improve rural infrastructure and to implement farmers' welfare measures; and (4) the government would implement agricultural insurance programs to increase farmers' incomes and to maintain rural social order. It was estimated that the total benefit that farmers received from government programs of Taiwan between 1973 and 1990 was NT$331 billion (Fu and Shei, 1999: 225).

As described in Table 5.4, in 1952, the industrial sector accounted for only 19.7% of Taiwan's GDP. In the 1950s, Taiwan adopted an import substitution policy to encourage the development of light industries, especially consumer goods industries. With US aid, Taiwan was able to start economic and industrial development in the 1950s. By 1958, the government began to adopt a number of policies. The government relaxed foreign exchange control and import restrictions to encourage international trade, and used tax and financial measures to promote savings, investment, and exports. The share of the industrial sector in GDP increased to 28.2 in 1962. The average annual growth rate of exports in real terms was 26% from 1963 to 1973 (Chen, 1999: 232). The rapid export growth of labor-intensive goods in textile, plastic products, plywood, and electronic industries helped Taiwan to achieve rapid industrialization. In the 1960s, Taiwan also began to develop heavy industries such as artificial fiber, plastic, steel, machinery, automobile, and ship building. The share of the industrial sector in GDP increased from 30% in 1963 to 41.6% in 1973. In the 1970s, the government further encouraged the development of heavy industries. The focus was on capital-intensive industries. The share of the industrial sector in GDP increased from 41.6% in 1973 to 46.7% in 1987. The share of the industrial sector in GDP tended to be stabilized after the previous rapid growth period. After 1982, the share of agricultural sector in GDP became relatively stable, even though it still tended to decline. After 1987, the New Taiwan Dollar appreciated, many of Taiwan's import barriers were lifted, and developing countries, especially Mainland China, began to compete with Taiwan in the international market. Also as Taiwan became industrialized and enriched, the service sector began to experience rapid growth. All these contributed to a steady decline of the share of the industrial sector in GDP of 46.7% in 1987 to 36.3% in 1995.

Table 5.5, which is based on Galenson (1999: 270–1), shows the sectoral distribution of employment and unemployment rates between 1975 and

Table 5.5. Sectoral distribution of employment and unemployment in Taiwan, 1975–1994, in percentage

	1975	1980	1985	1990	1994
Agriculture	30.3	19.5	17.5	12.8	10.9
Industry	40.8	48.3	46.6	46.4	44.5
Services	28.9	32.2	35.9	40.8	44.6
Unemployment rates	2.4	1.2	2.9	1.8	1.6

1994. The rates of unemployment between 1975 and 1994 were low. The sectoral distribution of employment experienced great changes. Almost one-third of the labor force was still engaged in agriculture in 1975, even though industry was the predominant sector. The share industrial employment increased from 40.8% in 1975 to 46.4% in 1990, while the share of employment by the service sector increased from 28.9% in 1975 to 40.8% in 1990. By 1994, only 10.9% of labor force was employed by the agricultural sector, in comparison to 30.3% in 1975. By 1994, industrial employment was overtaken by the services. Until the early 1990s, the primary national focus was on export of goods and the service sector received only residual government attention. Since then, attention was shifted to a better and fuller supply of services and more domestic-led growth. During the era of rapid industrial growth, public services and environmental pollution had been largely neglected. As Taiwan became democratic and people expected improvements in their standards of living to match the development success, the government had to pay more attention to public services and environmental issues.

Taiwan has also experienced great structural changes within the industrial sector. The share of food and food processing, textiles, and wood and paper declined in the total industrial output, while that of machinery and electronic goods rose. The rise of Taiwan's status as a manufacturer of electronic and information technology equipment of all kinds changed the common perception about Taiwan's labor-intensive miracle. In 1995, Taiwan was the third largest producer of these goods in the world, ahead of Germany and behind Japan and the US. A successful capital-intensive industry was Taiwan's man-made fiber (MMF) industry. The success of this capital-intensive industry in its early stage of industrialization mattered greatly for Taiwan to sustain its national growth. Since the late 1950s, the government played a crucial role in setting up the industry. The MMF sector (consisting of four subsectors, polyester, nylon, acrylic, and rayon) has grown by supplying intermediate inputs to the downstream export sectors. The MMF sector is more capital-intensive than the downstream sector. In the early stage of export-led growth, Taiwan exported mainly labor-intensive goods. The development of the MMF sector was important for Taiwan to successfully climb the economic ladder.

According to Chu and Tsai (1999), the development processes of Taiwan's MMF industry is as follows:

(1) In the 1950s, the cotton and textile sectors went through the import substitution stage and grew quickly in the early 1950s; but they began to stagnate in the late 1950s because of the saturation of the domestic market. However, the government planned to promote diversification into MMF production in the early half of the 1950s. Mainly due to the government's efforts to cause private interests, secure foreign technical co-operation, guarantee local supply of inputs, and secure foreign exchange allotment and favorable financing, the first MMF venture, China Manmade Fiber Corporation (CMMF), was established to produce rayon in 1957. The development of Taiwan's MMF sector benefited from accumulated capital and knowledge during the import substitution stage.
(2) In 1964, the China Development Corporation, a public development agency, joined with the CMMF's rayon project to form the United Nylon Corporation to produce nylon. The CMMF began to produce polyester in 1964 as well. All these projects were strongly supported and assisted by the government. The success of these investment projects led the eventual industry leader, Formosa Plastics, to enter into large-scale production of rayon and acrylic fiber in 1968, and polyester in 1969. By 1970, there were already 16 MMF plants, most of which were textile companies that were integrating into the upstream production.
(3) During 1971–1975, Taiwan's MMF industry experienced rapid growth. In these 5 years, the total capacity of the MMF industry was expanded fivefold from 8000 to 40,000 tons per year.
(4) During 1976–1983, the hastily built industry suffered from the downturn in the world market and the second oil crisis. The total output growth of the industry slowed considerably.

(5) From 1984 to present, the industry became more mature and has experienced a stable growth. The industry began to rely increasingly on expanding markets in Mainland China as the source of growth. Moreover, some firms started upgrading efforts. Since the 1980s, the rayon and acrylic staples have displayed stagnation in output growth. The nylon and polyester products experienced growth, although the speed of expansion has slowed down. It should be remarked that the first investments in all the four MMF subsectors were accomplished with comprehensive government assistance. Numerous entries took place only after these initial investments stabilized operations. Since its development from the 1960s, the average growth rates of the MMF industry have been high. After more than two decades of fast growth, Taiwan's MMF sector has become the second-largest producer in the world, next only to the US.

5.5 Trade Dynamics

According to Schumpeter, the overall growth in an economy is based on a continuing series of innovations. Innovation includes new products or processes as well as opening of new markets. Schumpeterian economic theory of innovation foretells that if industries lose cost-competitiveness in one region because of rising unit costs, production is transferred to an economically less advanced region. At the same time, the more advanced country builds up new, more capital- and technology-intensive production lines. Bass (2000) applied the Schumpeterian vision to examine export dynamics in Taiwan. The dynamics of exports can be described as a process of Schumpeter's creative destruction. Each phase experienced a further diversification of the export structure and an upgrading of capital intensity in production and the technology content of commodities. Export dynamics means a continuous upgradation in the structure of exports. This is reflected in that the share of sophisticated commodities in export rises, new markets are opened, and export volume is expanded. In 1961, Akamatsu introduced the term "flying-geese" to describe a well-observed pattern of economic development. The flying-geese pattern of economic development describes a dynamic process in which a group of economies, closely interacting with each other, develops together as a whole, led by a predominant economy as the growth center, followed by progressively less developed economies in a hierarchical pattern homologous to the pattern formed by a flock of "flying geese" (Chen, 1998: 241). In the global economy after World War II, the predominant economy is the US. The US economy led the flock of East Asian flying geese, with Japan as the second leader. Behind Japan followed the Asian NICs. In the third rank are members of ASEAN. In the fourth rank are the coastal provinces of China. In the fifth rank are Vietnam and the rest of China. In the 1960s, Japan began to speed up its FDI with Asian NICs as its primary target. Japan's labor-intensive industries moved to NICs, enabling the latter countries to initiate take-offs. In the 1970s, Japan moved to capital- and technology-intensive industries, while the NICs took over these labor-intensive industries and became the world's major exporters of textiles, electronic products, and other light manufactures. By 1985, Japan's capital- and technology-intensive FDI began to move to the US, Europe, and ASEAN, while NICs began to move labor-intensive light manufacturing to ASEAN members and China.

In 1950, Taiwan's foreign trade was made up of agricultural commodities, but these gave way to processed agricultural products. Soon after simple manufactures replaced processed agricultural goods came technology-based products, which have become increasingly more advanced (Chaponnière and Lautier, 1998). In the first 4-year plan of 1953, textiles and clothing were ranked as spearhead industries. The number of cotton spinning spindles expanded at an average annual rate of 15% during the period from 1957 to 1975. From 1952 to 1965, Taiwanese exports annually grew by 11% on average, and from 1965 to 1980 by 29%. The average growth rate of exports was annually 13% from 1985 to 1995 (Bass, 2000). Exports of clothing first surpassed those of textiles from 1968 (Farnie, 2000). In 1966, export zones were established to attract foreign, especially Japanese, capital. In 1979, Taiwan ranked 22nd in areas of origin in world merchandise trade flows. The dominant form of a trading company is small and specialized. These small enterprises and small local manufacturers themselves handled two-thirds of Taiwanese exports in the 1980s. Now the share has declined to about half of Taiwanese exports (Bass, 2000). As increasing returns to scale economies have become more dominant, small enterprises in Taiwan have lost some of their export competitiveness.

The dynamics of factor-intensive export structure are illustrated in Table 5.6, based on Chen (1999). The degree of labor intensity of each

Table 5.6 Highly factor-intensive exports, 1985–1995, in percentage

	1985	1988	1991	1993	1995
Labor intensive	45.9	46.3	40.1	39.0	37.3
Capital intensive	24.5	23.5	29.8	29.0	31.8
Human capital intensive	18.7	22.6	27.2	31.3	36.1

product is measured by the ratio between the amount of domestic labor utilized by the product and the domestic factor income the product contains. The degree of capital intensity is measured by the ratio of domestic capital to labor used directly and indirectly in the production process. The degree of human capital intensity is measured by the relative amount of labor with college or higher education in the directly and indirectly utilized domestic labor of an industry. The share of highly labor-intensive export declined from 45.9% in 1985 to 37.3% in 1995. The proportion of products with high capital intensities in Taiwan's export increased from 24.5% in 1985 to 36.1% in 1995. The share of products with high human capital intensities in Taiwan's exports increased from 18.7% in 1985 to 36.1% in 1995.

During the period 1950–1962, export was increased, based on processed agricultural commodities. Taiwan imported manufactured consumer goods and producer goods and experienced import substitution growth, based on export of processed agricultural commodities. In the 1950s, Taiwan followed the popular development strategy of overvalued domestic currency and high tariffs and strict quantitative import control. It exported only a few traditional agricultural products such as sugar and rice. In the late 1950s, the domestic market was saturated with light industrial products and there was low capacity utilization. Domestic competition became severe and there were pressures for prices to be reduced for textiles, leather, manufacturers, rubber, wood and paper products, and cement (Lin, 1979). Some factories lowered prices and reduced qualities, while others brought foreign trademarks to expand sales. The industrial stagnation in the late 1950s demonstrated the limits of inward-looking development strategies for the island. In 1957, the Provincial Association of Industries asked the Ministry of Economic Affairs to allow the organization of industrial cartels to restrict competition and to reallocate foreign exchange to promote industrial exports (Schive, 1999). There were some bankruptcies and total exports decreased due to a contraction of sugar exports (which comprised more than 50% of total exports). In 1958, the government united exchange rates and adopted various policy reforms to stimulate exports. The reforms included correcting the overvalued currency, exempting export businesses from business tax and reducing their income tax, allowing exporters to draw back customs duties paid on imported raw materials that were processed into exported goods, and so on (Chen and Ku, 1999).

The US assistance (US Aid) was a decisive factor in Taiwan's economic policy formation. It is held that US Aid and the IMF economists played a crucial role in persuading domestic policy-makers to reduce the scope of direct control and to rely more on the market mechanism, between 1950 and 1965. In 1959, the US Aid Mission set out "an accelerated economic development program" for Taiwan. Director Wesley C. Haraldson proposed an eight-point program of action by the government. The eight-point proposal included non-inflationary fiscal and monetary policy, tax reform, liberalized exchange controls, unification of foreign exchange rates, establishment of a utilities commission and of investment banking machinery, and the privatization of government enterprises (Jacoby, 1973). Later, the eight-point proposal was elaborated into Taiwan's own 19-point program in 1959–1960. US Aid amounted to about US$100 million annually. It compromised more than 30% of domestic investment each year. It was the main financial resource of domestic investment before 1961. Foreign investment other than US Aid was very rare before 1960. The US Aid investment from 1951 to 1965 was distributed such that the public sector received 67%, the private sector 6%, and the public–private sector mixes the rest (Kuo, 1994). The investment in the public sector was mainly used for expanding infrastructure, such as electricity, transportation, and communications. The investment in infrastructural construction through US Aid also made contributions to the growth of the private sector. US Aid had played a key factor in the economic development of Taiwan mainly because Taiwan's government effectively utilized the timely help (totaling US$1.465 billion over the period 1951–1965).

Taiwan's government wanted to attract more capital. The additional points included actions to improve the environment for private and foreign investment, liberalization of trade regulation, full utilization of government production facilities, elimination of subsidies, an increase in public utility rates, and keeping military expense at the 1960 level (Schive, 1999). The Mission would provide additional program loans if the program was implemented promptly. In 1960, the Statute for the Encouragement of Investment was promulgated as the action scheme of the 19-point proposal to offer tax and other incentives to investors. The Statute was to make investment environment more attractive, encourage savings and attract foreign capital. It was repeatedly revised according to changes in domestic and international environments. It was revised three times in the 1960s to incorporate tax cutting, tax consolidation, industrial land acquisition, and privatization of public enterprises. In the 1970s, it was revised eight times to incorporate export promotion, industrial restructuring, and industrialization. In the 1980s, it was revised seven times to encompass more and more types of industries and businesses. In the early 1960s, the Stock Exchange was established. Foreign exchange controls were liberalized and savings were encouraged. Import control was also gradually relaxed. Tax incentives were granted to a variety of industries.

Taiwan's trade-oriented development was started by a series of policy reforms adopted around 1960. These reforms included the simplification and devaluation of the New Taiwan dollar and the promulgation of the Statute for the Encouragement of Investment (Schive, 1999). In order to encourage export and make Taiwan more attractive to foreign investors, the government in 1965 enacted the Statute for the Establishment and Management of Export Processing Zones. Firms that could operate in EPZs had to belong to the approved industries or to meet certain other conditions. In the late 1960s and the early 1970s, the government tended to admit labor-intensive and high-value-added industries (such as precision machinery, electronics, optical equipment, and plastic products) to EPZs. The statute allows firms in EPZs to enjoy all privileges and tax incentives provided to export producers in Taiwan, but without the red tape. Administration was greatly simplified. One agency could handle official transactions from investment application to foreign exchange settlement. Firms in EPZs do not need to pay custom duties, commodity tax, and sales tax. In 1966, Taiwan's first EPZ was established in the port city Kaohsiung. Between 1966 and 1970, the EPZ in Kaohsiung received 22.9% of Taiwan's total FDI (Schive, 1999).

Comparative advantages changed when surplus labor was exhausted in the late 1960s. The government held that exports built on imported raw materials had reached a plateau in the late 1960s and it was important for Taiwan to upgrade the industrial structure for further economic development. Since the late 1960s, Taiwan made efforts to develop heavy industries with the objective of import substitution, known as second-stage substitution to differentiate it from the stage of import substitution in which light industries were encouraged to produce consumer goods as a substitute for imports. Between 1963 and 1969, Taiwan's exports increased by 21% on average per year. It is estimated that 55% of this growth was due to expansion of world market demand and market share in traditional commodities. Taiwan experienced export substitution growth, based on export of processed agricultural and industrial commodities (such as clothing, toys, yarns, footwear, sports-related products). It imported food, and manufactured consumer goods and producer goods. It is held that the second-stage import substitution helped to reduce dependency on imported capital goods and raw materials. It was considered a necessary step in strengthening export industries and sustaining economic growth. When measures such as devaluation of domestic currency and trade liberalization were proposed, industrialists and official decision-makers were hesitant about the initiative. They feared that Taiwan-made products could not compete with foreign goods. There were also fears that devaluation would worsen the economy's terms of trade and cause import inflation.

Foreign investors were often unfamiliar with Taiwan's administrative procedure and investment environment. To attract foreign investors, Taiwan started to establish the EPZ in 1966. Two more were established in 1970 and 1971. Government regulations were simplified and foreigners were allowed to take advantage of cheap labor and "tax holidays" (to labor-intensive investments up to 1972–1973). The EPZs offered industrial sites, buildings, and transportation facilities at reasonable prices. The EPZs had attracted a large share of FDI. The EPZs were designed to be export oriented and to have comparative advantages in Taiwan. The available facilities and administrative efficiency in the EPZs helped Taiwan to successfully shift from the import-promotion era to the export-promotion era in the 1960s. After a few years, the EPZs began to play a significant role in stimulating Taiwan's economic growth. In 1973, three EPZs (Kaohsiung, Nantze, and Taichung) were in operation, employing 78,000 workers

(55,000 in Kaohsiung, 15,000 in Nantze, and 8000 in Taichung) by 222 factories. The total investments in the three zones exceeded US$148 million. Exports from the three zones increased from US$8 million in 1967 to US$405 million in 1973. The share of these zones' exports in Taiwan's total exports was 9% in 1973. At this time, most FDI in and outside EPZs took place in labor-intensive operations, especially in electronic and electrical appliances. They also created many job opportunities and increased local purchases and production. By the late 1970s, the EPZs employed almost 80,000 people, about 80% of whom were females. In the 1970s, the government also allowed the establishment of bonded factories with similar status as the EPZ, in addition to the freedom to locate in any area on the island. This enabled foreign firms to take advantage of the labor supply in the whole island.

Taiwanese firms' success was largely dependent on "follower strategy," based on low cost and narrow product focus. Taiwanese firms usually did not pioneer new products and would produce the goods after Japanese or American firms had proved their potential market. Like early Japanese companies, Taiwanese firms could benefit from the leader's experience and save R&D costs. Since the second half of the 1970s, as labor-intensive production expanded rapidly, and domestic demand for machinery and equipment and intermediate materials increased, there was a substantial accumulation of capital and foreign exchanges. This gradually leveled out the relative scarcity of capital to labor. As management had become more sophisticated and technology improved, the industrial structure was gradually upgraded. Taiwan reached the stage of secondary import substitution where the increase in domestic production replaced imports of intermediates and capital goods (Fei *et al.*, 1985). Taiwan thus relied much less on the foreign supply of intermediates and capital goods. In the 1980s, there was a substantial increase in the level of inward FDI and a change in the nature of those investments. The size of average annual approved investment flows increased from US$183 million in the 1970s to US$870 million in the 1980s. Although electronic and electrical appliances remained the most important target sector in the 1980s, its share in total FDI inflows decreased from 27.4% in 1981–1985 to 20% in 1986–1990. In the manufacturing sector, chemicals and machinery experienced a rapid growth. This trend reflects a shift from purely export-oriented production investments to production targeted at Taiwan's market.

There was also a growing importance of finance and service industries in the late 1980s. Although foreign investment in these sectors was severely restricted before, their share in total FDI flows reached more than 30% in the late 1980s. By 1990, accumulated approved inward FDI reached US$13.3 billion (Hoesel, 1996).

In the 1980s, Taiwan experienced mounting trade surplus. In the early 1980s, the domestic economy was seriously affected by the slowdown of the world economy. Taiwanese companies became regional players in the 1980s. They began to set up offshore manufacturing plans in ASEAN countries in order to compensate for increasing labor costs at home. This process was speeded up with the progressive opening of China, where the overseas Chinese have become important investors. By the early 1990s, Taiwan had obtained self-confidence about its economy. Economic liberalization proceeded around a virtuous circle. As the economy was opened up increasingly, more and more people benefited from liberalization. Taiwan's traditional comparative advantage in labor-intensive production disappeared and the average unit labor cost in Taiwan increased. The high level of education also brought about a serious shortage of low-skill labor. Borrowing technology from other countries had become a less-successful competitive strategy than in the past because some Taiwan industries had gradually approached global technological frontiers (Amsden, 1992). To deal with the changed economic reality, the government shifted its economic policy to promote Taiwan as a regional operations center for MNEs. The purpose was to attract MNEs to establish their regional centers on the island and to engage in high-value-added activities. It was held that strategic alliances between the MNEs and domestic companies would speed up upgrading of Taiwan's industry in terms of technology transfer and manpower development. Taiwan also improved its infrastructure, for instance, by building a new airport and seaport facilities and constructing a high-speed railway system. The government also lowered the required minimum investment amount, simplified the application procedures, and offered new tax privileges for MNEs in priority sectors. Between 1990 and 1996, exports in office machines, automatic data processing machines, and electric machinery increased threefold (Bass, 2000: 119). In the 1990s, exports of all labor-intensive commodities decreased and exports of high-technology products increased.

5.6 Economic Linkages Between Taiwan and Mainland China

Before 1979, there were virtually no commercial ties between the ROC and the PRC. In 1979, Beijing changed its Taiwan policy of calling for liberation to peaceful reunification. From October 1987, when Taipei lifted the ban on its citizens visiting their relatives on the mainland, Taiwan began a new relationship with the mainland. In April 1993, representatives of China's Association for Relations Across the Taiwan Strait (ARATS) and Taiwan's Straits Exchange Foundation (SEF) held a historical conference in Singapore. The changes in the mainland's policies of economic reform and the open door represented both a competitive threat and a beneficial economic opportunity. Since China's rapid expansion of exports took place in the labor-intensive and low-technological sectors, Taiwan lost its international comparative advantage in these sectors. The mainland also provided a huge potential market for Taiwan's capital and capital-intensive and (medium-) technology-intensive products. Cultural, linguistic, political, and historical ties and geographical distance also meant possible low transactional costs.

As shown in Table 5.7, which is based on Chan (1998: 60), there was a steady increase in the number of visitors from Taiwan to the mainland. Taipei began to legalize these visits in late 1987. As shown in Table 5.7, the number of Taiwanese visitors to the mainland increased every year since 1988. There was even an increase of 74.5% in 1990 — the year after the Tiananmen Square crackdown. The accident did not dampen Taiwan people's interest in the mainland.

Beijing unilaterally ended its ban on Taiwanese investment and trade in 1979. It took Taipei 6 years to lift its own ban in those areas. When Taiwanese restrictions on investing in Mainland China were revoked from

Table 5.7 The number and annual change rate of Taiwan's tourists to China

	1988	1989	1990	1991	1992	1993
Number of visitors	430,766	530,534	925,768	995,714	1,511,990	1,541,628
Change rate, %	–	23.2	74.5	7.5	52.0	2.0

1990, Taiwanese enterprises wanted to invest in Mainland China because of low labor costs. Moreover, since 1985 Taiwan continually had trade surpluses with the US, which had caused the US to pressurize to adjust the trade balance. The increase in the NT dollar's value undermined the competitiveness of manufacturing in Taiwan and the profitability of Taiwanese exporters. In addition to the similarities in culture, tradition, and language as well as favorable locations, the remarkable trade growth mainly resulted from comparative and complementary economic advantages. Taiwan's capital and technology match well with China's ample labor resources and low cost of production. Taiwanese entrepreneurs made direct investments in China in export-orientated industries where lower labor and input costs were important. To maintain international competitiveness, Taiwanese heavily invested in China as an attractive outlet for much of Taiwan's manufacturing and exporting activity. As shown in Table 5.8, which is based on Deng (2000), cross-trade increased dramatically through the 1990s. After 1995, China replaced the US as Taiwan's most important export country. However, it is difficult to estimate the total amount of Taiwanese capital flowing into China because of its indirect nature. It was estimated that the amount of Taiwanese investment approved by China was, for instance, US$980 million in 1990, US$9970 million in 1993, US$5141 million in 1996, and US$2982 million in 1998. In monetary value, Taiwanese investment in China ranked second after Hong Kong. The typical investor has changed from an individual business person to large financial groups. Investment characterized by labor-intensive, low-value-added, and short-term has been gradually replaced by capital- and technology-intensive industries with long-run operational horizons such as

Table 5.8 Taiwan's indirect trade with China via Hong Kong (in US$ millions)

	Total trade volume		Exports to China		Imports from China	
	Amount	Ratio (%)	Amount	Ratio (%)	Amount	Ratio (%)
1990	4937	4.1	4171	6.2	765	1.4
1992	10,816	7.1	9697	11.9	1119	1.6
1994	16,512	9.3	14,653	15.7	1859	2.2
1996	23,810	10.2	20,718	17.9	3092	3.0
1998	23,978	10.5	19,867	17.9	4111	3.9
1999	25,758	11.1	21,231	17.5	4526	4.1

computers, construction equipment, and petrochemicals. For instance, in 1998, about 29% of Taiwan's PC-hardware production was manufactured on the mainland (Deng, 2000). The total cross-Strait trade reached nearly US$26 billion in 1999 and Taiwanese investments in China was about US$41 billion. China has become a powerful competitor of Taiwan in the international market. Taiwan's general international competitiveness has experienced a decline in recent years. Rising land, wage costs, and environmental protection have forced export-oriented enterprises to move offshore. On the other hand, China's exports of manufactured goods have grown consistently over these years.

Taiwan's economic dependence on China has been on the rise. On the other hand, Taiwan's trade dependence on the US is declining. Although Taiwan attempted to stimulate exports to the US, policies targeted at the US market did not enhance the macroeconomic situation in Taiwan as a whole. Table 5.9, based on Leng (1996: 121), illustrates Taiwan's trade with Mainland China, the US, and Japan as percentage of total trade during the period 1981–1995. Taiwan's major imports from the mainland were agricultural and industrial materials, such as Chinese herbal medicines, corn and cooking oil, marine products, minerals, and raw materials for textiles. Taiwan's exports to China were mainly manufactured or semi-manufactured products, such as synthetic fiber materials and products, polystyrene and its copolymers, polyvinyl chloride, electric machinery, and machinery and equipment for industry.

Taiwanese companies used Hong Kong as dummy investors to overcome legal obstacles for investment in Mainland China. This was particularly so prior to 1990. In 1991, big business groups began to enter the China market. They formed joint ventures with Chinese firms and multinational corporations. Their investment projects are aimed at the mainland's domestic market. Direct investment by Taiwanese enterprises has contributed to the

Table 5.9 Taiwan's trade with China, the US, and Japan as percentage of total trade

	1981	1984	1987	1990	1993	1995
China	3.5	3.1	3.1	5.8	10.2	12.3
The US	36.1	48.8	44.1	32.4	24.8	21.9
Japan	11.0	10.5	13.0	12.4	19.9	20.2

productive potential of mainland enterprises. Nearly 60% of cumulative foreign investments in 1995 came from Hong Kong, of which much was from disguised Taiwanese sources. Taiwanese investments in Mainland China have significantly stimulated export volumes and have contributed to the upgrading of Mainland China's export structure. China has become a powerful competitor of Taiwan in the international market, especially with exports of nondurable consumer goods in which Taiwan traditionally excelled. China has been rapidly gaining ground in those capital goods and durable goods that Taiwan had internationally comparative advantage.

Officials of the government in Taiwan have attempted to "slow down" rapid expansion of commercial ties. To reduce trade with and investment in the mainland, Taipei launched its "go South" strategy in 1994. The government encouraged investment in Southeast Asia to shift the emphasis of Taiwanese business away from China. In fact, the bulk of Taiwan's overseas investment between 1959 and 1980 was concentrated in that region, which had a potentially large market and many had bilateral agreements with Taiwan to guarantee Taiwanese investment. However, Taiwanese companies have language and religion barriers and Chinese tend to be "disliked" in the region. Taipei adopted several policy measures to promote trade with Southeast Asia. Irrespective of the government's efforts, the flow of Taiwanese capital to Southeast Asia sharply declined in the early 1990s mainly because of the growth of investment in China. In August 1996, President Lee Teng-hui called on Taiwan's companies to scale back their mainland investments. He warned that greater interdependence would make Taiwan vulnerable to political pressure from Beijing. In July 1997, the Ministry of Economic Affairs announced its Review Guidelines for Investment and Technological Cooperation in the Mainland Area. The guidelines widened the scope of prohibited investments. In early 1998, Taiwan re-emphasized its "go South" strategy even in the wake of the Asian financial crisis (Deng, 2000; Kung, 2001).

In May 1996, Formosa Plastics Group, Taiwan's biggest manufacturer and largest employer, announced a project of building a US$3.8 billion power plant in southern China. The initial phase of the project would have included the installation of two 600,000-kilowatt generators at a cost of about US$1.2 billion. If the company had built its planned six thermal power plants in Fujian, its core petrochemical business would be moved to the mainland. This would have marked the start of a large-scale shift to the mainland. Because of the project's economic and political significance, China immediately provided many preferential inducements to Formosa Plastics. In the May announcement, Formosa Plastics announced its goal of building a thermal power plant in Fujian province with an investment of US$3.8 billion. At the end of May 1996, Wang Yu-ching, founder and chairman of Formosa Plastics, announced that Formosa Plastics would increase the size of the plant from the initial 3.6 to 6 million watts. This would bring a total investment of US$6 billion to the mainland. Taiwan's policy-makers were shocked by the announcement. Taipei had no legal means to stop the project. The project was mainly financed by Formosa Plastics' overseas subsidiaries, which were legally allowed to invest freely on Mainland China without reporting it to the government so long as the parent company's stock share does not exceed 20%. However, Taipei would force the company to give up the project not on legal grounds, but in the name of national security concerns. The Ministry of Economic Affairs strongly pressurized the company to give up the project. Finally, the proposal was abandoned (Deng, 2000).

5.7 Income Distribution and Social Welfare

> In hearing litigations, I am like any other body. What is necessary is the cause the people to have no litigations.
>
> *Confucius*

If we follow Confucius' attitude towards litigations in thinking of poverty, we might say that what is important is to find out the cause that the people have no poverty. In Confucian tradition, man is born naturally equal in the sense that each man's social position is singly determined by one's own quality as being human and has nothing to do with any external factor such as family background or race. Confucian tradition holds that love that arises from benevolence manifests itself in different degrees of intensity. Love begins with self-cultivation and should be cultivated with different degrees of intensity. Love starts from its (supposed) most intimate and stable basis-love of one's parents and the rest of the members of the family. Love originates with the bonds of a common parentage and extends to other relationships until it culminates in the stage of benevolence toward all mankind. In Confucian tradition, love is not extended to such an extreme scope so that it includes one's own enemies. In *The Great Learning*, we read: "There are few men in the world, who love, and at the same time know the bad qualities of the object of their love, or who hate, and yet know the excellencies of the object of their hatred." Confucius held benevolence and (emotional) love to be the most important components of society; but this does not mean that he extended kindness to any situation. He said: "Some one said, What do you say concerning the principle that injury should be recompensed with kindness?" The Master said, "With what then will you recompense kindness? Recompense injury with justice, and recompense kindness with kindness." Confucian tradition holds that economic and ethical elements should have a harmonious relation. In the essay "Equalization" in *Many Dewdrops of the Spring and Autumn Annals*, Tung Chung-shu (179–104 BC) summarized Confucius' economic principle on the distribution of wealth as follows (Chen, 1911):

> It is said by Confucius, "We are not troubled with fears of poverty, but are troubled with fears of a lack of equality of wealth." Therefore, when there is here a concentration of wealth, there must be emptiness there. Great riches make the people proud; and great poverty makes them wretched. When they are wretched, they would become robbers; when they are proud, they would become oppressors; it is human nature. From the nature of the average man, the sages discovered the origin of disorder. Therefore, when they established social laws and divided up the social orders, they made the rich able to show their distinction without being proud, and the poor able to make their living without misery; this was the standard of the equalization of society. In this way, wealth was sufficient, and the high and low classes were peaceful. Hence, society was easily governed well. In the present day, the regulations are abandoned, so that everyone pursues what he wants. As human wants have no limit, the whole society becomes indulgent without end. The great men of the high class, notwithstanding they have great fortune, feel bad for the insufficiency of their wealth; while the small people of the low class are depressed. Therefore, the rich increase their avarice for money, and do not wish to do good; while the poor violate the laws every day, and no way can stop them. Hence, the society is difficult to govern well.

In *Li Ki* Confucius set forth his ideas of distribution according to productivity as follows: "To teach the people to make the doing of their duties the first thing, and their salaries an after consideration. A superior man will not for words of small importance receive a great salary, nor for words of great importance a small salary." In Confucian tradition, it is believed that distribution of wealth has an impact on people's minds and thus influences social justice and stability. To maintain a proper distribution of wealth that guarantees each individual a basic living is a kingly way of governing. Mencius said: "This condition, in which people nourish their living and bury their dead without any feeling against any, is the first step of Royal Government." This proper distribution is not enforced equalization, but natural distribution under constraints of social justice. Hsün Tzu said: "Where ranks are all equal, there will not be enough goods to go around; where power is equally distributed, there will be a lack of unity; where there is equality among the masses, it will be impossible to employ them." In Confucian tradition, income is not supposed to be equal among all the people since this would result in social decline and economic stagnation; on the other hand, income gaps between groups should not be "too" enlarged since this would lead to social instabilities and injustice. The KMT government considered social welfare a luxury that could not be easily offered. Provision of social welfare was perceived as an unhealthy dependence on the state. The KMT government never provided significant government funds to social security for the unemployed, disabled, and aged.

The demand for state-supported welfare schemes is growing. Welfare in Taiwan was traditionally provided by the extended family, rather than by the state. The ability of families to bear this burden has been eroded by economic development, demographic changes, and geographical and social mobility. Who should take care of the elderly has become a serious problem. The primary type of family unit is the nuclear family of a couple living with their children. In addition, increasing numbers of women are employed full-time. On the other hand, the proportion of the population aged 65 or over has been steadily increasing. As technological change has reduced household work and costs of support for dependents in terms of both time and money are increasing, the burden of looking after the elderly increases. In a democratic society, the voters tend to add pressure on the state to redistribute some of this burden among all citizens through enhanced welfare schemes. Taiwan's population is aging rapidly. More and more people have succumbed to lengthy illness requiring expensive care. Not until 1980 did Taiwan's government promulgate legislation for the elderly: the ROC Welfare Law for the Aged. Since then, policies and laws have tried to preserve family care. The government passed the National Health Insurance Law, effective from March 1, 1995. It calls for mandatory participation and covers everyone. Taiwan has the highest divorce rate in Asia. Its crime rate rose from 317.3 cases per 100,000 of the population in 1985 to 933.4 in 1996.

Taiwan's economic miracle was associated with environmental deterioration. Prior to the 1980s, the government failed to make sufficient efforts protect environment, industries (especially, high polluting industries such as plastics, petrochemicals, leather goods, and pesticides) failed to assume their responsibilities, and individual citizens lacked environmental consciousness. However, social awareness of environmental issues and discontent with government and corporate management began to grow in the 1980s. Although education and public health are well developed in Taiwan and social insurance is expanding to cover an increasing number of people, the government's welfare effort has not been high (Ku, 1997). Under the pressure of democratization since the 1980s, the Taiwanese state has made efforts to expand welfare. The first national universal social program, National Health Insurance, was introduced in 1995.

5.8 Poverty in Taiwan

Poverty may be due to various political, economic, psychological, social, and cultural reasons at different stages of economic development under different historical conditions. For instance, the reasons for poverty may vary in agricultural, communist, industrial, and post-industrial economies. The correlation between levels of national economic development and poverty vary greatly across the globe. Famine may be caused by various factors and the common predicament of mass starvation does not imply any one common fundamental cause. Droughts, floods, general inflationary pressure, and sharp recessionary loses of employment can deprive large parts of the population of their basic means of survival. Famines may occur when aggregated production is improved. Issues about poverty cannot be fully understood if the analytical framework does not treat society as a dynamic whole. For example, it is impossible to explain the economic mechanisms of poverty in an agricultural economy without genuine dynamics of population and class structures. In addition to production structures and consumption components, population dynamics, capital accumulation, knowledge creation and utilization, institutions and moral codes are essentially important factors in explaining phenomena associated with poverty. Institutions, customs, and other cultural factors play an essential role in affecting wealth distribution and poverty.

Absolute poverty was a major social problem in Taiwan. When Taiwan was experiencing rapid economic growth, levels of poverty incidence were greatly reduced. Today, levels of absolute poverty in Taiwan are relatively low. Kuznets (1955) held that inequality in income typically increases in the early stages of development and declines later, but this pattern did not seem to be confirmed by Taiwan's economic development. Taiwan was noted as an economy that has grown rapidly without increasing income inequality (Fei *et al.*, 1979; Schultz, 1999). It was observed that inequality decreased slightly from 1964 to 1975 and then increased from 1980 to 1993. However, by international standards the gap was not large. It was argued that massive labor absorption, development of small-scale enterprises, and industrial decentralization played a significant role in reducing income inequality (Kuo, 1983). Warr and Wang (1999) developed a time-series data set on the headcount measure of poverty incidence for Taiwan over the 20-year period 1976–1995. They tried to identify the relationship between economic growth and poverty incidence. Using the Taiwanese government's official poverty threshold levels for rural and urban areas in 1984 as the basis of its absolute poverty threshold, they showed that economic growth in Taiwan has been associated with dramatic reductions in poverty incidence.

The US is faced with the recently escalating problem of poverty. Indeed, the problems of defining what constitutes an adequate calorie intake and of measuring what people actually eat lead to differing estimates of the number of persons suffering from hunger in the world. For instance, nutritionalists and economists have different ways of defining poverty (e.g. Osmani, 1992; Sen, 1992). The human body needs energy for performing both internal functions (chemical and mechanical works within the body) and external work on the environment. Bodily functions are maintained by nutritional requirements. The concept of absolute poverty is commonly defined as the failure to satisfy a minimum standard of nutritional requirement. To the extent that such a failure constrains the physiological and behavioral performance of human beings, it has also had a bearing on the welfare-theoretic notions of "capacities" and "quality of life." In estimating the prevalence of undernourishment in a region, it is common to choose a critical limit reflecting nutritional requirements and then to calculate the percentage of the population falling below the limit. The basic units of a nutrition-based poverty line are nutrients, though the requirements may be stated not in terms of calories, proteins, and so on, but rather in terms of food of various kinds. As economists delved into the question of nutrition, they soon discovered that there were no readymade answers for them. Nutrition is still an area of active research and enquiry, characterized by disagreements about the interpretation of measurements and the validity of theories. Although they are essentially important for analyzing processes of poverty and assessing its magnitude, the relevant nutritional issues are matters of ongoing debate among nutritionists.

It is difficult to define the level of poverty from social and humanistic points of view. The definition itself involves issues about human perception and emotions. To determine how a society should weigh its member's suffering or happiness is an important issue in understanding the measurement of poverty. It seems that we cannot determine the weight by pure rationality. In practice, the measurement often reflects customs, political conflicts, and human perception in general. As early as in 1776, Adam Smith (1776) recognized the cultural-related character of necessity: "By necessaries I understand not only the commodities which are indispensably necessary for the support of life, but what ever the custom of the country renders it indecent for creditable people, even the lowest order, to be without. A linen shirt, for example, is, strictly speaking, not a necessary of life. The Greeks and Romans lived, I suppose, very comfortably though they had no linen. But in the present times, through the greater part of Europe, a creditable day-laborer would be ashamed to appear in public without a linen shirt, the want of which would be supposed to denote that disgraceful degree of poverty which, it is presumed, nobody can well fall into without extreme bad conduct. Custom, in the same manner, has rendered leather shoes a necessary of life in England. The poorest creditable person of either sex would be ashamed to appear in public without them."

5.9 Economic Consequences of Social Welfare

> Who says of Weisheng Gao that he is right? One begged some vinegar of him, and he begged it of a neighbor and gave it to him.
>
> *Confucius*

Many elementary aspects of being poor, such as hunger, inadequate healthcare, unhygienic living conditions, and the stress and strain of precarious living, are related to income and wealth distribution. It is thus necessary to schematically present the determinants of the income and wealth of particular households or groups of people within a society.

Smith argued that a capitalist, in making an investment that raised the country's output, is led by an invisible hand to promote an end that is not a part of his intention. Smith's point is that by pursuing his own interest the capitalist frequently promotes that of the society more effectively than when he really intends to promote for the public good. It is worthwhile to mention that from the economic literature we may conclude that the impact of social welfare (transferring income from some groups to other groups) on economic growth is situation-dependent. It is known that Malthus (who was concerned with growth of supply-driven economy) held that social welfare might neither benefit the poor nor enrich the rich. He argued that by redistributing income from the rich to the poor, the saving rate of the economy tends to decrease, thus reducing capital accumulation. In contrast to Malthus, Keynes (who was concerned with growth of demand-driven economy) held that redistribution policy would benefit the poor and would not harm the rich. He argued that by redistributing income, the saving rate of the economy tends to decrease, thus raising the level of aggregate demand in the economy. The economic performance of the system as a whole will be improved.

Zhang (2002) has recently proposed a two-group growth model with income transfers. In particular, the model is constructed to provide some insights into economic mechanisms of welfare economies. Many viewpoints have been proposed to justify the existence of welfare states. According to Sugden's (1984) "conditional co-operation" thesis, people are prepared to contribute their "fair share" to help the needy only if they perceive others to be doing likewise, and as such some level of compulsory contributions to welfare through the tax system may have advantages over a purely voluntary system. Miller (1988) examined the question of whether it is possible to explain the existence of welfare states in terms of the altruistic concern that people generally feel for the welfare of their compatriots. The existence of altruism means that people have the willingness to be taxed to provide welfare for others. It is argued that the welfare of the society is improved by redistribution through the government tax policy because everyone would be happier when some resources are transferred from the well-endowed to the needy. But it is pointed out that if people are altruistic, it is possible for them to make private arrangements to express their altruism through charity. It is argued that the liberal institution is superior to the welfare state in two ways. People can express genuine altruism without being forced to do. People donate the amount of their own choice without being asked to do so. Miller also provided other explanations for the existence of welfare states. For instance, the welfare state may be seen as an insurance scheme taken out by the rich to buy off the discontented poor. The welfare state is also considered as a device used by the poor, through majority voting, to benefit from the income transfers. It is argued that the welfare institution is the creation of a professional class that lives off its proceeds. The welfare state is seen also as a scheme of mutual insurance against remote and often unpredictable events. This study is not concerned with people's motives and beliefs that they would contract voluntarily into a welfare state. We see now what will happen to the economic system if the altruist rich transfers his income to the poor.

The understanding of the dynamics of national growth and differences of living conditions and wealth between different groups of people is one of the essential aspects for understanding modern socio-economic evolution. The issues related to economic growth and distribution are the main concerns of classical economists such as Ricardo and Marx. But there are only a few dynamic (mathematical) models with endogenous savings and income and wealth distribution. Zhang's model examined a dynamic interdependence of two groups with different productivity and preferences. Assuming that altruism affects income transfers between the two groups, Zhang showed how altruism and differences in preference structures and productivity between the two groups may affect national wealth accumulation, income and wealth distribution, and consumption levels over time. Because the model is technically complicated, we now provide a brief description of the findings of the model. It is shown that as altruism is strengthened, (1) the altruists' per capita capital, per capita consumption, and per capita income are reduced; (2) the altruism-receiving group's per capita consumption, and per capita income may be either reduced or increased; and (3) the national wealth and income may be either increased or decreased. It is well known that steady-state values of per capita variables in the neoclassical growth theory are dependent on the propensity to save. When one group transfers incomes to another group, the "aggregated savings" behavior would be changed when the two groups have different propensities to save. This change in savings behavior (due to altruism) may result in increases or decreases of the national output and wealth.

We described the case that altruism has no impact on working incentives and human capital of the altruism-receiving group. But possible influences of altruism are also dependent on the way in which wealth and income are spent. For instance, when the poor receives money from the rich, economic conditions would be different, depending on whether the poor spends the received money on education or eating. As mentioned by Keynes, if some labor force is unemployed, then monetary transfers from the rich to the poor would economically benefit the rich as well. Since we assume the full employment of labor force, to provide insights into the economic mechanism by Keynes, we may consider a case that the monetary transfer from the rich to the poor would increase the poor group's working efficiency. We now examine what will happen to the two groups' living conditions when the altruism-receiving group changes its work efficiency after receiving altruist contributions from the other group. It is proved that when the altruist group strengthens altruism and the altruism-receiving group increases the work efficiency, then (1) the altruists' per capita capital, per capita consumption, and per capita income may be either increased or reduced; (2) the altruism-receiving group's per capita consumption and per capita income are increased; and (3) the national wealth and income are increased. This corresponds to Keynes' argument. If we assume that altruism makes the poor less efficient (which may be interpreted as Malthus' assumption), then the national wealth and the altruist group's wealth are definitely reduced. If the reduction in the altruism-receiving group's productivity is high, we conclude that the altruism receiving group's per capita consumption and wealth are reduced. In other words, Malthus' view that no one would benefit from strengthening altruism is justified.

Zhang's model provides some insights into how altruism and differences in preference structures and productivity between the two groups affect national wealth accumulation, income and wealth distribution, and consumption levels over time. There are different viewpoints about man's nature and interrelations between beliefs and action. It is argued that altruism may not be a preexisting "stock." For instance, Aristotle held that virtues are neither innate nor contrary to nature. But from the sustainable point of view, altruism may be conducted in a large scale in the long term only when altruism has positive consequences not only for the altruism-receiving groups but also for the altruist groups. As far as society as a whole is concerned, it seems important to find out what kinds of altruist behavior would promote welfare of different individuals and increase productivity of the society. It is well known that Adam Smith advocated that the government should intervene in market economy so that all the social groups of the people would benefit from economic development. In the Zhang model, Smith's viewpoint can be interpreted as that "altruism" would benefit all the groups if it were targeting at improving human capital through spreading education. Our analysis may also provide insights into Malthus' viewpoint that altruist may neither benefit the poor nor enrich the rich. Keynes' viewpoint about government's redistribution policy and economic growth is a proper example that "social altruism" is in harmony with economic development and economic benefits of the different groups. It may be held that our analytical results provide insights into the viewpoints held by Smith, Malthus, and Keynes. Alfred Marshall (1890: 9) held that "The supreme aim of the economist is to discover how this latent asset (being capable of more unselfish service than they generally render) can be developed more quickly and turned to account more wisely." The Zhang model shows that there is no unique correspondence between altruism and economic consequences. In other words, altruism may either cause economic benefits or loss to the altruist group as well as to the altruism-receiving group. The model also provides some conditions under which Hayek was right when arguing "But the abolition of absolute poverty is not helped by the endeavour to achieve 'social justice'; in fact, in many of the countries in which absolute poverty is still an acute problem, the concern with 'social justice' has become one of the greatest obstacles to the elimination of poverty."

Equality is not a clearcut concept. It is multifaceted and often ambiguous. It can take different forms and apply to legal, political, moral, and economic domains. A society may have strongly egalitarian attitudes toward some matters and inegalitarian attitudes towards others. The US is still challenged with how the ideal of equality can be implemented. Government must at least minimally take care of some of the wreckage associated with capitalism: poverty, unemployment, and pollution. Liberals continue to give primacy to the institutions of private property and marketplace, but they have to face with challenges accumulated over the process of capitalism. In the US, the stress on success and less profound welfare system presses the unsuccessful or those without the means to win out legitimately to violate the rules of the game (Merton, 1957). Although every citizen has now the right to participate equally in the choice of elected representatives, public opinion is ambiguous about whether individual equality also requires an (relatively) equal distribution of social and economic benefits. If everyone is free to compete economically, it seems to eventually result in the social and economic inequalities. If rewards are equalized disregarding differences in ability and opportunity, society may turn out to be stationary or even decline. Capitalism and democracy tend to lead to equality in human spirits and enlarged inequality in economic conditions.

Chapter 6

Uncertain Future

> When right government prevails in the world, princes of little virtue are submissive to those of great, and those of little worth, to those of great. When bad government prevails in the world, princes of small power are submissive to those of great, and the weak to the strong. Both these cases are the rule of Heaven. They who accord with heaven are preserved, and they who rebel against Heaven perish.
>
> *Mencius*

In his essay *of the Rise and Progress of the Arts and Sciences* published more than 200 years ago, the British philosopher and historian, David Hume (1711–1776, 1994: 66) observed:

> In China, there seems to be a pretty considerable stock of politeness and science, which, in the course of so many centuries, might naturally be expected to ripen into something more perfect and finished, than what has yet arisen from them. But China is one vast empire, speaking one language, governed by one law, and sympathizing in the same manners. The authority of any teacher ... was propagated easily from one corner of the empire to the other. None had courage to resist the torrent of popular opinion. And posterity was not bold enough to dispute what had been universally received by their ancestors. This seems to be one natural reason, why the sciences have made so slow a progress in that mighty empire.

Hume's contemplation illustrates why individualistic aspects of Confucianism was not advocated after multiple states were integrated into a single China. Classical Confucianism was created when the area of contemporary China was composed of multiple competitive and independent states. Except his home state, Confucius traveled to and worked in some foreign states. He had opportunities to observe tradition, state management, and strength and weakness of these states. Like Europe in the nineteenth century, no single state established in the contemporary territory of

Mainland China was able to dominate all the other states in Confucius' time. Confucius showed "local" loyalty to the country where he was born; but he was far more concerned with "global identity" than "national identity." Patriotism or any kind of "clubism" is never advocated in Confucianism. Confucius' political thought was concentrated on harmonious co-existence of differences rather than enforced co-existence of differences.

As mentioned before, the ancient Confucian principles are almost the same as the democratic principles. But this does not imply that the Chinese had actually respected individualism and established institutions for freedom. One may quote Smith (1776: 129) to characterize traditional Chinese governing as follows: "To found a great empire for the sole purpose of raising up a people of customers, may at first sight appear a project fit only for a nation of shopkeepers. It is, however, a project altogether unfit for a nation of shopkeepers; but extremely fit for a nation whose Government is influenced by shopkeepers." The behavior and knowledge of the contemporary Mainland Chinese government exposes what Smith reveals. Humanistic aspects of Confucianism had never been practiced in China. The situation described by Chu Hsi (1130–1200) is contemporarily valid for Mainland China as many hundred years ago: "The way of Confucius had not been put into practice for a single day" (Chan, 1973).

There are multiple interdependent forces in Taiwan's economic and political development. The dynamism of autonomous economic force and the changeable role of the state in developing economic foundations and creating an environmental for social and political change have not been isolated from each other. In his later years, Chiang Ching-kuo successfully led Taiwan towards speeding up democratization. Notwithstanding the lack of individualistic aspects in Dr Sun's principles, the nationalist character in these principles helped the KMT to govern the island. In a speech delivered at the opening of the 14th National Congress of the KMT on August 16, 1993, the then President Lee Teng-Hui stated (Hu, 1994: 4): "Today we stand at a turning point in history. Over two thousand years ago, the Chinese had such democratic thoughts as 'the people rank higher than the nobility' and 'the people are the foundation of the state.' In recent years, we in Taiwan have successfully adopted the Western political philosophy of government of the people, for the people and by the people, and created on Chinese soil the first ever democratic society based on party politics. This achievement, unprecedented in Chinese history, marks the beginning of a new historic era." Although the CCP forced the KMT to the island and had the power over the mainland, it lost the final battle to KMT in the sense that the KMT succeeded in governing by enriching the people and democratizing the island.

Taiwan has become modernized. Modernity is a multivalent and richly vague complex (Hall and Ames, 1999). The notion of modernity is vague in the sense that it may be interpreted in multiple, sometimes even contradictory, ways. The cultural crisis of modernity in the West and East Asia shows that the world has failed to develop any coherent rational models of cultural accommodation. Bell (1978) maintains that capitalism has from its beginning contained three contradictions that have shaped its development. The conflict of *asceticism and acquisitiveness* refers to the tension between the self-disciplined work ethic and the need to acquire, own, and consume. The contradiction between the bourgeois tradition and modernism refers to the conflict between the need to ground one's intellectual and social life in the conservative past and the need to experience changes in almost all aspects of elite culture. The third conflict is found in the separation of *morality and law*. These contradictions can be interpreted by the Chinese *yin–yang* principles. Bell claimed that acquisitiveness, modernization, and legal mechanisms have come to dominate Western capitalist societies. It is argued that asceticism, conservative past, and moral mechanisms dominated Confucian civilization before modern times. Modernization of Confucian regions is to shift from the traditional pole towards the Western pole — each pole can never be perfect.

There are psychologically deep reasons for the conflicts mentioned by Bell. Jung (1989: 73) asserted: "No culture is ever really complete, for it always swings towards one side or the other. Sometimes the cultural ideal is extraverted, and the chief value then lies with the object and man's relation to it: sometimes it is introverted, and the chief value lies with subject and his relation to the idea. In the former case, culture takes on a collective character, in the latter an individual one." Confucius saw the dynamics of mind over generations (generation gaps in modern terms) in the following way: "Anciently, men had three failings, which now perhaps are not to be found. The high-mindedness of antiquity showed itself in a disregard of small things; the high-mindedness of the present day shows itself in wild license. The stern dignity of antiquity showed itself in grave reserve; the stern dignity of the present day shows itself in quarrelsome perverseness.

The stupidity of antiquity showed itself in straightforwardness; the stupidity of the present day shows itself in sheer deceit."

6.1 Sustainable Economic Development or a Paper Tiger?

> When a man's knowledge is sufficient to attain, and his virtue is not sufficient to enable him to hold, whatever he may have gained, he will lose again. When his knowledge is sufficient to attain, and he has virtue enough to hold fast, if he cannot govern with dignity, the people will not respect him. When his knowledge is sufficient to attain, and he has virtue enough to hold fast; when he governs also with dignity, yet if he try to move the people contrary to the rules of propriety: full excellence is not reached.
>
> *Confucius*

What the *Great Learning* says may be applied to explain the Asian economic crisis: "To see men of worth and not be able to raise them to office; to raise them to office, but not to do so quickly: this is disrespect. To see bad men and not able to remove them; to remove them, but not to do so to a distance: this is weakness. To love those whom men hate, and to hate those whom men love: this is to outrage the natural feeling of men. Calamities cannot fail to come down on him who does so." The 1997 financial crisis that began in Thailand and spread quickly to the Philippines, Malaysia, Indonesia, Singapore, South Korea, and other areas in Asia has raised doubts about economic miracles of the other Asia regions (Backman, 1999). "Better learn from East Asia," an advice often given to low-income countries before the middle of 1997, was suddenly swapped to "the miracle was built on sand" (Garran, 1998) as the common viewpoints about East Asian industrialization among many observers and writers after the crisis. Taiwan did not suffer immediately from the financial and economic crises of the Asian region perhaps owing to its flexible networks and a flexible private sector based on small- and medium-scale businesses. However, it could not have prevented economic crises in last few years.

Taiwan's economic miracle resulted from a proper combination of many factors. It had enjoyed the infrastructure left by the Japanese, the Korean War, the US aid, and the evolving global economic system. It has developed a free-market economic system and adopted economic policies such as aggressive import substitution and then an export-oriented economic development strategy. The KMT had played an active role in the island's economic life. Taiwanese entrepreneurs were allowed to freely use their wealth, talents, and efforts to advance their own material well-being. Taiwan has achieved the economic miracle not only because of its internal efforts but also because of the fortunate "accessible ground" during the cold war. As the cold war ended and countries like Mainland China and India have entered global markets, Taiwan is faced with new challenges.

The government had a harmonious relationship with business in the early years of Taiwan's economic development. The harmony was sustained by strict social control and maintenance of social order through the imposition of martial law. Since martial law was lifted, the relationship between the government and business relationship has rapidly changed. The government no longer has the power to influence business communities that the KMT government formerly had. Taiwan hoped to become an Asia-Pacific "Regional Operations Center" (APROC). Fulfillment of this goal would help the globalization of Taiwanese companies and obviate problems associated with the alternative policies based on enterprise relocation. However, Taiwan does not yet have adequate infrastructures to transform itself into a comprehensive regional operations center, embracing communications and financial services, as well as transportation facilities. It is difficult to foresee whether Taiwan is able to compete with Hong Kong, Singapore, and even Shanghai in the region for some time to come. Shanghai's huge potential and security factors make Taiwan less attractive as the region's financial center. In comparison to Hong Kong and Singapore, Taiwan's competitiveness is weak. Taiwan is far from providing the full institutional and informational framework required. In Taiwan, most upstream industries, such as energy, heavy machinery, shipbuilding, and steel, have been governed by the public sector. These industries have now proved to be the most inefficient sectors in the economy. The use of state-owned enterprises as an instrument to develop selected industries became an impediment for further development of the Taiwanese economy. The state-owned enterprises account for just over 10% of Taiwan's GNP in recent years. Taiwanese form of familism capitalism might be fragile in a new era of globalization in which economies of scales work in many strategic industries. The SMEs form flexible production networks relying heavily on extensive subcontracting. The Taiwanese SMEs are sensitive to changes in demand generated by manufacturing networks. Heavy reliance on export markets is easily affected by the dynamics of the regional economy. Taiwan has access to the China market and personal connections among about 25 million overseas Chinese in some of the fastest growing economies in the world: China, Hong Kong, Vietnam, Singapore, Malaysia, Indonesia, and Thailand. However, its relations with other overseas Chinese communities are unstable because of increasing interactions between Mainland China and these communities.

Taiwan is now faced with challenges from the mainland — on the other hand, it is trying to extend its living space in the mainland. It attempts to take the best from the USA and the mainland. Like the KMT in the 1950s, the CCP learned painful lessons from the Cultural Revolution. Like the KMT in the 1960s, the CCP is now improving itself rapidly. Whether Taiwan can sustain its economic development is much dependent on the government's sincerity for democracy and its relationship with the mainland. The *Great Learning* taught the Chinese: "By gaining the people, the kingdom is gained, and, by losing the people, the kingdom is lost. On this account, the ruler will first take pains about his own virtue. Possessing virtue will give him the people. Possessing the people will give him the territory. Possessing the territory will give him its wealth. Possessing the wealth, he will have resources for expenditure. Virtue is the root; wealth is the result. If he make the root his secondary object, and the result his primary, he will only wrangle with his people, and teach them rapine. Hence, the accumulation of wealth is the way to scatter the people; and the letting it be scattered among them is the way to collect the people. And hence, the ruler's words going forth contrary to right, will come back to him in the same way, and wealth, gotten by improper ways, will take its departure by the same."

6.2 Political Flexibility and Respect for Law

> The superior man is easy to serve and difficult to please. If you try to please him in any way which is not accordant with right, he will not be pleased. But in his employment of men, he uses them according to their capacity. The mean man is difficult to serve, and easy to please. If you try to please him, though it be in a way which is not accordant with right, he may be pleased. But in his employment of men, he wishes them to be equal to everything.
>
> *Confucius*

The KMT learned about the significance of science and technology and accumulated managerial skills through its own painful experiences in the mainland. It was "fortunate" for Taiwan to speed up its industrialization under the leadership of the KMT. Mencius (371–289 BC) said: "To give the empire to another man would be easy, to find a man who shall benefit the empire is difficult." History records that neither the KMT nor the CCP had accumulated sufficient moral quality and governmental skills to lead modernization of the mainland in the 1940s. However, the experiences and knowledge that the KMT had accumulated through "playing" (accurately fighting and killing) in the mainland had sufficiently enabled it to govern the small island in an effective way. After the KMT moved to Taiwan, Taiwan was rapidly industrialized with Chinese culture, colonial experience, US-guaranteed peaceful environment, and the KMT's accumulated human capital. In this sense, the mainland paid the "learning costs" for Taiwan's modernization. Taiwan has rapidly become the most developed democracy in the Chinese-speaking world partly because the KMT was represented by the minority of the mainlanders in early times, Taiwan had the political need to distinguish itself from the mainland, and "mountain-people and pirates" had a strong preference for not being controlled — which should not be equalized with freedom.

Because of its special cultural, political, and historical geography, Taiwan has become the quickest of all the parts of China to become industrialized and democratized. Since the lifting of martial law in 1987, Taiwan has made remarkable progress in democratization. Because of its achievements at civil liberties and improvement of political rights, Taiwan received the status of "free country" in a 1997 Freedom House Publication. Taiwan's rapid democratization was lauded as a "political miracle," parallel to its economic miracle of the 1970s. It is now a center, rather than periphery, of Chinese modernization. Over the last two decades, Taiwan's modernization experience has had a powerful influence on the hearts and minds of the people in the mainland. Since its economic reform more than two decades ago, Mainland China has closely followed the example of Taiwan, rather than the opposite. Irrespective of its small size, it has shown a sustainable way for the mainland to become modernized. Under the authoritarian era, Chiang Kai-shek and his son Chiang Ching-kuo made major policies. Politicians of the KMT maintained a patron–client relationship, while the technocrats were in charge of substantial economic planning. Major social forces, such as peasants, labor, and the opposition, exerted no important constraints on state policymaking capacity. The KMT is no longer in power. Its defeat by the CCP was shameful in the sense that it left a poor, uneducated, and chaotic China to the CCP. However, its defeat by the DDP was actually a symbol of its success because it left an enriched, educated, and democratized Taiwan to the DDP. Chiang Kai-shek (Barlow, 1987: 106) once said: "If when I die I am still a dictator I will certainly go down into the oblivion of all dictators. If on the other hand I succeed in establishing a truly stable foundation for a democratic government, I will live forever in every home in China." Although it does not seem that he will have any opportunity to live in every home in China, he succeeded in establishing a stable foundation for a democratic government in Taiwan by securing economic success and spreading education.

Sophisticated division of labor and professionalism tend to result in the following situation as described by Weber (1991): "specialists without spirit, sensualists without heart." As society becomes more "sophisticated," it tends to need co-existence of multiple political parties rather than the political monopoly. The political "monopoly" does not seem to be socially sustainable for an internationally open society, except under some special circumstances. This is not only due to well-observed facts that absolute power is corrupt in the long term. In a democratic system, it is the "aggregated" happiness that determines who will govern. A (common) happy life is characterized by variety and dynamics. A well-educated and rich population can hardly feel happy with any single, even if it was capable and moral, power in the long term. There is a strong desire for variety for the sake of variety in human nature. Demand for political change is an internal mechanism of democratic society. The Taiwanese live under quasi-tropical climate and were controlled by non-Taiwanese governments in history. Until 10 years ago, the rulers in Taiwan had not brought justice to the people in Taiwan. The Chiang family did bring about the economic miracle, but not social justice to the Taiwanese people. The Taiwanese traditionally distrusted authority and appreciated freedom. However, natural passion for freedom does not necessarily mean abiding by the law, which is the foundation for a civilized democratic society. Hsün Tzu (298–238 BC) said: "A man who has no laws at all is lost and guideless. A man who has laws but does not understand their meaning is timid and inconsistent. Only if a man abides by laws and the same time comprehends their wider significance and applicability can he become truly liberal and compassionate." Taiwan was once known in China as a place for rebellion. It takes time for the DDP to change the political culture of distrust for public authority.

Modern economics shows that institutions play a decisive role on economic development (Davis and North, 1971; North, 1990). These institutions include formal ones such as chambers of commerce, guilds, and the state, and informal ones such as customary practices and codes of conduct. The formal ones may provide market information and regulate transactions by using bureaucracies and legal systems. North argues that as an economy evolves, formal institutions will replace informal ones. Taiwan has implemented a rule of law and abridged arbitrary personal rule. The chief early obstacles to rationalization of the system of laws were the temporary provisions and martial law. The former granted the president vast unchecked powers and the latter left the military authorities enormous power. After these extra-constitutional measures were terminated, Taiwan has significantly improved the transparency of legal procedures and their implementation. Development of a competitive party system and a free press has improved the uniform application of rules and laws. Nevertheless, there are still many problems for effective and consistent enforcement of the law in Taiwan's legal system (McBeath, 1998: 109). The law in Taiwan tends to be ambiguous. This makes the legal environment unpredictable. Taiwan is faced with government corruption, organized crime, vote buying, and drug trafficking. It is still far from establishing a system of law that can be called to be fairly administered and rigorously enforced. In a speech delivered at the opening of the 14th National Congress of the Kuomintang on August 16, 1993, Premier Lien Chan wrote: "(Taiwan's) greatest cause for concern is lack of respect for the rule of law. Democratic government means government by the law; this is basic common sense, but is also a truth that is easy to disregard. Our people speak out their support for democracy and fight for rights; but at the same time, they are unwilling to accept the controls of law and justice, and their burden of responsibilities to society. There is an increasing tendency to make any and every issue into a political issue, leading to widespread skirting of the law, playing with the law, and violation of the law."

Since President Chen Shui-bian came to power, the economy has stumbled badly. From his May inauguration to November 2000, Taiwan's stock market plunged 50%. Public support for Chen plummeted from 80% in March 2000 to 40% in November 2000. His party's electoral support came mainly from pro-independence and environmental groups, which were ignored by the KMT. The DDP used environment, anti-corruption, and independence to win the election. These problems have a common character: easy to criticize but complicated to solve even in the short term. A politician who gets power by targeting this kind of questions in a democratic society tends to lose support when coming to power. It is difficult for Chen to deliver campaign promises to those who had supported him. To find a lover is one thing; to manage a family with children is quite another. The DDP became a ruling party for the first time. The DDP is not to observe and criticize, but has to analyze, understand, and make decisions. The DDP has no experience governing at a Taiwan-wide level. Many DDP cabinet members now heading ministries have only a city or county background at best. Since the KMT brought many talented administrators to Taiwan, it is the first time that Taiwan is governed by a party lacking experienced administrators. The DDP has to learn new knowledge and accumulate new skills to fit for the new position. Chen won the presidential election by a slim margin. He won because the KMT split. He is now faced with political instability and growing pessimism among investors. His pragmatic but "Taoism-influenced" way may not be fit for governing people who want to be collectively among the frontiers of the world.

6.3 Taiwan and the Mainland

> Good government obtains, when those who are near are made happy, and those who are far off are attracted.
>
> *Confucius*

One might wonder about how democratic Taiwan should deal with the mainland according to traditional Confucianism. Confucius provided the following principles: "With sincere faith he unites the love of learning; holding firm to death, he is perfecting the excellence of his course. Such a one will not enter a tottering state, nor dwell in a disorganized one. When right principles of government prevail in the empire, he will show himself;

when they prostrated, he will keep concealed. When a country is well governed, poverty and a mean condition are things to be ashamed of. When a country is ill governed, riches and honor are things to be ashamed." For Confucius, the rightness is the principle of unification. One might well understand long-term implications of Confucius' above saying if one considers the impact of Albert Einstein's immigration to the US from Europe. Einstein's passage through foot not only benefited the US but also played a positive role on Europe in the long term. Confucius' thought can also be applied to relations between Taiwan and the mainland. Not to reunify with the mainland is to play a positive role for the mainland's economic development and democratization.

"He who exercises government by means of his virtue," Confucius says, "may be compared to the north polar star, which keeps its place and all the stars turn towards it." If the mainland government has any sense of what Confucius called "being filial," it would first improve itself as government before even thinking of reunification. According to Confucian tradition, a region governed by the right principles, even if it is small, should not give up its rights to any other region governed by wrong principles. When the prince Wen of Teng once asked Mencius about whether his small Kingdom, located between Qi and Chu, should serve Qi or Chu, Mencius replied: "This plan which you propose is beyond me. If you will have me counsel you, there is one thing I can suggest. Dig deeper your moats; build higher your walls; guard them along with your people. In case of attack, be prepared to die in your defence, and have the people so that they will not leave you, this is a proper course." In order to build and protect Taiwan as a democratic region, the government should carry out benevolent policies that the people would truly love the island. For Mencius, the people will not leave the country if it is governed by right principles. When the prince Wu of Zou asked why his officers were killed but none of his people would die in their defense in a battle between Zou and Lu, Mencius replied: "If you put in practice a benevolent government, this people will love you and all above them, and will die for their officers." Peking government's "one country and two systems" proposal itself shows that it has neither decent socio-economic principles nor modern military forces to reunify the two sides across the Taiwan Straits. "There are instances of individuals without benevolence," observes Mencius, "who have got possession of a single state, but there has been no instance of the whole empire's being got possession of by one without benevolence."

Confucius assured: "Those whose courses are different cannot lay plans for one another." Different people might believe or follow different ideologies. Zhang (2000) demonstrates that the Confucian principles are fundamentally the same as the democratic principles. It is argued that Mainland China's socialism is an anti-democratic (and such anti-Confucian) ideology and should not have a lasting impact on Confucian civilization. Chinese peoples have paid high prices for each step towards freedom and democracy in modern times. "The strongest cause for the feeling of nationality ... ", John Stuart Mill (1806–1873) explains, "is identity of political antecedents; the possession of a national history, and consequent community of recollections; collective pride and humiliation, pleasure and regret, connected with the same incidents in the past." Most people in Taiwan and the mainland identify with the same cultural antecedents and possess the same history. Except the last two decades, the Chinese over the world might have more collective humiliation than collective pride in the last century. "A man must first despise himself," according to Mencius, "and then others will despise him. A family must first destroy itself, and then others will destroy it. A kingdom must first smite itself, and then others will smite it." In Taiwan, Dr Sun's Three Principles of the People is presumed to represent the Chinese orthodox tradition, while the PRC's communism is treated as a heresy, which has destroyed Chinese culture. The mainland does not have a democratic culture for Taiwanese people to feel for national identity. Reunification between the democratic island and the socialist mainland is meaningless for Chinese civilization.

When Chiang Kai-shek escaped to the island in 1949, he believed that he would recover the mainland. He bragged: "(during) the first year in Taiwan we are going to make preparations for attacking the Communists; (during) the second year we will launch our attack; (in) the third year we shall make a clean sweep of the Communist bandits in the mainland; and in the fourth year we will recover our mainland" (Wu, 1995: 65). Since then, neither has the ROC has recovered the mainland nor has the PRC liberated Taiwan. Before it overtook power through election, the DDP regarded cross-Straits relations as a state-to-state relationship. Its policy was based on the assumption that Taiwan would become independent. In early 1988, the party released its first formal policy for Taiwan to declare independence (Leng, 1996: 42–3): (1) agreement of the KMT on party-to-party negotiations with the CCP; (2) Taiwan being sold out by the KMT; (3) the PRC using force to unify China; and (4) refusing democratic reforms by the KMT. By 1990, the DDP began to promote Taiwan's independent sovereignty, holding that the ROC's sovereignty was limited to the Taiwan area. In October 1991, the DDP's Fifth Congress was held. The congress made the following resolutions concerning Taiwan's independence (Leng, 1996: 43): (1) Taiwan's sovereignty is separated from the PRC's; (2) Taiwan should establish itself as a new nation; and (3) Taiwan should establish diplomatic relations with the RPC according to international law. In fact, the congress made its policy for the National Assembly election scheduled for December 1991. The party's poor performance in the election showed that the public did not support the independence cause declared by the DDP.

After being elected Taiwan's president, Chen Shui-bian, the long-time opposition leader, came to power in March 2000. The historical transition of power went smoothly, showing Taiwan's political maturity. Chen's victory was a progressive symbol of democratization in Taiwan. The event when Chen was elected to the top post in Taiwan represented not only a landmark in its evolution from a military-dominated autocracy to a full-fledged democracy, but also a landmark in Chinese civilization. In his inaugural address, Chen said: "while upholding the principles of democracy and parity, building upon the existing foundations, and constructing conditions for cooperation through goodwill, we believe the leaders on both sides possess enough wisdom and creativity to jointly deal with the question of a future 'one China'." He also stated: "As long as the Chinese Communist Party regime has no intention to use military force against Taiwan, I pledge that during my term in office, I will not declare independence, I will not change the national title, I will not push for the inclusion of the so-called 'state-to-state' description in the Constitution, and I will not promote a referendum to change the status quo in regards to the question of independence or unification. Furthermore, the abolition of the National Reunification Council or the National Reunification Guidelines will not be an issue." There is almost no essential change in the new government's policy toward China. The new government has not embraced the one-China principle.

With the reconciliation between the US and the PRC, Taiwan experienced increasing diplomatic isolation as a number of its former allies switched official recognition to Beijing. In the late 1970s, the PRC carried out a series of reforms towards a more market-orientated economy. The PRC has potentially huge markets as attractive factors for states to accept it as the sole legitimate government of China. In response to its growing diplomatic isolation, the ROC's government accepted a more flexible approach. It accepted different terms such as Chinese Taipei that were acceptable to Beijing. The approach secured the ROC's representation in international bodies such as the Asian Development Bank and the Asia Pacific Economic Cooperation (APEC) forum. However, the ROC did not get back into the United Nations. Under President Lee Teng-hui, the ROC continued its efforts to increase diplomatic recognition. Most of the leading European and North American states upgraded their representation in Taiwan during the last two decades. On the other hand, China has increased its efforts to isolate Taiwan. The isolation policy is successful as China has been able to maintain social stability and achieve rapid economic growth. The diplomatic strategy of the PRC to isolate Taiwan internationally has been effective in reducing the number of countries engaged in arms sales to the island. Today, the US is essentially the sole source for Taiwan's military to import arms. Taiwan's relationship with the mainland has been dependent on its military capacities. Great power military support, a strong airforce, and a modern navy have been an essential part of the Taiwanese nation-building formula. Taiwan has become the world's largest arms buyer since the Gulf War. Of the US$3.5 billion in arms sold to Taiwan between 1993 and 1995, the US share was US$3.2 billion. Between 1995 and 1997, the total value of all arms transfer deliveries to the island was US$12.5 billion. The orders and deliveries in 1998 totaled US$6.3 billion (MaClaran, 2000: 624). Taiwan's economic miracle has enabled it to become one of the biggest arms buyers in the world and one of the most important customers for the US defense military. Taiwan's rapid military modernization has ensured that Taiwanese military forces are among the best equipped in the world. One might wonder about the discipline of Taiwanese soldiers. The well-equipped KMT army was defeated by the poorly equipped PLA owing to its lack of loyalty and discipline.

The pace of economic interaction with the mainland is becoming a serious issue for the DDP. The party may want to separate the sovereignty issue from economic ones. On the other hand, the CCP would not separate political and economic issues. Taiwan's internationally medium-level technologies could not easily find markets as in the 1970s and the 1980s. Developing countries like India and China are rapidly taking up the Taiwanese market. Taiwanese companies fear loss of the market to rivals if they do not move their production lines to the mainland. The DDP-led municipal government in Hsinchu has proposed hiking taxes on high-tech businesses at the industrial park near Taipei; and meanwhile, the new government strongly discourages Taiwanese businesses to invest in the mainland. Recently, Taiwan tycoon Winston Wong (son of Formosa Plastics chairman, Wang Yung-ching) planned a US$1.63 billion computer-chip plant in Shanghai. Taiwan's companies have invested more than US$40 billion in China, roughly 40% of its total foreign investments. The information industry, the core of Taiwan's technological advantage and economic growth, has started moving offshore. For the DDP government, this may be a nightmare. Wong's Shanghai investment and other projects in computer-chip manufacturing that are already following accelerate Taiwan's dependence on the mainland. China is now Taiwan's third largest trading partner, buying 17% of Taiwan's exports and sharing 4% of the island's imports. It is generally agreed that trade benefits both sides, even though it may not strengthen the island's political position. Irrespective of Chen's inclination towards independence, the new government approaches the mainland even closer, perhaps to expand the space for Taiwan's long-term survival. Taiwan's Ministry of Education even recently approved the establishment of Taiwan curriculum schools in the mainland. This would enable Taiwanese communities to stay in the mainland in the long term. Although the mainland offers favorable conditions to Taiwanese businesses, the mainland also makes life difficult for those investors who favor Taiwan's independence.

The great majority of Taiwan's population no longer appears to want unification with the mainland under any terms at present, even though Beijing itself shows no sign of relinquishing its claims over what it views as its province. Table 6.1, based on Leng (1996: 50), provides public opinion polls on independence and unification in Taiwan. Only one-fourth of the Taiwanese people want unification. The majority prefers status quo. Taiwan has to identity itself because the mainland has not established any Chinese cultural identity at all — the CCP even criticized the key element

Table 6.1 Public opinion polls on independence and unification (in percentage)

	June 1989	June 1992	July 1995
Unification	20.5	29.9	20.0
Independence	2.1	6.4	14.0
Status quo	57.5	41.6	46.0
No comment	19.7	22.2	20.0

of the Chinese soul, Confucianism, at a national level in the so-called Cultural Revolution. However, the reality is that much of Taiwan's future prosperity will depend on its access to the mainland. Cheap and effective mainland labor force is important for Taiwan's international competitiveness; a potential huge market in the mainland absorbs Taiwan's second-rate products; its fluency in both Chinese dialects and Mandarin provide its easy access to Chinese markets around world. Partly because of its own success, it has become difficult for Taiwan to further penetrate markets in North America and Japan. Moreover, as the Chinese tend to accumulate "similar" human capital, the traditional comparative advantages of the Taiwanese may be lost to the mainland.

Taiwan has actually benefited from *de factor* independence, privileged access to the Chinese economy, and the advantages of its connections to the US, Japan, and the region in general. Three regions, the US, Mainland China, and Japan, seem to have strong influences on Taiwan's future. Taiwan's economic strength and education have given its leaders and people much greater confidence in being either a global citizen, a Chinese, or a Taiwanese. Taiwan has become more independent in its views and less inclined to support US policies when these do not benefit Taiwan's own interests. Its economic success tends to have a negative impact on US interests. Taiwan has followed Japan's examples by constantly upgrading its economy and has already moved into some areas of high technology in direct competition with American industries. Billions of dollars are also invested from Taiwan in the US. Moreover, the impact of replacement of the Soviet Union-influenced generation by the America-influenced generation on China's political system seems to change the political system. The economic integration of Taiwan into the greater China economy is already under way. In a historical perspective, between the two sides there are no deep conflicts in deep issues such as historical issues, perception of the world, common interests, cultural values, ideal societies, religions, and long-term ideologies.

Taiwanese trade with and investment in China has increased to such a great extent that many in Taiwan have begun to worry that increasing economic ties could be used to force Taiwan into reunification. In the 1960s and 1970s, when Taiwan's economy was relatively "simple," the government succeeded in providing public goods and intervening directly in the market system to achieve the national goal. Since the late 1990s, as the economy has become complicated, the government has not established any clear vision to guide the market. Taiwanese companies fear loss of the market to rivals if they fail to move their production lines to the mainland in time. The fact that Taiwan is heavily dependent on the China market enables the mainland to manipulate Taiwan's domestic economy. This has increased Taiwan's political vulnerability.

6.4 Being Oneself, Being Taiwanese, Being Chinese ...

> I do not know any dress of the scholar.
>
> *Confucius (the* Li Chi*)*

Similar to the US (in terms of institutions, customs, languages, and cultures in relations to Europe), Taiwan is mainly an immigrated existence. It does not use a native language as national language and has maintained its modern culture with immigrated (somehow adjusted) ideologies and religions. An immigrated culture has advantage in that it can improve principles, customs, and institutions of the original culture(s) to fit its own survival and avoid negative aspects of the original culture(s). Almost all the political and economic fundamental principles that are essential for Western civilization were created in Europe. However, in modern times it is not Europe but the US that has most effectively applied these principles. When Europeans immigrated to the United Sates, they brought European cultures with them. This is similarly true with Taiwan's modern development.

Since diffusion and application of new thought tend to result in "redistribution" of incomes, (academic) reputation, and political and social power, there are conflicts among various interest groups in association with new ideas. The contrast between the slowness that Mainland

China started to speed up industrialization and the economic miracles that overseas Chinese have achieved in modern times is partially due to possible complicated consequences that introduction of Western ideas might bring about in the mainland (Zhang, 1988). Mainland China could have identified a national consensus for industrialization only after the Cultural Revolution had left China in abject poverty. China's economic reform was started with the death of Chairman Mao and Taiwan's democratization was speeded up as the Chiang family lost power. It will take some years for Mainland China to identify a national consensus for rapid democratization. Max Planck (1858–1947), the German physicist who won the 1918 Nobel Prize for discoveries in connection with quantum theory, once remarked (Zeidler, 1986): "A new scientific truth does not triumph by convincing its opponents … but rather because its opponents eventually die, and a new generation grows up that is familiar with."

Confucian attitudes towards "club-formation," such as nationalism, racialism, regionalism, groupism, or familism are illustrated by Confucius' following statement: "The superior man is catholic and not partisan. The mean man is a partisan and not catholic." This Confucian value is reflected in what Fei (1992: 11) observed: "From both the economic and political standpoints, the external manifestation of Western nationalism has been far from healthy since its very beginnings in the sixteenth century. In contrast, the cultural nationalism, as developed historically in China over two thousand years, has always been tinged with an internationalism of 'all men are brothers' and 'the world is for all.' This is quite different from the Western nationalism that began with an antagonistic tone with such ideas as 'those who speak French are Frenchmen and have the divine right to kill Englishmen who seek French soil.' "

The Taiwanese has lived on the island for a long time. Many Taiwanese do not look to a land across the ocean as their home. Even the so-called "mainlanders in Taiwan" who came only after 1949 have lived on the island for over half a century. They have set down roots on the island and have children on the island. They have already taken Taiwan as their own country and have treated Mainland China as another part of the world. National identity is the central issue of Taiwan's political consensus. According to Confucius: "There is harmony but not a single identity among the gentlemen; there is a single identity but not harmony among the mean." When we examine identity issues among Taiwanese, we have to examine their beliefs, values, and sentiments. Reasons cannot provide us sufficient bases to identify people's identities. A man may have a single identity or multiple ones at the same time. One may have multiple even competing identities over a lifetime. One changes identities because one's emotion, knowledge, and ability to judge human affairs are changeable. According to the *I Ching*, different people would change identities in different ways: "The superior man produces his changes as the leopard does when he changes his spots — their beauty becomes more elegant. Small men change their faces — they show themselves prepared to follow their ruler." There is no universal standard that can determine who is Chinese when people from New York, London, Taipei, and Peking all claim the same label.

People in Taiwan developed a sense of sharing a common fate. The new Taiwanese consciousness seems to be shared by all the Mainlanders, Taiwanese, and aborigines. In a global environment, all the people in Taiwan need to harmonize. In the *Art of War*, Sun Tze said: "For the men of Wu and men of Yue are enemies; yet if they are crossing a river in the same boat and are caught by a storm, they will come to each other's assistance just as the left hand helps the right."

A main reason that one is rarely aware of influences of Confucianism on Confucian regions' modernization is that Confucianism does not ask for racial, national, or group, or any other concrete identity. What Confucianism is concerned with are righteousness, principles, duties, and self-cultivation. Loyalty to organization is not the purpose but a consequence of individual cultivation. In Confucianism, national or racial identity is important but should be formed, following righteousness. Confucius said: "The superior man, in the world, does not set his mind either for any thing, or against any thing; what is right he will follow." In modern times, Chinese men are commonly perceived as being family-centered. It is often mentioned that Confucianism advocates for a family-centered or seniority-determined system. The familism typically observed in overseas Chinese communities is perhaps a rational election of the Chinese under foreign "control." The ancient Chinese classic, the *Record of Rites* (Chao, 1983: 78), classified: "Filial piety is of three grades: the highest is to honor the parents by achievements, the lesser is to not disgrace oneself, thus casting reflections on the parents, and the least is to be able to support the parents." If we consider the PRC and the ROC as two separate branches of Confucian civilization in modern times, using the above Confucian standard, we conclude the PRC was not a filial son of Confucian culture because it failed to follow the essence of Confucianism and destroyed Chinese culture. The ROC has made positive contributions to Chinese civilization by showing that democracy can be achieved in Confucian cultural soil.

It is a universal principle among rational human beings that rich men rarely want poor, uneducated relatives. This might be the key factor for the "identity crisis" among the Taiwanese. In this sense, if Mainland China can become rich and politically proper, the identify crisis would vanish (perhaps, except for those people who hold American passports). Listen to what Charles Lamb (1833) said about poor relations: "A poor relation is the most irrelevant thing in nature, a piece of impertinent correspondency, an odious approximation, a haunting conscience, a preposterous shadow, lengthening in the noontide of your prosperity, an unwelcome remembrancer, a perpetually recurring mortification, a drain on your purse, a more intolerable dun upon your pride, a drawback upon success, a rebuke to your rising, a stain in your blood, a blot on your scutcheon, … an apology to your friends."

Ethnic, racial, or national identity in Taiwan is not a simple matter. Without proper education, there cannot be solid identification — the external symbol is chaotic. One person may identity oneself as being culturally Chinese and being politically, for instance, American. Some people on the island identify themselves as part of the Chinese nation (when nationality is defined in terms of shared identity and feelings of affinity). Some acknowledge their Chinese origin but identity themselves as Taiwanese. There are also people who consider Taiwan as their nation (Wachman, 1992; Tu, 1994). According to the public opinion polls in 1997, 36.9% of the people of Taiwan consider themselves Taiwanese; 34.8% consider themselves Taiwanese and Chinese; and 23.1% consider themselves Chinese (Scalapino, 2001: 5).

To maintain their Chinese identity, the mainlanders imposed the Mandarin language and a household registration system that required the mainlanders, their wives (but not their husbands), and their offspring, even those born in Taiwan, to be registered as residents of their home provinces on the mainland. Different from the mainlanders, the Taiwanese tried to identify their native roots and establish a "Taiwanese consciousness" and a "Taiwanese national" identity. Consciousness of distinction between

Taiwanese and mainlanders in the Taiwan tends to decline in recent years. Different groups are gradually integrated on equal terms into a democratic society. Taiwan does seem to have a national identity supported by, at least, native-born Taiwanese who now account for about 85% of the island's population. Their desire for a unique national identity makes significant contribution to democratization on Taiwan. Since Taiwan's conflicts with the mainland are not ideological or religious in historical perspectives, the majority of Taiwanese people desire to preserve the status quo of *de factor* independence to maximize their welfare. Taiwanese people would not call for formal independence since they do not want to lose cultural connections with, economic opportunities from, and political freedom from the mainland. Now, the majority of Taiwanese people do not want to reunify with China partly because of China's poverty and the CCP's unacceptable ideology and improper behavior. A Chinese proverb says: "in all the important human affairs, long-term unification would lead to separation and long-term separation would lead to unification."

The "symbols" do not have permanent meanings. They are changeable as history progresses. Crisis, fluctuations, and chaos of racial and national identity are a part of Chinese modern life. Irrespective of being ambiguous or even meaningless, the symbol of "being Chinese" is perhaps the only lasting attractor that connects the Chinese over the world. Many Chinese communities over the world may not care about the CCP, but their education and life experience are enabling them to feel what Qu Yuan (340–278 BC) felt:

> Gazing with longing eyes, I stand, oh!
> When may I come back to my homeland?
> A bird flies nowhere but home-bound; oh!
> A dying fox turns its head to its mound.

The KMT was committed to the notion that there was only one China and Taiwan was a part of China. Many opposition activists hold that Taiwan must sever territorial and political links with the mainland. They argue that Taiwan should be a new and independent state. Conflicts between these two fundamental positions raise questions related to the nature of the constitutional arrangement and national title. To be mainlanders or Taiwanese is a symbol to validate an objective structure of differences in economic, social, and institutional relations and consciousness. Bourdieu

(1979: 164) asserted: "Every established order tends to produce (to very different degrees and with very different means) the naturalization of its own arbitrariness. Of all the mechanisms tending to produce this effect, the most important and the best concealed is undoubtedly the dialect of the objective chances and the agents' aspirations, out of which arises the sense of limits, commonly called the sense of reality, i.e., the correspondence between the objective classes and the internalized classes, social structures and mental structures, which is the basis of the most ineradicable adherence to the established order." People in contemporary Taiwan were described to have "been nurtured and cultivated to acquire the characteristics of an ocean. Their former conservative character, like that of traditional China's, has been remoulded into another only concerned with goals and caring nothing about principles" (Myers, 1998: 28). Tu (1998: 94) has said that the backdrop for discussing Taiwanese consciousness is "the changing meaning of being Chinese today. ... Although Taiwan ... embraces modernism or even post-modernism by transcending nationalism and culturalism, as an economy and polity it must negotiate strenuously and wisely with Mainland China by mobilizing all the symbolic capital it can for its physical survival and spiritual well-being." For Tu, to be Chinese is not even a (relatively) fixed symbol but something to bargain about according to situations. Tu argued (1998: 95): "And it will certainly be detrimental to Taiwan's peace and prosperity to formulate a primarily anti-Sinitic cultural identity for the sake of international (mainly American) politics of recognition."

Taiwan's economic development and recent rapid democratization miracles were associated with increases in pollution, social disorder, and black and gold politics (influence of organized crime and the super-rich in politics). These negative externalities appear to have been insignificant in comparison to positive externalities derived from industrialization and political democratization in the past; but they are increasingly preventing Taiwan from further modernization. Since we are mainly concerned with interdependence between economic development, democracy, and Confucianism, we did not pay sufficient attention to negative consequences along with the positive sides of Taiwan's economic and political development. Wittgenstein (Wright 1998:12) illuminated: "It might be said that civilization can only have its epic poet in advance. Just as one can only foresee one's own death and describe it as something lying in the future, not report it as it happens. So it might be said: If you want to see the epic of a whole culture written you will have to seek it in the works of its greatest figures and hence see it at a time when the end of this culture can only be *foreseen*, for later there is no one there any more to describe it."

Like a single individual, a race, a nation, or a group of people cannot achieve any lasting achievements if it "progresses" merely by imitation — an imitator is one who has lost his child-mind in Mencius' sense. Confucius once remarks: "It is all over!" Perhaps, it is not the end but only the beginning of fulfilling one cycle of cultural/racial evolution — the fulfillment of Chinese industrialization and democratization. Each cycle of the Chinese civilization is started by knaves, neglected, debilitated, pirates, escapers, invaders, or defeaters. The politically civilized rarely makes any revolutionary change but constantly talks about reforms in a clear fashion but with confusing meanings. Rational as it is claimed to be, the Chinese man rarely learns from history, but repeats it. Racial stupidity repeats, so does racial learning and wisdom.

Bibliography

Aldcroft, D.H. (1998) Education and Development—The Experience of Rich and Poor Nations. *History of Education* 27.

Amsden, A. (1992) Taiwan in International Perspective, in *Taiwan's Enterprises in Global Perspective*, edited by Wang, N.T. New York: M.E. Sharpe.

Backman, M. (1999) *Asian Eclipse: Exposing the Dark Side of Business of Asia*. Singapore: John Wiley & Sons.

Balassa, B. (1981) *Economic Policies in the Pacific Area Developing Countries*. London: Macmillan.

Barlow, J. (1987) *Sun Yat-sen*. New York: Chelsea House Publishers.

Bass, H.H. (2000) Export Dynamics in Taiwan and Mainland 1950–2000—A Schumpeterian Approach, in *Asia Pacific Dynamism, 1550–2000*, edited by Latham, A.J.H. and Kawakatsu, H. London: Routledge.

Bau, T.H. (1992) Beijing–Taipei Interaction as a Two-Person Conflict (1949–1988), in *Taiwan—Beyond the Economic Miracle*, edited by Simon, D.F. and Kau, M.Y.M. New York: M.E. Sharpe.

Bauer, J.R. and Bell, D.A., editors (1999) *The East Asian Challenge for Human Rights*. Cambridge: Cambridge University Press.

Bell, D.A. (1978) *The Cultural Contradictions of Capitalism*. New York: Basic Books.

Bell, D.A. and Jayasuriya, K. (1995) Understanding Illiberal Democracy: A Framework, in *Towards Illiberal Democracy in Pacific Asia*, edited by Bell, D.A. et al. New York: St. Martin's Press.

Bergère, M.C. (1998) *Sun Yat-sen*, translated from the French by J. Lloyd. Stanford: Stanford University Press.

Book of Poetry, translated by Yuanchong Xu and revised by Shengzhang Jiang, published in the Chinese English bilingual series of Chinese classics. Hunan: Hunan Publishing House, 1993.

Bourdieu, P. (1979) *Outline of a Theory of Practice*. Cambridge: Cambridge University Press.

Bradley, O. and Blair, C. (1983) *A General's Life*. New York: Simon and Schuster.

Brook, T. and Blue, G., editors (1999) *China and Historical Capitalism—Genealogies of Sinological Knowledge*. Cambridge: Cambridge University Press.

Bullard, M.R. (1997) *The Soldier and the Citizen—The Role of the Military in Taiwan's Development*. Armonk: M.E. Shape.

Campbell, W. (1903) *Formosa Under the Dutch*. London: Kegan Paul.

Capra, F. (1982) *The Turning Point—Science, Society, and the Rising Culture*. New York: Simon and Schuster.

Chan, S. (1998) Peace by Pieces? Mainland–Taiwan Transactions Flows, in *Beyond the Developmental State: East Asia's Political Economies Reconsidered*, edited by Chan, S., Clark, C., and Lam, D. London: Macmillan.

Chan, W.T. (1973) *A Source Book in Chinese Philosophy*, translated and compiled. Princeton: Princeton University Press.

Chang, C. (1963) *The Development of Neo-Confucian Thought*. New Haven: College and University Press.

Chang, C.C. (1992) The Development of Taiwan's Personal Computer Industry, in *Taiwan's Enterprises in Global Perspectives*, edited by Wang, N.T. New York: M.E. Sharpe.

Chang, K.N. (1958) *The Inflationary Spiral: The Experience in China, 1939–50*. Cambridge: Technology Press of MIT.

Chao, K. (1986) *Man and Land in Chinese History—An Economic Analysis*. California: Standford University Press.

Chaponnière, J.R. and Lautier, M. (1998) Industrial Policy for Catching Up—The Case of Taiwan, in *Latecomers in the Global Economy*, edited by Storper, M., Thomadakis, S.B., and Tsipouri, L.J. London: Routledge.

Chen, E.K.Y. (1997) The Total Factor Productivity Debate—Determination of Economic Growth in East Asia. *Asian-Pacific Economic Literature* 11, No. 1, May.

Chen, H.C. (1911) *The Economic Principles of Confucius and his School*. New York: The Faculty of Political Science of Columbia University.

Chen, H.Y. (1994) Taiwan's Economic Relations with Southeast Asia, in *Taiwan in the Asia-Pacific in the 1990s*, edited by Klintworth, G. Canberra: Allen & Unwin.

Chen, J.P. (1990) *Confucius as a Teacher—Philosophy of Confucius with Special Reference to its Educational Implications*. Beijing: Foreign Languages Press.

Chen, M. (1995) *Asian Management Systems: Chinese, Japanese and Korea Styles of Business*. London: Routledge.

Chen, P. (1999) The Role of Industrial Policy in Taiwan's Development, in *Taiwan's Development Experience: Lessons on Roles of Government and Market*, edited by Thorbecke, E. and Wan, H.J. Boston: Kluwer Academic Publishers.

Chen, T.J., editor (1998) *Taiwanese Firms in Southeast Asia—Networking Across Borders*. Cheltenham: Edward Elgar.

Chen, T.J. and Ku, Y.H. (1999) Second-Stage Import Substitution—The Taiwan Experience, in *The Political Economy of Taiwan's Development into the 21st Century*, edited by Ranis, G., Hu, S.C., and Chu, Y.P. Cheltenham: Edward Elgar.

Cheng, C.Y. (1991) *New Dimensions of Confucian and Neo-Confucian Philosophy*. Albany: State University of New York Press.

Cheng, R.L. (1994) Language Unification in Taiwan: Present and Future, in *The Other Taiwan—1945 to the Present*, edited by Rubinstein, M.A. New York: M.E. Sharpe.

Chiou, C.L. (1994) Emerging Taiwanese Identity in the 1990s: Crisis and Transformation, in *Taiwan in the Asia-Pacific in the 1990s*, edited by Klintworth, G. Canberra: Allen & Unwin.

Chou, Y.S. and Nathan, A. (1987) Democratising Transition in Taiwan. *Asian Survey* 27, 277–99.

Chu, J.J. (1994) The Rise of Island–China Separatism, in *Taiwan in the Asia-Pacific in the 1990s*, edited by Klintworth, G. Canberra: Allen & Unwin.

Chu, J.J. (1995) Taiwan: A New Regional Center in the Making, in *The Changing Capital Markets of East Asia*, edited by Cao, K. London: Routledge.

Ch'u, T.T. (1965) *Law and Society in Traditional China*. Taipei: Rainbow-Bridge Book Co.

Chu, W.W. and Tsai, M.C. (1999) Linkage and Uneven Growth: A Study of Taiwan's Manmade Fiber Industry, in *The Political Economy of Taiwan's Development into the 21st Century*, edited by Ranis, G., Hu, S.C., and Chu, Y.P. Cheltenham: Edward Elgar.

Clark, C. (1989) *Taiwan's Development: Implications for Contending Political Economy Paradigms*. London: Greenwood Press.

Cohn, E. and Johnes, G., editors (1994) *Recent Developments in the Economics of Education*. Vermont: Edward Elgar Publishing Company.

Confucius (1992) The Confucian Analects, in *The Four Book* translated by James Legge and revised and annotated by Zhongde Liu and Zhiye Luo. Hunan: Hunan Publishing House.

Copper, J.F. (1990) *Taiwan: Nation-State or Province?* Colorado: Westview.

Copper, J.F. (1998) *Taiwan's Mid-1990s Elections—Taking the Final Steps to Democracy*. London. Westport.

Dahl, R. (1993) *Democracy and its Critics*. New Haven: Yale University Press.

Dardess, J.W. (1983) *Confucianism and Autocracy: Professional Elites in the Founding of the Ming Dynasty*. Berkley: University of California Press.

Davidson, J.W. (1903) *The Island of Formosa—Past and Present*. New York: Macmillan.

Davis, L.E. and North, D. (1971) *Institutions of Change and American Economic Growth*. New York: Cambridge University Press.

Deng, G. (1999) *The Premodern Chinese Economy—Structural Equilibrium and Capitalist Sterility*. London: Routledge.

Deng, P. (2000) Taiwan's Restriction of Investment in China in the 1990s. *Asian Survey* XL, No. 6, 958–80.

Deuchler, M. (1992) *The Confucian Transformation of Korea*. Cambridge, MA: Harvard University Press.

Doctrine of the Mean (1992) in *The Four Book* translated by James Legge and revised and annotated by Zhongde Liu and Zhiye Luo. Hunan: Hunan Publishing House.

Donnelly, J. (1999) Human Rights and Asian Values—A Defense of "Western" Universalism, in *The East Asian Challenge for Human Rights*, edited by Bauer, J.R. and Bell, D.A. Cambridge: Cambridge University Press.

Drucker, P. (1998) *Managing in a Time of Great Change*. New York: Truman Talley Books.

Durkheim, E. (1956) *Education and Sociology*, translated by S.D. Fox. Glencoe: The Free Press.

Ernst, D. (2000) Inter-organizational Knowledge Outsourcing: What Permits Small Taiwanese Firms to Compete in the Computer Industry? *Asia Pacific Journal of Management* 17, 223–55.

Farnie, D.A. (2000) Four Revolutions in the Textile Trade of Asia 1914–1994, in *Asia Pacific Dynamism, 1550–2000*, edited by Latham, A.J.H. and Kawakatsu, H. London: Routledge.

Fei, J.C.H. (1992) Taiwan's Economic Development and its Relation to the International Environment, in *Taiwan's Enterprises in Global Perspectives*, edited by Wang, N.T. New York: M.E. Sharpe.

Fei, J.C.H., Ranis, G., and Kuo, S. (1979) *Growth with Equity: The Taiwan Case*. Oxford: Oxford University Press.

Fei, J.C.H., Ohkawa, K., and Ranis, G. (1985) Economic Development in Historical Perspective: Japan, Korea and Taiwan, in *Japan and Developing Countries: A Comparative Analysis*. Oxford: Basil Blackwell.

Findlay, R. and Wellisz, S., editors (1993) *Five Small Open Economies*. New York: Oxford University Press.

Fisher, I. (1930) *The Theory of Interest*. Macmillan: New York.

Francks, P. (1992) *Japanese Economic Development—Theory and Practice*. London: Routledge.

Francks, P. (1999) *Agriculture and Economic Development in East Asia: From Growth to Protectionism in Japan, Korea and Taiwan*. London: Routledge.

Friedman, E., editor (1994) *The Politics of Demoncratization: Generalizing East Asian Experiences*. New York: Westview Press.

Fu, T.T. and Shei, S.Y. (1999) Agriculture as the Foundation for Development: The Taiwanese Story, in *Taiwan's Development Experience: Lessons on Roles of Government and Market*, edited by Thorbecke, E. and Wan, H.J. Boston: Kluwer Academic Publishers.

Fukuyama, F. (1995) *Trust—The Social Virtues and the Creation of Prosperity*. London: Hamish Hamilton.

Fung, Y.L. (1952) *A History of Chinese Philosophy*, vol. I, translated from the Chinese origin by D. Bodde. Princeton: Princeton University Press.

Fung, Y.L. (1953) *A History of Chinese Philosophy*, vol. II, translated from the Chinese origin by D. Bodde. Princeton: Princeton University Press.

Galenson, W. (1999) The Labor Market in Taiwan: Manpower, Earning, and Market Institutions, in *Taiwan's Development Experience: Lessons on Roles of Government and Market*, edited by Thorbecke, E. and Wan, H.J. Boston: Kluwer Academic Publishers.

Garran, R. (1998) *Tigers Tamed—The End of the Asian Miracle*. St. Leonards: Allen & Unwin.

Gleick, J. (1987) *Chaos: Making a New Science*. New York: Viking.

Gold, T.B. (1986) *State and Society in the Taiwan Miracle*. New York: M. E. Sharpe.

Gold, T.B. (1988) Colonial Origins of Taiwanese Capitalism, in *Contending Approaches to the Political Economy of Taiwan*, edited by Winckler, E.A. and Greenhalgh, S. New York: M. E. Sharpe.

Gold, T.B. (1998) Taiwan Society at the *Fin de Siècle*, in *Contemporary Taiwan*, edited by Shambaugh, D. New York: Clarendon Press.

Great Learning, translated by James Legge and revised and annotated by Zhongde Liu and Zhiye Luo, published in the Chinese English bilingual series of Chinese classics. Hunan: Hunan Publishing House, 1992.

Grieder, J.B. (1981) *Intellectuals and the State in Modern China—A Narrative History*. New York: The Free Press.

Haggard, S. (1990) *Pathway from the Periphery*. New York: M.E. Sharpe.

Halbersen, H. and Ferdinand, P. (1996) Domestic Political Change, in *Take-Off for Taiwan?* edited by Ferdinand, P. London: The Royal Institute of International Affairs.

Hall, D.L. and Ames, R.T. (1999) *The Democracy of the Dead—Dewey, Confucius, and the Hope for Democracy in China*. Chicago: Open Court.

Hall, D.L. and Ames, R.T. (1987) *Thinking Through Confucius*. Albany: State University of New York Press.

Hall, D.L. and Ames, R.T. (1995) *Anticipating China: Thinking through the Narratives of Chinese and Western Culture*. Albany: State University of New York Press.

Hall, D.L. and Ames, R.T. (1998) *Thinking from the Han—Self, Truth, and Transcendence in Chinese and Western Culture*. Albany: State University of New York Press.

Hall, I.P. (1997) Creativity without Diversity? The Anomalous Case of the Japanese University, in *The Vitality of Japan*, edited by Clesse, A., Inoguchi, T., Keehn, E.B., and Stockwin, J.A.A. New York: St. Martin's Press.

Hayek, F.A. (1944) *The Road to Serfdom*. London: Routledge.

Hayek, F.A. (1990) *New Studies in Philosophy, Politics, Economics and the History of Ideas*. London: Routledge.

Hermalin, A., Liu, P.K.C., and Freedman, D. (1994) The Social and Economic Transformation of Taiwan, in *Social Change and the Family in Taiwan*, edited by Thornson, A. and Lin, H.S. Chicago: The University of Chicago Press.

Ho, S.P.S. (1978) *Economic Development of Taiwan, 1860–1970*. London: Yale University Press.

Hoesel, R. (1996) Taiwan: Foreign Direct Investment and the Transformation of the Economy, in *Foreign Direct Investment and Governments: Catalysts for Economic Restructuring*. London: Routledge.

Hong, S.G. (1997) *The Political Economy of Industrial Policy in East Asia—The Semiconductor Industry in Taiwan and South Korea*. Cheltenham: Edward Elgar.

Howe, C. (1996) The Taiwan Economy—The Transition to Maturity of the Political Economy of its Changing International Status. *The China Quarterly*, No. 148, 1171–95.

Hsing, Y.T. (1999) Trading Companies in Taiwan's Fashion Shoe Networks. *Journal of International Economics* 48, 101–20.

Hsu, W.H. (1980) From Aboriginal Island to Chinese Frontier: The Development of Taiwan in 1683, in *China's Island Frontier: Studies in the Historical Geography of Taiwan*, edited by Knapp, R.G. Hawaii: University Press of Hawaii.

Hsün Tzu (1963) *Basic Writings*, translated from the Chinese origin by B. Watson. New York: Columbia University Press.

Hu, J.C. (1988) *A Concise History of Chinese Economic Thought*. Beijing: Foreign Languages Press.

Hu, J.C., editor (1994) *Quiet Revolutions*. Taipei: Kwang Hwa Publishing Co.

Hume, David (1994) *Political Essays*, edited by Knud Haakonssen. Cambridge: Cambridge University Press.

Hung, S.C. (2000) Institutions and Systems of Innovation: An Empirical Analaysis of Taiwan's Personal Computer Competitiveness. *Technology in Society* 22, 175–87.

Huntington, S.P. (1968) *Political Order in the Changing Societies*. New Haven: Yale University Press.

Huntington, S.P. and Nelson, J. (1976) *No Easy Choice: Political Participation in Developing Countries*. Cambridge, MA: Harvard University Press.

I Ching or Book of Changes (1993) translated by James Legge and revised and annotated by Qin Ying. Hunan: Hunan Publishing House.

Iwao, S. (1955) Sugar and Tea Trade Between Taiwan and Persia During the Dutch and the Cheng Period, in *Collection of Writings on Economic History* 1, 38–53. Taipei: Bot.

Jacoby, N.H. (1973) *U.S. Aid to Taiwan: A Study of Foreign Aid, Self-Help, and Development*. New York: Praeger.

Jansen, M. (1965) *Changing Japanese Attitudes Toward Modernization*. Princeton: Princeton University Press.

Jung, C.G. (1989) *Psychological Types*, a revision by R.F. Hull of the translation by H.G. Baynes. London: Routledge.

Ka, C.M. (1995) *Japanese Colonialism in Taiwan: Land Tenure, Development, and Dependendency, 1895–1945*. Taipei: SMC Publishing Inc.

Keeves, J.P., editor (1997) *Educational Research, Methodology, and Measurement: An International Handbook*, 2nd edition. Oxford: Elsevier Science Ltd.

Kerr, G.H. (1965) *Formosa Betrayed*. Boston: Houghton Mifflin.

Kerr, G.H. (1974) *Formosa: Licensed Revolution and the Home Rule Movement, 1985–1945*. Honolulu: The University of Hawaii Press.

Klintworth, G. (1995) *New Taiwan, New China: Taiwan's Changing Role in the Asia-Pacific Region*. Sydney: Longman Australia.

Kraus, R. (1990) *Recreation and Leisure in Modern Society*, 4th edition. New York: Harper Collins Publishers.

Ku, Y.W. (1997) *Welfare Capitalism in Taiwan—State, Economy and Social Policy*. London: Macmillan.

Ku, Y.W. (2000) Social Development in Taiwan: Upheavals in the 1990, in *Social Development in Asia*, edited by Tang, K.L. Dordrecht: Kluwer Academic Publishers.

Kung, I.C. (2001) Taiwanese Business in Southern Asia, in *Chinese Business in Southeast Asia—Contesting Cultural Explanations, Researching Entrepreneurship*, edited by Gomez, E.T. and Hsiao, H.H.M. Surrey: Curzon Press.

Kuo, C.T. (2000) Taiwan's Distorted Democracy in Comparative Perspective, in *Taiwan in Perspective*, edited by Lee, W.C. Boston: Brill.

Kuo, S.W.Y. (1983) *The Taiwan Economy in Transition*. Boulder: Westview Press.

Kuo, S.W.Y. (1994) The Taiwanese Economy in the 1990s, in *Taiwan in the Asia-Pacific in the 1990s*, edited by Klintworth, G. Canberra: Allen & Unwin.

Kuo, S.W.Y. (1999) Government Policy in the Taiwanese Development Process: The Past 50 Years, in *Taiwan's Development Experience: Lessons on Roles of Government and Market*, edited by Thorbecke, E. and Wan, H.J. Boston: Kluwer Academic Publishers.

Kuznets, S. (1955) Economic Growth and Income Inequality. *American Economic Review* 45, 1–28.

Lamp, C. (1883) Poor Relations, in *100 Best English Essays*, selected and translated by Gao Jian, 2001. Beijing: China's Publishing Company of Foreign Languages.

Lao Tzu (1963) *Tao Te Ching*, translated with an Introduction by D.C. Lau. London: Penguin Books.

Lasater, M.L. (1993) *U.S. Interests in the New Taiwan*. Boulder: Westview Press.

Latham, A.J.H. and Kawakatsu, H., editors (2000) *Asia Pacific Dynamism, 1550–2000*. London: Routledge.

Lee, W.O. (1991) *Social Change and Educational Problems in Japan, Singapore and Hong Kong*. London: Macmillan.

Leng, T.K. (1996) *The Taiwan–China Connection: Democracy and Development Across the Taiwan Straits*. Boulder: Westview Press.

Levy, B. (1991) Transaction Costs, the Size of Firms and Industrial Policy: Lesson from a Comparative Case Study of the Footwear Industry in Korea and Taiwan. *Journal of Development Economics* 34, 151–78.

Li Chi or The Book of Rites, translated by James Legge, 1928, Sacred Books of the East, vol. 28, The *Li Ki*. London: Oxford University Press.

Li, K.T. (1988) *The Solution of Policy Behind Taiwan's Development Success*. New Haven: Yale University Press.

Lim, C.H. (1992) The Confucian Tradition and its Future in Singapore—Historical, Cultural and Educational Perspectives, in *Asian Traditions and Modernization—Perspectives from Singapore*, edited by Yong, M.C. Singapore: Times Academic Press.

Lin, C.Y. (1979) *Industrialization in Taiwan, 1946–1972*. New York: Praeger Press.

Lin, H.T. et al. (1990) *Taiwan History*. Taipei: Chung-wen (in Chinese).

Lin, O.C.C. (1998) Science and Technology Policy and its Influence on Economic Development in Taiwan, in *Behind East Asian Growth: The Political and Social Foundations of Prosperity*. London: Routledge.

Lipset, S.M. (1959) Some Social Requisites of Democracy: Economic Development and Political Legitimacy. *American Political Science Review* 53, 69–105.

Lipset, S.M. (1990) *Continental Divide: The Values and Institutions of the United States and Canada*. New York: Routledge.

Lipset, S.M. (1996) *American Exceptionalism: A Double-Edged Sword*. New York: W.W. Norton & Company.

Liu, C.Y. (1993) Government's Role in Developing a High-Tech Industry: The Case of Taiwan's Semiconductor Industry. *Technovation* 13, No. 5.

Long, S. (1991) *Taiwan: China's Last Frontier*. London: Macmillan.

Low, L., Heng, T.M., and Wong, S.T. (1991) *Economics of Education and Manpower Development: Issues and Policies in Singapore*. Singapore: McGraw-Hill Book Co.

Lu, D. (1994) Confucian Heritage and Singapore's Economic Policy, in *The Universal and Particular Natures of Confucianism*. Korea: The Academy of Korean Studies.

Lux, K. (1990) *Adam Smith's Mistake—How a Moral Philosopher Invented Economics & Ended Morality*. London: Shambhala.

MaClaran, J.P. (2000) U.S. Arms Sales to Taiwan: Implications for the Future of the Sino-U.S. Relationship. *Asian Survey* XL, 622–40.

Maddison, A. (1989) *The World Economy in the 20th Century*. Paris: OECD.

Maguire, K. (1998) *The Rise of Modern Taiwan*. Aldershot: Ashgate.

Mainzer, K. (1996) Thinking in Complexity—The Complex Dynamics of Matter, Mind, and Mankind, 2nd edition. Berlin: Springer.

Mao, Y.K. (1991) Agricultural Development and Policy Adjustments in Taiwan. *Industry of Free China*, September, 33–52.

Marsh, R.M. (1996) *The Great Transformation—Social Change in Taipei, Taiwan Since the 1960s*. New York: M.E. Sharpe.

Marshall, A. (1890) *Principles of Economics*, 1990. London: Macmillan.

McBeath, G.A. (1998) *Wealth and Freedom: Taiwan's New Political Economy*. Aldershot: Ashgate.

Mencius (1992) The Works of Mencius, in *The Four Book* translated by James Legge and revised and annotated by Liu and Zhiye Luo. Hunan: Hunan Publishing House.

Merton, R.K. (1957) *Social Theory and Social Structure*. Glencoe, IL: The Free Press.

Miller, D. (1988) Altruism and the Welfare State, in *Responsibility, Rights, and Welfare: The Theory of the Welfare State*, 163–88, edited by Moon, J.D. London: Westview Press.

Ministry of Education (1984) *Education in the Republic of China*. Taipei.

Morishima, M. (1978) The Power of Confucian Capitalism. *The Observer* (London), June.

Morishima, M. (1982) *Why Has Japan Succeeded?* Cambridge: Cambridge University Press.

Morris, P. and Sweeting, A. (1995) *Education and Development in East Asia*. New York: Garland Publishing, Inc.

Myers, R.H. (1998) A New Chinese Civilization: The Evolution of the Republic of China on Taiwan, in *Contemporary Taiwan*, edited by Shambaugh, D. New York: Clarendon Press.

Nicolis, G. and Prigogine, I. (1977) *Self Organization in Nonequilibrium Systems*. New York: Wiley.

North, D.C. (1990) *Institutional Structure and Institutional Change*. New York: Cambridge University Press.

NSC (1988) *Yearbook of Science and Technology*. Taipei: National Science Council.

Osmani, S.R., editor (1992) *Nutrition and Poverty*. Oxford: Clarendon Press.

Prigogine, I. (1980) *From Being to Becoming*. San Francisco: W.H. Freeman.

Prigogine, I. (1997) *The End of Certainty—Time, Chaos, and the New Laws of Nature*, written in collaboration with I. Stengers. New York: The Free Press.

Prigogine, I. and Stengers, I. (1984) *Order Out of Chaos: Man's Dialogue with Nature*. Boulder: New Science Library.

Qu, Y. (1995) *Poetry of the South*, translated by Y.Z. Xiu and revised by F.B. Yang Hunan Province: Hunan Publishing House.

Ranis, G. (1979) Industrial Development, in *Economic Growth and Structural Change in Taiwan*, edited by Galenson, W. Ithaca: Cornell University Press.

Ranis, G., Hu, S.C., and Chu, Y.P., editors (1999) *The Political Economy of Comparative Development into the 21st Century*. Cheltenham: Edward Elgar.

Ravich, S.F. (2000) *Marketization and Democracy—East Asian Experiences*. Cambridge: Cambridge University Press.

Redding, G. (1993) *The Spirit of Chinese Capitalism*. Berlin: Walter de Gruyter.

Redding, G., editor (1995) *International Cultural Differences*. Sydney: Dartmouth.

Reilly, M., editor (1974) *Play as Exploratory Learning—Studies of Curiosity Behavior*. London: Sage Publications.

Riggs, F.W. (1952) *Formosa Under Chinese Nationalist Rule*. New York: Macmillan.

Robins, F. (1998) *Taiwan's Economic Success, in Emerging Economic Systems in Asia—A Political and Economic Survey*, edited by Sheridan, K. St Leonards: Allen & Unwin.

Ross, I.S. (1995) *The Life of Adam Smith*. Oxford: Clarendon Press.

Rowen, H.S. (1998) The Political and Social Foundations of the Rise of East Asia: An Overview, in *Behind East Asian Growth: The Political and Social Foundations of Prosperity*. London: Routledge.

Scalapino, R.A. (2001) Taiwan: Opportunities and Challenges, in *Taiwan's National Security*, edited by Tan, A.C., Chan, S., and Jillson, C. Singapore: Ashgate.

Schive, C. (1992) Taiwan's Emerging Position in the International Division of Labor, in *Taiwan: Beyond the Economic Miracle*, edited by Simon, D.F. and Kau, M.Y.M. Armonk: M.E. Sharpe.

Schive, C. (1999) How Was Taiwan's Economy Opened Up? The Foreign Factor in Appraisal, in *The Political Economy of Taiwan's Development into the 21st Century*, edited by Ranis, G., Hu, S.C., and Chu, Y.P. Cheltenham: Edward Elgar.

Schultz, T.P. (1999) Income Inequality in Taiwan 1979–95: Changing Family Composition, Aging and Female Labor-force Participation, in *The Political Economy of Taiwan's Development into the 21st Century*, edited by Ranis, G., Hu, S.C, and Chu, Y.P. Cheltenham: Edward Elgar.

Sen, A. (1992) *Inequality Reexamined*. Oxford: Clarendon Press.

Shepherd, J.R. (1993) *Statecraft and Political Economy on the Taiwan Frontier 1600–1800*. Standford: Standford University Press.

Simon, D.F. (1992) Taiwan's Emerging Technological Trajectory: Creating New Forms of Competitive Advantage, in *Taiwan—Beyond the Economic Miracle*, edited by Simon, D.F. and Kau, M.Y.M. New York: M.E. Sharpe.

Simon, D.F. (1996) Charactering Taiwan's Technological Future—The Impact of Globalization and Regionalization. *The China Quarterly*, No. 148, December, 1196–223.

Simon, D.F. (1998) Charting Taiwan's Technological Future: The Impact of Globalization and Regionalization, in *Contemporary Taiwan*, edited by Shambaugh, D. New York: Clarendon Press Oxford.

Slote, W.H. and De Vos, G.A. (1998) *Confucianism and the Family*. New York: State University of New York Press.

Smith, A. (1759) *The Theory of Moral Sentiments*, edited by Raphael, D.D. and Macfie, A.L. 1982. Indianapolis: Liberty Press.

Smith, A. (1776) *An Inquiry into the Nature and Causes of the Wealth of Nations*, edited by Cannan, E, 1976. Chicago: The University of Chicago Press.

Smith, W.W. (1959) *Confucianism in Modern Japan: A Study of Conservatism in Japanese Intellectual History*. Tokyo: Hokuseido Press.

So, A.Y. and Chiu, S.W.K. (1995) *East Asia and the World Economy*. London: Sage Publications.

Stevenson, H.W. (1998) Human Capital: How the East Excels, in *Behind East Asian Growth: The Political and Social Foundations of Prosperity*. London: Routledge.

Stromberg, R.N. (1996) *Democracy—A Short, Analytical History*. New York: M.E. Sharpe.

Sugden, R. (1984) Reciprocity: The Supply of Public Goods Through Voluntary Contributions. *The Economic Journal* 94, 772–87.

Sun Tzu (1992) *The Art of War*, translated by Lionel Giles and revised and annotated by Y. Cheng and H.S. Zhang. Hunan: Hunan Publishing House.

Sun, Y.S. (1922) *The International Development of China*, reprinted in 1975. New York: Da Capo Press.

Sun, Y.S. (1983) *The Three Principles of the People*, translated by F.W. Price. Taipei: China Publishing Company.

Tai, H.C. (1969) *Socio-Economic Impact of Land Reform in Taiwan*. Taipei: Chia-Hsin Cement Cultural Foundation.

Tai, H.C. (1989) *Confucianism and Economic Development: An Oriental Alternative?*. Washington: The Washington Institute Press.

Tan, K.Y.L. (1999) Economic Development, Legal Reform, and Rights in Singapore and Taiwan, in *The East Asian Challenge for Human Rights*, edited by Bauer, J.R. and Bell, D.A. Cambridge: Cambridge University Press.

Tao, Y.C. (1969) *The Tariff System of the Republic of China*. Taipei.

Temple, R. (1986) *The Genius of China—3000 Years of Science, Discovery, and Invention*. New York: Touchstone Book.

Thorbecke, E. (1979) Agricultural Development, in *Economic Growth and Structural Change in Taiwan*, edited by Galenson, W. Ithaca: Cornell University Press.

Tien, H.M. (1991) *The Great Transition: Political and Social Change in the Republic of China*. Taipei: Shih-pao (in Chinese).

Tien, H.M. (1992) Taiwan's Evolution Toward Democracy: A Historical Perspective, in *Taiwan: Beyond the Economic Miracle*, edited by Simon, D.F. and Kau, M.Y.M. New York: M.E. Sharpe.

de Tocqueville, A. (1948) *Democracy in America*, vols I and II. New York: Alfred A. Knopt.

TSDB (1995) *Taiwan Statistical Data Book*. Taipei: Council for Economic Planning and Development.

Tsiang, G.R.J. (1999) Human Capital Creation and Utilization in Taiwan, in *Taiwan's Development Experience: Lessons on Roles of Government and Market*, edited by Thorbecke, E. and Wan, H.J. Boston: Kluwer Academic Publishers.

Tsurumi, E.P. (1977) *Japanese Colonial Education in Taiwan, 1895–1945*. Cambridge, MA: Harvard University Press.

Tu, W.M., editor (1991) *The Triadic Chord—Confucian Ethics, Industrial East Asia and Max Weber*. Singapore: The Institute of East Asian Philosophies.

Tu. W.M., editor (1994) *The Living Tree—The Changing Meaning of Being Chinese Today*. California: Stanford University Press.

Tu, W.M., editor (1996) *Confucian Traditions in East Asian Modernity—Moral Education and Economic Culture in Japan and the Four Mini-Dragon*. Cambridge, MA: Harvard University Press.

Tu, W.M. (1998) Cultural Identity and the Politics of Recognition, in *Contemporary Taiwan*, edited by Shambaugh, D. New York: Clarendon Press.

Varga, A. (1998) *University Research and Regional Innovation: A Spatial Econometric Analysis of Academic Technology Transfers*. Boston: Kluwer Academic Publishers.

Wachman, A.M. (1992) *Taiwan—National Identity and Democratization*. New York: M.E. Sharpe.

Wachman, A.M. (1994) Competing Identities in Taiwan, in *The Other Taiwan – 1945 to the Present*, edited by Rubinstein, M.A. New York: M.E. Sharpe.

Wade, R. (1990) *Governing the Market: Economic Theory and the Role of Government in Taiwan's Industrialization*. Princeton: Princeton University.

Waldrop, M.M. (1992) *Complexity—The Emerging Science at the Edge of Order and Chaos*. New York: A Touchstone Book.

Wang, H.H. (1998) *Technology, Economic Security, State, and the Political Economy of Economic Networks—A Historical and Comparative Research on the Evolution of Economic Networks in Taiwan and Japan*. New York: University Press of America.

Warr, P.G. and Wang, W.T. (1999) Poverty, Inequality and Economic Growth in Taiwan, in *The Political Economy of Taiwan's Development into the 21st Century*, edited by Ranis, G., Hu, S.C., and Chu, Y.P. Cheltenham: Edward Elgar.

Weber, M. (1951) *The Religion of China—Confucianism and Taoism*, translated from German original by H.H. Gerth with an introduction by C.K. Yang. New York: The Free Press.

Weber, M. (1991) *The Protestant Ethic and the Spirit of Capitalism*, translated from German by T. Parsons. London: Harper Collins Academic.

Wei, H.C. and Christodoulou, C. (1998) The Changing Relationship Between the Taiwanese Government and Small and Medium-Sized Enterprises. *Asian Studies Review* 22, No. 2, 239–60.

Wo, J.H. (1991) Education and Economic Growth in Taiwan—A Case of Successful Planning. *World Development* 19, 1029–44.

Woronoff, J. (1986) *Asia's "Miracle" Economies*. New York: M.E. Sharpe.

Wright, G.G., editor (1998) *Ludwig Wittgenstein—Culture and Value*. Oxford: Blackwell.

Wu, H.H. (1995) *Bridging the Strait—Taiwan, China, and the Prospects for Reunification*. Hong Kong: Oxford University Press.

Ye, J.Y. (1986) On Policy for Peaceful Reunification. *Beijing Review* 3, February.

Young, A. (1992) A Tale of Two Cities: Factor Accumulation and Technical Change in Hong Kong and Singapore, in *NBER Macroeconomics Annual 1992*, edited by Blanchard, O.J. and Fisher, S.F. Cambridge, MA: The MIT Press.

Young, A. (1995) The Tyranny of Numbers—Confronting the Statistical Realities of the East Asian Growth Experience. *Quarterly Journal of Economics*, August, 641–80.

Yu, T.S. (1999) A Balanced Budget, Stable Prices and Full Employment: The Macroeconomic Environment for Taiwan's Growth, in *Taiwan's Development Experience: Lessons on*

Roles of Government and Market, edited by Thorbecke, E. and Wan, H.J. Boston: Kluwer Academic Publishers.

Zeidler, E. (1986) *Nonlinear Functional Analysis and its Applications: I: Fixed-Point Theorems*, translated from German original by P.R. Wadsack. New York: Springer-Verlag.

Zeigler, H. (1988) *Pluralism, Corporatism, and Confucianism: Political Association and Conflict Regulation in the United States, Europe, and Taiwan*. Philadelphia: Temple University Press.

Zhang, W.B. (1990) *Economic Dynamics—Growth and Development*. Heidelberg: Springer-Verlag.

Zhang, W.B. (1991) *Synergetic Economics*. Heidelberg: Springer-Verlag.

Zhang, W.B. (1996) *Knowledge and Value—Economic Structures with Time and Space*. Umeå Economic Studies, Umeå: Umeå University.

Zhang, W.B. (1998) *Japan versus China in the Industrial Race*. London: Macmillan.

Zhang, W.B. (1999a) *Confucianism and Modernization*. London: Macmillan.

Zhang, W.B. (1999b) *Capital and Knowledge—Dynamics of Economic Structures with Non-constant Returns*. Heidelberg: Springer-Verlag.

Zhang, W.B (2000) Adam Smith and Confucius—*The Theory of Moral Sentiments* and *The Analects*. New York: Nova Science.

Zhang, W.B. (2001) Economic Growth with Creative Leisure—A Theoretical Insight into Singapore's Manpower Policy, in *Singapore Economy in the 21st Century*, edited by Department of Economics, National University of Singapore. Singapore: McGraw-Hill.

Zhang, W.B. (2002) Singapore's Modernization — Westernization and Modernizing Confucian Manifestations. New York: Nova Science.

Zhang, W.B. (2003) American Civilization Portrayed in Ancient Confucianism. New York: Algora.

Index